C000062531

Abuse of Power:

Because Councils Can

Foreword

This book exposes the stories of two women who challenged a City Council in Ireland on its actions. The executive powers and infinite resources available to Council officials enabled the eviction of one woman from her home and removal of the other from employment.

Bríd Cummins was an articulate and talented journalist and artist from Co. Tipperary, who started her working life as a civil servant, before retraining as a journalist and working for the *Reuters* news agency.

This book lays bare the facts surrounding the unnecessary and avoidable eviction of this lady by Galway City Council. Bríd Cummins was challenged by disability following an accident. Using unfettered access to legal services and using powerful legislation, Galway City Council advanced a neighbourhood dispute through the courts for an eviction order. In battling these powers, the lone voice of this vulnerable and single woman, living on her own, was lost.

The city of Galway, traditionally known for its friendliness and hospitality, ultimately turned out to be a cold and harsh place for Bríd Cummins. Council executives used the power of the Courts to instruct that Bríd be turned out on to the streets of Galway on a cold and wet winter night approaching Christmas.

Further still, they ordered the homeless services in the city to not provide emergency shelter; after they evicted her. When Council officials called to her rented property on Munster Avenue, Galway, to retrieve the keys and lock her out, she was found dead.

The author Julie Grace is a former local authority employee who worked in the Housing section at Galway City Council. During her ten years interacting with colleagues and with the public, she witnessed many executive decisions and actions, which ranged from the good and positive to the irregular and unprofessional.

Initially Julie worked at Galway Corporation as a revenue collector, moving on to work in Estate Management/Community Development, and as a Tenant Liaison Officer with Galway City Council during her last working years. She is a widely experienced and knowledgeable practitioner in all aspects of social housing. She now works as a independent professional Mediator.

After ten years of an unblemished record of public service, Julie was directed by her superiors in Housing at City Hall to carry out actions that she believed were not ethical or fair. Despite her historical dedication, commitment and unblemished good name, Galway City Council terminated her career as a public servant prematurely at 52 years of age. She believes this arose because she refused to engage in the abuse of the powers of the council and the resources of the public purse.

This book aims to highlight how executive decisions have the capacity to cause untold human misery for ordinary citizens. Politicians and the State have devolved decision-making powers to local public servants in Ireland, but who is accountable for flawed decisions? Who regulates the decision-makers? What sanctions apply on bad actions in public office? Why are public funds always available to defend the misdeeds of local public servants? Why are known misdeeds not challenged by political masters? When is a vulnerable council tenant allowed an equal footing to challenge wrongdoings of local authority executives? Where is the governance? Where does the buck stop? The answers are difficult to find in 2014 Ireland.

The writing of this book has involved a detailed examination of the *'Report to Councillors'* (compiled by council officials after Bríd's death).

The research undertaken in compilation of this book has relied on previously published sources, radio and television reporting, newspaper articles and matters of public record from the author's own civil action against Galway City Council in the High Court in 2010.

This book seeks to open a public discourse in questioning the following:

1. What does a public servant do when they are ordered to carry out a direction that they know is morally and ethically wrong?

2. When a citizen needs to question or challenge a decision of a local authority (such as a housing allocation), how do they gain a fair hearing?

3. Why does the Irish Government continue to condone, fund and rubber-stamp grossly inequitable decisions of local authority officials, in actions against the Irish citizen?

Dedication

This book is dedicated to all persons whose lives have been irretrievably damaged by bad and wrongful decisions of public servants, and who did not have any choice, other than to suffer in silence.

"The problem of power is how to achieve its responsible use rather than its irresponsible and indulgent use - of how to get men of power to live for the public rather than off the public".

Robert Kennedy (1964) 'I Remember, I believe, Pursuit of Justice'

7

Introduction

Bríd Cummins was born in 1956 in Clonmel Co. Tipperary. The youngest of seven children, Bríd was born into a hard working and well-respected family. After briefly working as a civil servant, she trained as a journalist, and worked for *Newsweek* and *Reuters*. She subsequently lived in Brussels, working for the European Parliament. In her early 30's, Bríd moved to live in Galway and got involved in the vibrant arts community and in writing poetry.

After a freak accident in a swimming pool in the 1990's, her health suffered badly, which for Bríd resulted in a remaining life of disability, psychiatric illness and intermittent occasions of employment. Bríd lived in private-rented accommodation in Galway City for a number of years, and eventually secured accommodation from the local authority. Due to her disabilities it was less than ideal for her needs, but it provided security of tenure for her, and there was the expectation of the flat being improved by way of repairs. Later on, Bríd sought out her statutory rights from the council for a housing transfer to more appropriate accommodation. She pleaded her circumstances in multiple applications, but Council officials refused to transfer her.

The powers of local authorities in Ireland are maintained by the generosity of the public purse. I believe the citizens of Ireland are entitled to know of the potentially serious negative consequences for an ordinary unconnected person in challenging wrongdoing. Integrity and common decency can come with a high personal price. In the wrong hands, power can be a potent and lethal weapon.

Who makes up 'The Council'?

At times there can be confusion about who 'the Council' actually are. The Council is made up of elected Councillors whose function is to vote on policies for the direction of council activities. The executives and officials are public servants who are charged with implementing these policies.

City and County Councillors are elected in local elections every five years. Their function is to represent the interests of the people at official city-level and influence the policies of the council in annual-budget setting. Owing to the party political makeup of Councillors, it is rare for executive powers to be challenged. In practice, this results in many of the powers that were once entrusted with elected persons, is held and exerted by the top executives.

In my experience working inside a local authority, I found that there were three typical categories of Councillors:

Type 1: Those aiming to promote and protect their private / commercial interests

Type 2: Those desiring a public profile, hoping to use this official role as a stepping stone into national politics

Type 3: Those seeking to represent the people who elected them, for the common good

Type 1 Councillors operate in a very smooth, quiet way. Characteristically they ingratiate themselves to the key officials making decisions. They tend to vote with the status quo at council meetings. They express great regard publicly for how 'hard' council officials work and 'doff the cap' to officials in public. They rarely represent any of the 'difficult issues' of the electorate and

9

avoid upsetting council officials. When they do ask for something, it's usually a 'big ask' and it is generally facilitated.

Type 2 Councillors operate and thrive by the media spotlight. They have their eye on the bigger stage, being the proverbial photo-call opportunists. They are very reluctant to ask many challenging questions of officials. They shy away from representing the marginalised and deprived. They are happiest representing the more affluent areas of the city, where something 'small' is required to keep residents happy. Examples include keeping minor environmental work up to date. They use language such as "and working positively with Council executives, I achieved...". Should a crisis arise, they typically won't get tainted with any of the political fall-out, adopting phraseology such as ... "moving forward", or "that is an issue", but never "a problem".

Type 3 Councillors are those who give of their best personal efforts to genuinely represent the people who elected them. They ask the uncomfortable questions. They challenge bad decisions. They enquire about overspends. They will not accept 'waffle' from an official as a reply. They probe and seek evidence. These individuals are intensely disliked by some council officials. They are categorised as 'The Troublesome Ones'.

In practice, officials can play an important and powerful role in projecting how an elected Councillor is perceived by the media.

Under the Local Government Act 2001, the Manager performs executive functions in accordance with a policy framework (for some key areas) established by the elected members. They are written, signed and dated orders termed 'Managers Orders', which formally sign-off executive decisions.

Under the Act, any member of a local authority is entitled on request to be supplied with a copy of any specified Order made by the County/City Manager. A Manager must also keep a register containing a copy of every Order, available for inspection. Orders made by a Deputy Manager, or by a Director of Services, or another employee under a delegation, where the Manager has delegated a responsibility, are subject to the same requirements.

The City Manager has overall responsibility for day-to-day management, including staffing matters.

Background history: Bríd's interactions with Galway Corporation

From documents presented to City Councillors by the City Manager, there is a case history that provides details about Bríd's interactions with Galway Corporation, later to become Galway City Council.

Bríd Cummins first applied to Galway Corporation for Housing accommodation on 6/11/1994.

On 1/2/1995, Bríd was visited at her rented accommodation in Shantalla by the Environmental Health Officer (EHO). At that time, when the council received an application for accommodation, it was then sent on the Western Health Board, where an officer would then visit an applicant at their address. The purpose of the visit was to establish the exact status of the applicant, using a check-list of criteria in line with the legislation, from a public health point of view. This area is governed by the 1966 Housing Act. It was stated on the EHO's report, that Bríd was in receipt of unemployment assistance, which notably also stated she was suffering from manic depression. They recorded that she was 'adequately housed'.

On 15/4/1995, the Social Work department of the Galway Regional Hospital telephoned the housing section of the Corporation, where the Social Worker was advised that there was no suitable accommodation available for Bríd, yet, and that she would have to wait a considerable amount of time for accommodation from the Corporation. Five days later, the Corporation wrote to advise Bríd that she was not being included on the city's Housing List. A month later, she was written to again to confirm the same position.

On 23rd May 1995, Bríd again applied to the Corporation for housing, as she had to leave the rented accommodation in Shantalla, because the owner of the property wanted her room for a relative. At this point, she gives further information about her needs, referring to her being a patient of Professor Tom Fahy at Galway Psychiatric Unit. Here she outlines the fact that she is suffering from depression, and that her general health is degenerating 'due to the stress of moving constantly'.

She stated in her letter:

> I find it hard to share accommodation. At this stage of my life (39) I feel I really need a home. I am just not able to cope anymore with such insecurity. Please let me know if I will be included on the housing list.

The Housing Officer at the time put her name on the housing list, and highlighted her health situation on the letter.

On the 17/11/95 Bríd had a visit from the EHO, who found her living at accommodation in Upper Abbeygate Street. She recommended that Bríd be re-housed on medical and compassionate grounds. The EHO referred this matter onto the Fire Officer, who condemned the building.

On the 1/12/1995, the Fire Officer stated that he was advising the Corporation of the position as an early warning, that Ms. Cummins was likely to be seeking re-housing on an emergency basis.

On 21/12/1995, the Psychiatric Social Worker from the Regional Hospital wrote to the Housing section of Galway Corporation asking that her housing application be given consideration:

> As her present circumstances are particularly difficult, it would greatly benefit Ms. Cummins if she were residing in more permanent accommodation, as she would be able to settle and limit the effect of this additional stress on her depressive condition.

On 7th Oct 1996, while renting privately at Glenard Crescent, Salthill, Galway, Bríd was offered the tenancy of a flat in Rahoon Park. Bríd's GP wrote to the Corporation to say:

> It is a third storey flat and consequently would be unsuitable because of her respiratory problems. She is very disappointed to lose this opportunity and would be grateful to be considered for another more suitable flat soon.

Bríd herself wrote at the same time to the Corporation, clarifying that she was seeking a ground or first floor flat.

On 25/8/1998, Bríd wrote a letter to the Mayor of Galway, Angela Lupton:

> Dear Mayor Lupton,
>
> I would like to plead for your assistance in finding me a home. I have been on the Corporation Housing list for several years and was told I would definitely be housed 2 years ago. Nothing has materialised. Bobby Molloy has written several letters on my behalf, as have my GP and social worker, all to no avail."

Where I am living, is a nice little one-bedroomed flat in a safe, quiet area. But it is very small, has no constant heat and the windows are rotten. The cooker doesn't work properly and it costs a fortune to heat the immersion for the bath.

I've had complex, serious medical problems for years, which have destroyed my life. I am very depressed, suicidal...

A new tenancy: Bríd secures council accommodation

This letter secured a response. On the 2nd September 1998, Bríd was appointed the tenant of 5a Munster Avenue, with the Corporation going some way towards fulfilling their statutory obligation. This house had originally been divided in two parts, one flat upstairs and one flat downstairs, sharing the same front door.

This property was intended for the purposes of providing accommodation mainly for single women for whom Rahoon Park (flats) may not be a viable option. At that time, there was a shortage of newer and more up to date accommodation. Arguably it was a good option in preference to private rented accommodation.

Munster Avenue is located in a quiet area, with easy access to the city and within walking distance to University College Hospital. Most of the houses on that terrace had been bought out by former tenants.

14

This flat would never be a life-long option, as the tenants of 5a or 5b Munster Avenue would not have a right to purchase it. At that time, apartments or flats did not come under the tenant purchase scheme criteria in Galway.

Bríd complains about the upstairs tenant

A year after she moved into the flat, Bríd Cummins wrote to the Corporation in October 1999 seeking a meeting with them "*to discuss.. the tenant of the flat upstairs.*" Bríd asserts that [the woman] was:

> ..Causing me a lot of disruption, with constant noise overhead and harassment. As you know, I am registered disabled with the National Rehabilitation Board and am undertaking an Information Technology course through Distance Learning. I have a lot of work to do and do not need this ongoing conflict.

> (Letter to Galway Corporation, Oct.1999, *Report to Councillors* (2005)).

Bríd claimed that because of the upstairs tenant living there for such a long time, the other tenant feels the house is hers and is very territorial. She claimed that the other tenant causes a racket when she has people to visit. She stated:

> She stomps up and down the stairs, listens at my door, bangs the door at the end of the stairs, and generally behaves in a very anti-social manner. Instead of having friends around to visit now, I go out to visit them as much as I can. It's very disruptive.

> When an official from the health board calls to see me, [she] listens to our conversation and then questions me about my business. There is no sound-proofing so it is possible to hear conversations, if you actually listen, although I always warn people not to speak too loud.

Bríd further complains that the noise is causing her distress, that she finds it difficult to concentrate when working on her computer. She states that her sleep is constantly disturbed because of the same pattern of behaviour, and with items being dropped on the floor over her head.

> I am exhausted from this and have spoken to [her] on several occasions about wearing outdoor shoes with high heels all the time. She denies that she does this, but she makes so much noise when walking back and forth overhead, that it's obvious she's wearing high heels indoors. Some of my visitors have actually thought there was a big man living overhead, the noise is so bad. She is actually a small, light woman. The obvious conclusion is that the noise is deliberate.

She goes on to say, that she believes she has:

> ...No privacy, I'm constantly afraid of what's going to happen next and am under tremendous pressure all the time. I have too much to deal with because of my health, and am in a lot of pain. I need to be able to rest, but cannot get any rest here'.

Bríd stated in the letter that in the year since she moved in to the flat, she has:

> ...Tried everything to be neighbourly, to be considerate, to work out some way that we could pull together, all to no avail.

She feels tormented and hopes that by putting her concerns to paper, and on record, that the Corporation would find a way to find a solution for her.

At this time, the Corporation workmen were carrying out a schedule of remedial works at the property, which had now been going on for over a year. Senator Margaret Cox wrote to the executive with responsibility in Housing, Ciarán Hayes, querying:

> If you have any idea of the due date for completion, I would appreciate it if you could let me know.
>
> Bríd is currently suffering a large amount of disruption from the antics of the upstairs tenant in 5 Munster Avenue. I will call you to discuss the matter next week, and would appreciate it if you could formulate a couple of possible solutions in the interim. (Source: Letter to Galway Corporation by Sen. Margaret Cox, 4/11/99)

Shortly afterwards, Bríd wrote to the Corporation outlining difficulties being suffered by her, accusing the upstairs tenant of engaging in intimidating, unreasonable and anti-social behaviour and again asks for a transfer. This letter is very significant, as it highlights use of the term 'anti-social behaviour' for the very first time in correspondence. It is in the context of Bríd Cummins making the allegation about the upstairs tenant.

On 7th December 1999, Bríd wrote to the local TD, Bobby Molloy, in his capacity as Minister of State for Environment and Local Government, seeking assistance.

> Dear Mr Molloy,
>
> After almost a year in this flat, the situation with the upstairs tenants has become almost intolerable. I have written and spoken to both Michael Owen in disability housing section, and Ciarán Hayes, Housing Officer, about this, but no improvement has taken place. The problem is that Josephine __ who rents the upstairs flat is very noisy and disruptive, particularly at night time. I am constantly kept awake as she drops heavy items on the floor above my head at all hours of the night.

For the past few weeks, I have been unable to continue with my IT course, which I am doing through Distance Learning with the NRB and NTDI. The stress has caused deterioration in my health to such an extent, that I am unable to function to my full capacity, even taking into account my disabilities. My neck, shoulder and right arm have been very painful and I have been in negotiation with the NRB and NTDI to get a proper work station which will be ergonomically safe, as all the equipment is on my kitchen table since I started the course last March.

But the exhaustion from the constant harassment and intimidation from [the tenant upstairs] has meant that I am now more disabled than ever and having my hip injected to keep myself mobile. It is very difficult to get any rest here, which I really need in order to continue with the course and have a decent quality of life. Talking to Ms [named], makes her worse, as she thinks she owns this house and that I am like an interloper.

Now, friends won't come here so much because she makes such a fuss, there's no comfort. I have to visit them. Also, of course, if I need to get some rest, I have to go elsewhere. This does not feel like a home at all, after all the time it took and all the distress I suffered, in order to get the work done. A purpose built unit to myself would suit me better, naturally if such a thing was available, preferably not too far out of town. I need a place that will suit my living and vocational needs. I miss Salthill and would love to get back out there, where I have so many friends and a sense of belonging and community. There is so much hostility here that I don't feel safe.

I was awarded a place at the GMIT to do a part time diploma in Art and Design which I had to defer until next year because of doing the IT course and it would mean that I would be in Cluain Mhuire on the Thursday. You may remember that I did a lot of artwork while in Glenard Crescent and I really wanted to develop that. Part of the IT course that I'm getting into now, includes desktop publishing, so there is some design work involved. I have had some of my work framed and had my first sale a couple of weeks ago, so that's a positive thing. However, again because there is a disruption from [the tenant upstairs], I cannot get on with any more painting or design work here.

It is like being tortured, having someone over my head all of the time, and of course sleep deprivation is torture, so I hope you can encourage Ciarán Hayes to do something to resolve the situation. I was loathe to move after all the time it took to get this place done, but now I feel I need a place to myself. I have so much work to do and I really want to get on with my life in peace. If [the tenant upstairs] is as disturbed as I believe she is, then there is no chance of me being able to that with her being above me. She has being living upstairs for a number of years and regards the house as hers, so I don't think anyone would survive living here for long with that kind of unreasonable and anti-social behaviour going on.

I am very unwell and need a lot of rest. If you need any medical evidence, ..my GP and the MO at the Western Board will supply same. This has been a tough year, especially with the death of my mother, but I believe that I have done well considering all the stress and distress I have suffered.

I completed the ECDL part of the course in six months and have achieved very good results and have requested that the NCVA part of the course be accelerated to enable me to finish next July, instead of the following December. Unfortunately, now I am feeling so low and in so much pain, that I am not sure if I will be able to go ahead with that. The workstation will make a difference to me physically, but there is nothing else I can do about the disturbance from the upstairs tenant, and that is a constant source of terrible stress. Having my sleep disturbed so often, sometimes for two or three nights at a time, is wearing me out.

I hope that you can help, as you have been such a great help to me so often. Thanks in advance, and best regards to yourself and Phyllis.

Yours sincerely,

Bríd Cummins

Complaints emerge against Bríd

On the 16th December 1999 Ciarán Hayes spoke with Bríd Cummins by telephone. He wrote a note to her file, recording that:

> I advised her that I had also received complaints against her. I explained that it is essentially a neighbourhood dispute and that it was up to the two women to resolve their differences. I have now spoken to both parties and asked that they both do what they can to address the problem.

On the 5th January 2000, Bobby Molloy TD wrote to the Acting Assistant Town Clerk:

> Dear Mr O'Neill, I enclose copy of a letter which I have received from Ms Bríd Cummins, 5a Munster Avenue, regarding her accommodation. I would appreciate if you could examine the matters raised by Ms Cummins in her letter and let me know if Galway Corporation can be of any assistance to her. I note from her correspondence that she would like to be considered for a transfer of accommodation and mentioned that she would like to move to the Salthill area if a suitable dwelling becomes available there. I would be grateful if you could let me know whether she would be considered for a transfer. I look forward to hearing from you..

On the 17/1/2000, the City Council replied to Minister Molloy, acknowledging receipt of his letter, advising:

The matter contained therein is being examined and I will revert to you in due course.

On 14/3/2000, a letter issued from the Council in follow up to Minister Molloy:

I am to inform you that I have spoken to both parties in the matter, and requested that they refrain from causing disturbance to each other. It is essentially a neighbourhood dispute, with both parties making allegations against the other.

With regard to the request for a transfer, I am to inform you that the Corporation does not have accommodation available in Salthill, furthermore, transfers are primarily granted on overcrowding or medical grounds.

Minister Molloy wrote back to the Council officials again regarding Bríd's wish to obtain a transfer of accommodation to transfer to Rahoon. (Rahoon and Salthill are adjoining districts in Galway City.) All of this time, Bríd maintains active written communications with City Hall, and numerous medical and political representations are made on her behalf.

On the 22/8/2000, Ciarán Hayes had a meeting in City Hall between the disputing tenants of 5 Munster Avenue. It is stated in his written notes afterwards that:

Following a full and frank exchange, the following was agreed:

1. Both parties had their differences

2. Both also had common interests such as music and art

3. Both were still seeking a transfer and notwithstanding the above, both would attempt to draw a line under past events and move forward.

In this regard they undertook to address issues that were causing annoyance and disturbances to each other.

On 23/6/2000, Minister Molloy wrote to Joe O'Neill seeking progression. He is not having much joy with a response.

On 27/9/2000, Minister Molloy wrote this time to Ciarán Hayes, who is now promoted to the position of Acting Asst Town Clerk. The Minister again enquires about Bríd's application for a housing transfer. A response issues:

> Ms Cummins is on our transfer list and will be considered for a transfer along with other applicants as suitable accommodation becomes available.

On 26/10/2000, the Council wrote to Bríd Cummins on foot of an enormous level of representation. They advise:

> Your request for a transfer will be dealt with along with all other transfer requests as soon as suitable accommodation becomes available.

This is very significant as Bríd is now deemed to be on the Transfer list for consideration for re-housing. Hopes must have been raised highly with Bríd at this stage, as the Minister with responsibility for housing can confirm to her that she is on the transfer list. It is now a matter of *when*; rather than *if* this will happen.

During November 2000, records show that Bríd made telephone calls to the Council regarding dampness and mould in the flat at 5a Munster Avenue. She reiterates dissatisfaction with the upstairs tenant. As the Tenant Liaison Officer for the functional area, I was tasked with visiting her flat. I established that there was visible proof to show that a section of wall (where an external door had been removed) was previously left un-plastered by the Council workmen. I reported this. Bríd also stated that she believed that there was a water leakage somewhere upstairs (in the other flat). This was inspected by the Council plumber, who found this was not so, but commented that if the outside wall was plastered, it would eliminate the problem.

Around this time, Bríd identified two terraced council properties locally that were vacant, but unfortunately it was apparent that neither would be suitable for her disability needs as they both had stairs.

During November, Bríd lodged numerous further complaints about the upstairs tenant and the effects it was having on her health.

A succession of letters and telephone calls from various representatives ensued over the following months. I was the receiver of some of those and I met with her on several occasions. She expressed deep dissatisfaction with the Council's Clerk of Works. For example, there is one instance noted to file on the 15th November 2000 where after contacting the Clerk of Works regarding the outstanding maintenance problems, he assured that "*the repairs at her flat will be done tomorrow morning*". These did not happen.

On 3rd April 2001, a legal firm Claffey & Daly Solicitors wrote to the City Council on behalf of Bríd Cummins requesting them to sort out the defects in the property:

> ..and despite many many attendances by the Corporation workmen, they have failed to make it properly and safely habitable.

This culminated in a formal letter being sent to Bobby Molloy, Minister for Housing and Urban Renewal at the Department of Environment and Local Government on the 18th April 2001, from Ciarán Hayes (Acting Asst Town Clerk) updating the position as follows:

I am to inform you that Ms Cummin's application for a transfer is being considered along with all other applications.

However, I am presently of the view that she is adequately housed. The issues raised regarding the alleged poor condition of the flat are being examined at present and I will revert to you in the matter in due course.

This is very strange communication. Mr Hayes previously advised the Minister that Bríd was on the Transfer List, but her status has now changed, seemingly on his executive discretion. His 'view' overrides any other factor.

Over this time, I as Tenant Liaison Officer recorded several complaints from Bríd regarding her dissatisfaction with her accommodation, with the way maintenance works were not being completed, which would all be part and parcel of my day's work. Minister Bobby Molloy TD made many written pleas for a transfer for Bríd, citing medical problems; however, he was not able to supersede the executive powers wielded by senior local authority officials.

On 5 September 2001, Bríd Cummins wrote to the new City Manager John Tierney, a fellow Co Tipperary native of Bríd's:

Dear Mr Tierney, I wish to draw your attention to my plight and ask you to intervene in my case.

Since 1998, I have been pleading with Galway Corporation, Maintenance Dept., and [The Clerk of Works] in particular, to clear the rubbish and rubble out of the rear garden of number 5 Munster Avenue, where I live in the ground floor flat, flatA.

There has been little progress made and it seems that there are no staff available to do the job. When the foreman ... was here on Monday last, he

24

told me no one seems to be making any decision about the garden or what is being done to clear it and make it viable for use as a garden. I cannot even walk out of my back door or hang clothes on the line. In recent weeks, there was an infestation of rats and the Walsh family next door at number 6 Munster Avenue were very concerned.

I contacted the environmental health inspector from the Western Health Board, who has sent a report to Galway Corporation. Mr [Foreman] called to see Mr and Mrs Walsh and said the garden would be cleared for once and for all, the manhole sealed. The manhole has been sealed, a bit of the garden has been dug, and that's all. Those weeds will take over again if they are not taken out. The soil, for the most part, is contaminated with domestic refuse and cannot sustain normal plant life. I have a letter from a professional gardener, whom I paid myself, to spray the weeds and dig part of the garden over the past two summers. It clearly states that the soil is not fit to be planted until the rubbish is cleared out.

The garden is a disgrace. It is a health hazard. It is dangerous. At present, it looks like a ploughed field. Someone needs to make a decision about this matter, whether to rake and bag the rubbish, put down slabs over the landfill, or take down part of the wall at the back and bring in a machine to clear out all the dirt to make the garden usable and safe.

I have serious injuries to my spine and neck and have been warned by my doctor, not to attempt to do the garden myself, as the last time I did that, I was unable to move for two days afterwards and needed extensive treatment which is of course very costly. My disabilities mean that I am very confined at times and my mobility is obviously very important to me. Dealing with Galway Corporation has proved so stressful for me that it has seriously affected my health and caused me serious financial distress.

The accommodation is unsuitable for my needs and I have supplied letters from my GP and from the MO of the Western Health Board, stating same in their expert medical opinion, Mr Ciarán Hayes has chosen to ignore the urgency of this matter. Mr Hayes persists in maintaining that I am adequately housed, despite the fact that he has never been inside my door, even though I have asked him to come here and see for himself how difficult things are for me. He forgets that he is a Public Servant, paid out of the Public Purse and needs to take a good look at how he does his job. He was the Housing Officer while I was being allocated the flat and knew that it was in a dreadful condition. He has known about the garden all along and still he does nothing to help me. I applied for a transfer to somewhere more suitable for my needs, a purpose-built unit, but Mr Hayes has refused to take the matter seriously. He is knowingly putting me at risk.

It seems to me that there is a culture of corruption, deceit, discrimination, and lack of humanity at work in Galway Corporation. I have been neglected because I am an outsider, because I am alone, because I am disabled and because I am poor. Therefore, it seems I am viewed as someone who does not matter, has no power, is not related to anyone important in Galway and am not a member of the Fianna Fáil party.

I would appreciate your intervention in my case as I am getting worn out from banging my head against the wall trying to get through to the engineer, who has not been inside my door either, despite my asking him to come as see for himself how bad things are in this flat. The work that I am asking Galway Corporation to do now, is what they should have done in 1998, when they spent months in 5 Munster Avenue. They completely renovated and decorated the flat upstairs, FlatB, which has been occupied by [the tenant upstairs] for about 13 years. She was given priority even though they were there to make my place habitable. It was in absolutely dreadful condition, but I was reassured by Mr [Foreman] that Galway Corporation would do all the work necessary to clean, decorate and turn it into a self-contained unit for me. I am still waiting for the work to be finished, and have been through hell from old leaks which Mr [Foreman] would have known about, but which were not repaired, and endless problems with electricity, again all things that needed to be seen to years before I came on the scene.

My first 8 weeks in this flat, the bathroom floor and back hallway were flooded because the pipes under the bath were rotten and had been for years. I had no telephone at the time and used to go across the road to the hackney office to telephone Galway Corporation. I usually spoke to Mr Tom [named]. He would sympathise and promise to send someone down straight away. I was foolish enough to believe him and would come back to the flat and wait. For 8 weeks, no one came. Then when I had had enough, and had started telephoning the Mayor, Minister Molloy, Senator Cox and anyone else I could think of, the men finally came from Galway Corporation to fix the leak.

I should not have to call on politicians or indeed go to the newspapers in order to get Galway Corporation to do the job it is supposed to do, that it is paid out of public money to do so. Is there anyone actually in charge, or capable of making a decision?

I would very much appreciate your intervention in my case before my condition deteriorates further and I am in a wheelchair or worse.

Yours sincerely,

Bríd Cummins

The procedure at that time for housing repairs was that when tenants telephoned the Council with housing maintenance requests, they would be put through to Housing, who would note the request and pass it on to the foreman for attention.

27

The foreman was the head of a maintenance crew, who worked outdoors. When I would meet him out on the ground, he often told me that he just didn't know what some of the lads were doing on the day to day and he spent a lot of time chasing them. He reported upwards to the Housing Engineer, who in turn reported directly to the Director of Services in Housing, Ciarán Hayes. In my experience, and from what I witnessed happening, there was often discrepancy between the paperwork completed and the specific performance of tasks.

In a report by an engineer of the Council, it is outlined how work men went out to Bríd Cummins address, but failed to get a reply.

> Our workmen could not access the building on 9/1/03 as the night latch was on the upper door lock. They tried knocking on the front door but did not get any reply. They sat outside from 8.15 until 11.30 am. At this stage they left for another job as there was no point wasting any more time.

Delegation of Executive Powers

On the 7th September 2001, the City Manager John Tierney forwarded Bríd's detailed letter down the management line to Ciarán Hayes, Director of Services, with a cover note 'Please discuss, by return' and he also copied the communication to Billy Dunne (Senior Engineer). Bríd had written to the highest executive level in Galway City Council in the form of the manager Mr Tierney, who sent it back down the line to Ciarán Hayes.

Mr Hayes had in the meanwhile been promoted to the new position of Director of Services for Housing, Economic Development and Planning in Galway City Council. These 'Directorships' within local authorities across Ireland were new upgraded positions created under a new national programme structure known as 'Better Local Government' (BLG). This initiative created many new positions at management and middle management levels.

It is well recognised throughout the system that very many council employees up and down the country moved into upgraded posts owing to 'years of service', as distinct from ability, qualifications, knowledge or experience. In his new position, the former housing officer Mr Hayes became responsible for all housing matters and staff in that department. The post also carried responsibility for oversight of the engineers and maintenance crew in that section.

After receiving Bríd Cummins's letter, Mr Hayes directed the council engineers to compile a report for him, calculating how much money had been spent to-date on the property at 5 Munster Avenue. Calculations submitted showed that almost €15,000 had been spent on the property between the years 1998-1999. This cumulative costing illustrated gross amounts for labour and material costs, but was short on work-detail specifics.

On 1/11/2001 Ciarán Hayes wrote back to Mr Tierney advising of the 'monies spent' on 5 Munster Avenue, and further confirms that his intention is now to *not* transfer Bríd Cummins.

> At this point, I am advised that all works required of Galway Corporation have been attended to. I am also of the opinion that the accommodation is suitable for Ms Cummin's needs and I am therefore not in a position to accede to her request for a transfer.

Unknown to herself, Bríd had committed the ultimate sin in the temple of local authority power – she challenged their authority. She had claimed to Council management that the workmen were not doing the housing maintenance jobs, where conversely the council were in a position to show figures of a financial spend.

I have firsthand experience of seeing how Council foremen and Clerks of Works could be very influential in the success or otherwise of transfers for tenants. One particular foreman for example, was well known for promising work to be done, sometimes for up to three people in three different locations at the same time on the next day. His standard response was: '*No hassle, I'll be there myself at 11o'clock tomorrow*'. His operations were well known by outdoor staff, for the impossibility of following through on tri-location. In fairness to him, he went overboard trying to appease the administrative staff in City Hall and caused himself enormous stress in his attempts.

Many of the engineers who came to work in the housing section could be quite inexperienced initially in the technical aspects of housing maintenance and construction. Oftentimes they would be dependent on the knowledge and experience of the foremen who they were meant to be supervising. Maintaining the cooperation of the maintenance crew could be challenging for various reasons. There was a wisecrack around relating to one worker when he returned from a period of considerable sick leave. He enquired of the foreman "*Did you miss me while I was gone*", to which the reply came; "*I did, but not as much as when you're supposed to be here*".

It is clear from the correspondence that Bríd is no longer being considered for a housing transfer, despite the Minister for Housing continuing to advocate for her.

On 6/11/01, Bríd wrote to the City Manager again, who again delegates to the Director of Services, who reports back that he believes the work is being done. She appeals:

The back garden has been left unfinished for the past 7 weeks. They dug a trench outside my back door and were supposed to come back the following morning so that I could walk out the back door and reach the garden and the clothes line.

This situation I remember well, because when the workmen had seemingly been called to another job, they had left the spades and tools stuck in the ground.

Bríd reports that the storage area has been left unfinished and is unusable, damp and cold. She said that when she spoke with Peter Sammon (Housing Officer) the previous week, "*he assured me that Galway Corporation never leaves a job unfinished*". She appeals for the flat to be made suitable:

..To feel at home in, otherwise I need alternative accommodation. This situation needs urgent attention and I am confident that you won't let me down.

This dialogue continues on for some further months and Minister Molloy pleads repeatedly for action on improving her accommodation needs. Even though he is a government minister, with responsibility in this area, he is unable to order or elicit the action being sought.

While Bríd is engaging directly with the City Council, beseeching repairs to be done to make the place more habitable, she again pleads for a transfer to more suitable accommodation, She is being distressed by the lack of actual repairs and is getting even more frustrated. Since she moved in to 5 Munster Avenue in 1998, she had been asking for the back garden to be cleared of refuse. Over three years later, this is still ongoing.

It would later emerge, that a more comprehensive second file was maintained covertly at a senior executive level in the City Council's housing section. Her attendance with a consultant psychiatrist should have merited her an automatic housing transfer based on medical and compassionate grounds, notwithstanding additional discretion for a positive consideration under the heading of 'exceptional circumstances'.

I believe that Bríd Cummins was terribly wronged.

Commissioning of an Independent Report

Various agencies advocated for Bríd to get a transfer of accommodation but the Council management insisted that she was 'adequately housed'. It appears from the records published in the Council's *Report to Councillors* that bizarre actions were coming into play.

From the time Bríd went into the flat, she highlighted the deplorable state of the back garden, due to rubbish and filth left there since the last tenant. As the tenant liaison officer for that area, I lobbied one of the foremen to clear the garden as promised. He said they would get in a mini-digger and clear it all out, to start again with a fresh garden. They discussed with Bríd how they would put down paving stones in one area for easy maintenance, and keep another area for grass and a few shrubs. Unfortunately it never happened.

Council records show a 27/01/01 standard form (written report) from a Council Environmental warden, giving Bríd's name as the 'The Alleged Offender' for the garden stating:

> Has been on to Housing on various occasions. Has let back garden and around the house go. Builders rubble, overgrown grass, general rubbish

32

gathering around house, has been warned to clean up, willing you meet you Annette [Warden] and see what can be done. Attracting rats.

I believe this was a misrepresentation of the facts against Bríd. After seeing that incorrect report, anybody similarly falsely accused would arguably be incensed for being unfairly associated with its deplorable state. In addition to the mixture of plastics, ash, old carpet and rubbish not being cleared away, Bríd was now being recorded as the 'alleged offender'. The situation was getting more ridiculous, yet the solution was very simple. It was the Council's responsibility to remove the rubbish before the change of tenancy. The back garden was surrounded by a high hedge, and over the years had become a dumping ground. Despite the simple solution, the effort got very protracted, with a lot of paper circulating for low-level issues.

At this point, Bríd was getting on well with her next door neighbours the Walsh Family, as they shared a common standard in tidiness and cleanliness and pride in their community surroundings. Bríd was the first person in a very long time to show initiative in improving the environs of number 5.

Bríd was not the only council tenant dissatisfied with the lack of repairs and maintenance. As a former public servant, she was aware of her entitlement, as well as the responsibilities of the local authority for service delivery.

Bríd initiates legal action against the Council for lack of repairs

In frustration, Bríd Cummins commissioned an independent chartered consultant engineer to carry out an independent inspection of her rented Council property on 4th February 2003. His report to her itemised a detailed list of identified problems and advised her in summary that:

> You are rightly concerned that the City Council are only painting the upper apartment at present and not actually doing anything to rectify the problem. If they complete the painting and let a new tenant in, then an ideal opportunity to repair may have been lost.
>
> OPINION: I am of the opinion that you are living in substandard and potentially very dangerous (electrically) housing conditions.

The Independent Engineer also recommended to Bríd in his report to request her solicitors to:

> Initiate urgent action with a view to compelling City Council to undertake the necessary repairs or to provide you with alternative accommodation. It is my opinion that the Housing Authority are in breach of the regulations...your Solicitor would have more knowledge than I with respect to the relevant legislation.

This independent report was challenged and contradicted by the City Council's own Housing Engineer, who disagreed with the report. He concluded in a written record addressed to Ciarán Hayes describing it as making *'a series of unsubstantiated claims'*.

> Our electrician checked the light socket that was causing the tenant concern on 4th April 2002.

34

These were directly opposing findings. After considering the advices in the independent engineer's report, Bríd's solicitor was instructed to initiate a 'Civil Equity Bill' against the Council. In April 2003, her new solicitor Jarlath McInerney lodged a formal action in Galway Circuit Court to force the Council to 'perform the statutory duties' she claimed they were failing to do. The Civil Equity Bill described the various failings in her property (cold, damp, leaking water, fears of the electrical system) and requests a full remedying of the property, *or* a transfer to suitable accommodation.

The particulars of her Civil Equity Bill stated:

> The Plaintiff has gone to numerous Politicians and has resorted to a number of solicitors in an attempt to resolve the problems created by the Defendants. While some works have been carried out, no proper action has been taken to address the underlying problem of the accommodation. The Plaintiff has been under severe stress as a result of all of the aggravation surrounding her attempts to secure better accommodation or to improve her existing accommodation.

> As a result of the aforesaid breach of duty, breach of statutory duty, negligence, nuisance, breach of contract and Tenancy agreement the Plaintiff has suffered exacerbation of a previous medical condition, anxiety, psychological injury, stress and special damages.

It is claimed in her submission, that she is 'extremely frustrated and has a very low mood as a result of the problems surrounding her accommodation. She has become depressed and it has been very difficult for her to maintain a proper psychological balance in the circumstances'. Her doctor stated that he has had to increase her medication at times, despite his preference that less medication should be taken.

The Council are requested to enter an appearance (reply) within ten days and in addition:

> ..If you intend to defend the proceedings on any grounds, you must not only enter an Appearance as aforesaid, but also within ten days...deliver a statement in writing showing the nature and grounds of your defence.

On 27th June Bríd's solicitors consented to the late filing of the defence and this delay continued on for nine months until 15th March 2004, when the Council solicitors Blake & Kenny wrote to the Plaintiff solicitors submitting their defence (providing a blanket denial of everything) and seeking notice for particulars (questions and answers).

Meanwhile, during this nine month delay, 'complaints' between the neighbours at 5-6 Munster Avenue continued to be logged by the Council. During this time, when the Council had not yet submitted a defence, they went about assembling a parallel action against her, on the basis of her declining to attend a meeting at City Hall to answer questions of alleged anti-social behaviour, where her neighbour had complained to the Council about her.

In March of that year I was called to a meeting with Ciarán Hayes, Director of Services in Housing, Peter Sammon (Housing Officer) and John Carr, Solicitor with Blake and Kenny. Ciarán Hayes led the meeting and announced his intention of moving to evict Bríd Cummins. The purpose of the meeting was to consult with John Carr, Solicitor, in relation to how the Council intended to deal with this tenant. Ciarán Hayes announced that he had decided to evict her. Peter Sammon appeared disinterested. I spoke up; to ask what grounds the Council had to move in this way, as there was no evidence at all against the tenant to substantiate an action of eviction.

At this point, Ciarán Hayes went distinctly quiet and looked to the solicitor to answer me. John Carr advised that they were considering as to whether they would use the 1966 or the 1997 legislation. (These legal avenues did not require prima facie evidence.) A heated debate then ensued, when I queried the wrongness of doing this, particularly pointing out that regarding the 1997 Act; in social housing and poverty circles, this legislation had been heavily criticised by housing professionals and agents with social consciences. Housing practitioners and legal experts in this area were expressing concerns about the unsafeness of this law after the legislation came into force in 1997.

The three men looked at me disparagingly; in silence. I expressed my deep reservations about proceeding with this course of action (which I recounted in full detail in the High Court in my action against Galway City Council in 2010). During this meeting at City Hall, I was a lone voice and was dismissed from the meeting at that point. The three men continued with their meeting.

I discovered in a memo later, that John Carr had advised the Council against using me to give evidence, as he deemed me to be 'argumentative, belligerent and not of much assistance' in this eviction process. I have never subscribed to the theory that 'might is always right', whereas I found the mindset of many public servants at Galway City Council was hardwired into believing that higher ranks are always right. John Carr was working without full knowledge of the tenant's situation.

Nora Walsh of 6 Munster Avenue instructed a solicitor of her own to represent her complaints against her neighbour; however she was not satisfied with the lack of progress being made in having Bríd

Cummins transferred. She telephoned the City Council and sought a meeting with Ciarán Hayes, requesting that I should also be in attendance as the Tenant Liaison Officer for the area.

In the meeting Nora asked Ciarán Hayes what he knew about this tenant. This was a question I had also asked of him many times previously. On different occasions in the past I asked Ciarán if there was supplementary information on Ms Cummins, and he assured me that I had all the information that was available. However, Nora's question now got a different response. He pointed towards an extensive file on his desk. This was first time I became aware of the existence of such a second file being maintained on Bríd Cummins. I realised that Ms. Cummins's history was being kept from me. It confirmed to me that Ciarán Hayes was denying me information on the tenant and I wondered what this was about. At that meeting, Nora pleaded with Ciarán Hayes to transfer Bríd Cummins. She cited many reasons. His response was:

> "No. Even if I bought this woman an apartment in Salthill, she still wouldn't be satisfied."

I did think at the time it was a strange remark. I was taken aback through the rest of that meeting on seeing the existence of the second file. The file available to me as Tenant Liaison Officer was much smaller. I do not know all of what was in that substantial file, because the first time I would physically handle it - was to be in the High Court in 2010 when it was presented to me under cross examination. This second file was covertly hidden from key personnel. I would have been able to advise at that time had I known the details that I was to later learn in the High Court, that Bríd having been a patient of Professor Tom Fahy, Consultant Psychiatrist would have met the Council's criteria for a transfer.

Ciarán Hayes proceeded to advise Nora Walsh that in order to 'deal with Bríd Cummins', he needed written evidence and suggested that Nora go to the Guards and make a formal complaint, and that I was to liaise with her on this matter as the tenant liaison officer. After the meeting, Ciarán asked me to drop Nora home. During this trip Nora told me that when she had asked for me to be present on her arrival for the meeting that day, Ciarán told her that I 'wasn't in the building'. I found this odd at the time, as we had spoken on the corridor a few minutes prior to her arrival.

The Council's minutes of that meeting, published in the *Report to Councillors* show that Ciarán Hayes told Nora that he was offering the legal services of the Council's solicitors, Blake and Kenny to her, if she wished to pursue an injunction option against Bríd Cummins. (Bríd was not offered a similar service, although she was a tenant and making parallel complaints against the Walshs.)

I contacted Nora again the next day and she confirmed to me that she did not want to involve the Guards. She wanted the Council to do their job and transfer Bríd somewhere else. Mr Paddy Walsh met with the City Manager John Tierney and Ciarán Hayes to progress this and the legal services of Blake & Kenny were offered to the private citizen neighbours once again. After this meeting, I was instructed to accompany Mr Walsh to the solicitor.

In August 2003, Bríd Cummins wrote a letter to the Senior Social Worker, Gerard Flanagan, at Galway City Council. In the records she thanks him for his recent letter (copy of this letter missing from *Report to Councillors* file). I believe the matter she was referring to, was her allegation of sexual abuse perpetrated against her by a Council workman. As the Council senior social worker, Mr Flanagan was in a powerful position. She tells him:

> My solicitor has served notice of a civil action ... regarding the refusal of the council to deal with the persistent water leaks in my flat. It is therefore, and has been a very stressful time for me. Perhaps you can help me in your capacity as Senior Social Worker, or are you prevented from helping a tenant who is suing your employer?
>
> ... I feel I have no financial security as well as no security at home, which is very stressful for me.

She requests the maintenance crew to come before the winter, if she is being refused more suitable accommodation, particularly highlighting the need for a new soot box to be installed over the stove in the living room.

> The chimney cleaner has to go up on the roof and then remove the pipe from the stove to clean it each time. He has recently been here twice and has repeated his assertion that Galway City Council need to install a soot box over the stove which would make more sense. His details and receipt for the 40 Euros I paid him are attached.

She also outlines how she has paid out €160 for the garden to be cleaned up, front and back.

> Could you please let me know if Galway City Council will help in maintaining their own property, as it is too much for me alone to afford and is causing friction with my neighbours, who bully me and harass me because of it even though they know my circumstances... if possible I would appreciate it if you could call to the flat to see it for yourself.

There is no reply to this letter according to the *Report to Councillors*.

Allegation of Sexual Abuse against Bríd Cummins

"The greater the power, the more dangerous the abuse"

Edmund Burke (1729–1797)

It is recorded that on 20th February 2003 Bríd Cummins made a statement to a Garda from Mill Street Garda station. She outlined to him how the now-vacant flat overhead at 5 Munster Avenue was being refurbished by Council workmen. She went up to the men and requested them not to make so much noise. She alleges that she was sexually assaulted by one of them. She told the Garda that she did not want to make an official complaint, but requested that the foreman be contacted so that this would not happen again.

My role as Tenant Liaison Officer involved working outside of the office for a large proportion of the day. During the summer of 2003, I was approached in town by a man from the Munster Avenue area. He asked for 'a quiet word' with me. He said that he knew he could confide in me and that I might be able to do something about a particular situation. He told me that he was disgusted with the way that Bríd Cummins was being treated by the Council.

He told me that he heard that Bríd Cummins had been sexually abused by one of the maintenance team working in her council-rented property. He presumed I had heard about it from working at City Hall and he knew it was being 'investigated' by the Council. I was shocked to say the least. He told me that "it was worse than that", because Bríd was being 'set-up' to make a fool of herself, as one of the lads had given her the wrong name of the perpetrator. He was upset in telling me the wrongly accused man's name being cited was a man called Michael. This young man said he was horrified for the 'poor tenant' and for Michael, as the co-workers in the maintenance section were entertaining themselves by his mistaken identification.

I queried why they would do this. He said "They are jealous of him; he is living out the country in a very nice house. He has a farm of land, and is single with plenty of money". He said the team were envious of him and his comfortable lifestyle, and perversely this was making the accusation seem more hilarious to them. I asked him if he knew who carried out the misdeed. He affirmed that he believed he did.

I gathered my thoughts after this shock and wondered could this account be true? I figured out where Michael would be working at the time and went to find him to speak with him. When I drove up, he saw me and left down his tools. I approached him and offered him a handshake. He broke down crying immediately. He said "Thanks Julie for coming to me". He asked if I'd heard that he was "in awful trouble" and that he was being accused in the wrong. I asked him what was he being accused of? He said "I've been accused of sexually assaulting Bríd Cummins, I'm now labelled as a pervert" and he continued crying. He was visibly shaken and traumatised. He told me he felt like "getting sick all the time" as he was "so ashamed". He said "it is more than that, but I can't tell you the rest".

He said that I was lucky when I went home from work that I had a husband and family; "I go home to an empty house". He said that he had family living nearby and they were very good to him, but he would be ashamed to tell them about this awful accusation. He was blubbering saying that on the one hand it was so unbelievable, but that he didn't know what to do. I suggested to him that he should see his GP, which he promised he would do on this way home from work.

I was perplexed as to why I was being left 'out of the loop' on this serious matter by my colleagues in Housing. When I returned to City Hall, I sought out Ciarán Hayes, Director of Services. I knocked on his door and asked if I could have a word with him. He gestured to come in. He enquired what this was in relation to. I said I understand that Bríd Cummins has made a complaint about a sexual offence against her. He said "I can't comment to you on that". He said that "The matter is being dealt with at the highest level here by the Senior Social Worker". He added; "Gerry Flanagan is looking after this and it would be inappropriate for me to have any discussion with you."

I replied "I hope he is getting the full facts, as I have been approached by a private citizen in this regard". He reiterated in a dismissive tone that it would be inappropriate for him to have any discussion with me. I walked away feeling a sense of overwhelming shock and incredulity that he didn't want to know what I had heard, particularly as he knew full well of my excellent rapport with the community.

I was highly concerned about why such a serious allegation was being delegated to a relatively new member of staff, who might not yet know the people involved. I wasn't contacted by the social worker Gerry Flanagan as part of his 'investigation' at any time. Best practise would ordinarily dictate that all of the Council employees working (in any shape or form) in any such case, would be questioned and statements would be taken.

After Bríd Cummins subsequently died, I was contacted by Michael. (I no longer worked for the Council at this time.) He was very upset that Bríd Cummins was so mentally unwell and nobody had told him. He remembered the details of her complaint about the incident very well and described in detail the facts around it.

Michael recounted that in actual fact, he was not working at all on the day of the incident. This was in part why the team found it so funny. They told him he did not have any choice but to go along with what they were saying. Michael told me that the scope of the 'investigations' by the Council and the Gardaí was merely to see did Michael carry out this deed; it did not enquire as to whether the offence took place. The torture of being falsely accused rested very heavily on Michael for a long time afterwards. The Gardaí eventually contacted Michael and confirmed to him that they were satisfied that he did not do what was alleged by Bríd Cummins.

Michael remains very upset to this day, as he believed that this was possibly one of the incident's that contributed to the woman's despair. He understood the significance of her being characterised as an unreliable person. Later when he discovered that the woman had been suffering from mental illness, he was extremely upset and directly questioned a senior housing official as to why he would treat a vulnerable woman the way he did. The executive denied all knowledge of her medical condition.

Although Michael had been named in the wrong, he said that he had fully forgiven her as he understood how this had come about. He said that when you don't know people well, it's easy to make a mistake. He firmly believes that this criminal act had taken place.

Unfortunately what was achieved was to further discredit Bríd by this flawed investigation, as there was information and misinformation surrounding this situation in the public domain. Memos of meetings between council officials and her neighbours confirm this.

In the records provided to Councillors in January 2005, notes of a telephone conversation between Ciarán Hayes and Nora Walsh are saved to file by Ciarán Hayes on 12/6/03. Historical incidents with Bríd Cummins (next door neighbour at 5a Munster Avenue) were noted. In addition to a new record of an alleged incident the previous week involving a door being swung at her, Ciarán Hayes also records that Nora Walsh advised him that Bríd Cummins told her that 'four council workers abused her'.

This same issue arose again on 18/2/2004, at a meeting held in City Hall between Paddy Walsh and his solicitor, in attendance with Galway City Council officials Frances Mullarkey (Senior Executive Officer) and Patricia Philbin. Amongst other issues at that meeting, the minutes show that Paddy Walsh stated that '*Ms Cummins has falsely accused five men of sexual assault, one of which is now in Ballinasloe following a breakdown*'.

Mr Walsh's solicitor asked "*if the whole matter in relation to complaints against GCC worker had been finished*". Frances Mullarkey explained that it was 'a separate issue' and was 'not willing to comment' on same.

It is regrettable that misinformation in this matter was circulated. The record could have been put straight, to avoid unnecessary fabrication and rumours.

Previous tenants of Bríd's Flat

The divided house at 5 Munster had a series of council tenants before Bríd Cummin's tenancy. I knew of two of them as I had collected their rent in my previous role. They are both since deceased, but were fortunate to be transferred by the council. I remember one elderly lady named 'Mary' very well. When she was transferred to a new apartment, Mrs Walsh next door had advocated on her behalf, as she believed this woman was no longer able to manage an open fire and needed a more modern, warm place to live.

Owing to her particular psychosis, this unfortunate woman would not sleep in the bedroom in her lovely new apartment. No level of reassurance could convince her otherwise. Instead she used to sleep in an armchair in her sitting room. Her former neighbour was very concerned that she would fall out of the chair, so gifted her a sofa to match the armchair she had already given her. Mrs Walsh kept a watchful eye, travelling up the town to visit her, until Mary passed away.

A subsequent tenant appointed to 5a Munster Avenue had a child living with her in the flat. Again recognising this was not an ideal arrangement for a woman with a child, her neighbour Mrs Walsh sought assistance from the then Corporation for this tenant to be transferred to a new house, which she was. I remember that younger woman telling me of the great surprise she got one Christmas Eve when her neighbour Mrs Walsh gave a generous present to the child.

Recognising that Bríd Cummins had mental health issues, the Walsh family wanted her transferred by the council. When Nora Walsh advocated for this and was granted a meeting with the Director for Housing in May 2003, the purpose of her meeting was to outline the difficult situation that had ensued next door.

Upstairs neighbour of Bríd Cummins: Josephine

I remember it was a fine summer's day in 2004 when I bumped into Josephine while shopping in Galway Shopping Centre. She was the former upstairs tenant at 5B Munster Avenue. She became very emotional when she met me and asked if we could sit down somewhere for a quiet word. She did not want to be seen speaking to me by any council official. I remember telling her it was early in the morning and that it was unlikely that any of them would be around the town shopping yet.

She told me that she was terrified to be seen speaking to me, as she recently had an unsolicited visit to her home from Frances Mullarkey of Galway City Council, demanding that Josephine make a statement for the Council in relation to Bríd Cummins, because they wanted to use it in court in order to evict her.

Josephine was shaking telling me this, stating that Frances told her that she was never to talk to me, adding that I was "bad news" and that the council "had to get rid'" of me. She claimed that Ms Mullarkey told her that she was unable to work with me, that I was "too soft" with tenants, and "not to be trusted". Josephine reassured me that she knew this to be untrue.

This 'bad mouthing' from my former line manager did not come as a total shock to me, as I had heard a similar story from another tenant some time previously. It upset me that falsehoods were being put about in relation to my previous employment, but there was not a lot I could do about it.

Josephine and I knew each other long before I came to work at City Hall. She reminded me of the times I collected her rent and laughed nervously reminding me that 'soft didn't come into the equation there'. She reminisced on her earlier life, recounting details of her early married days. She loved re-telling about the times when she had her first child, and of how young she looked back then. Once when she was on a visit to her home town in Co. Mayo, an elderly neighbour saw her carrying a baby, with a man in Garda uniform walking behind her. The woman queried Josephine's mother, on whether she "was minding a baby for somebody"? She figured that she must be, when there was a Garda in tow with her. The mother explained that the baby was Josephine's own, and the handsome Garda was her husband.

Josephine enjoyed that she kept her young looks for a good length of her life, and was still an extremely good-looking woman. In the midst of all her troubles, Josephine had an acerbic wit. While she was separated from her husband of many years, she often jokingly said "Well at least he replaced me with another good-looking girl!". She reminisced a lot about other very personal issues. She told me how proud she was that her children had turned out to be fine people, emphasising that she 'came from good stock' herself. Her privacy was paramount to her and she expressed her fears and embarrassment to me about having another one of 'those visits' from Ms Mullarkey or Ms Philbin at a time when her family might be visiting her.

On this particular day I knew by Josephine's demeanour that she had something significant bothering her. She broke down and told me that she was physically unwell now (a serious illness claimed her a short time afterwards). She did not like the attitude of the housing official she called 'Mullarkey', who had reminded her in "no uncertain terms" that the council were her landlords and that she was expected to comply with their request. It was explained to her, that they wanted to evict Bríd Cummins and needed her evidence for use in Court. Josephine was very anxious, and said that she didn't have anyone to confide in who might be able to help her through this 'nightmare'. Josephine said that she did not want to see Bríd Cummins evicted, that although they may have had their differences, "such was life".

Josephine admitted that a lot of what was said about one another was exaggerated, and that Number 5 Munster Avenue was a "horrible house to share", but at least it was secure and she "could always walk up town". She related how she liked her new accommodation on the far side of town, even though it was further out from the city centre. She described how she was nervous that the Council might interfere with her tenancy in her 'nice new bungalow' if she didn't give them what they were asking for.

Josephine said that she was shocked and frightened by the harshness of the demands being made of her by the council official. She said she felt that it was cruel to be trying to evict a woman like Bríd Cummins, whom she believed was not well. Josephine dearly wanted to be left alone in peace, and believed that she had made her situation very clear to Patricia Philbin and I, when we had met with her in February of that year. She said that she was bothered about why she was being singled out to give evidence against Bríd, and said that she believed it was because she was living alone and in a weak position to stand up to them. She confided that she was nervous of the council forcing her to go to court to speak against her former neighbour.

The next time I heard from Josephine, was some months later in December 2004. She had heard about the tragic death of Bríd Cummins on local radio. She was distraught and asked me to call on her. When I called to visit, she was still very shocked over her former neighbour's death and kept going over the events of previous months. Josephine was very upset that what she entrusted as an 'off-the-record-conversation' with Patricia Philbin, and subsequently in a home visit by Frances Mullarkey, was misrepresented in Court, and purported to be a serious account of anti-social behaviour as part of the Council's prosecution case in securing her eviction.

Josephine was beside herself with angst about Bríd Cummin's death. She expressed concern to me that her own family would "disown" her if they thought that she had been implicated in saying something that drove this woman to her grave. I reassured her that this was not the situation and it was outside of her control if Housing Officials deceived her. Knowing what had been done, I assured her that no blame was attributable to her. She told me that she was considering going to her Solicitor to see what she could do.

Her health was continuing to deteriorate. I received what was to be the final phone call from Josephine a short while later. She was in a high state of anxiety and said that she was petrified, after having a visit to her home from two male senior executives of the Council. She recounted the discussion, wherein she was asked not to comment to any media about the situation of Bríd Cummins, as it had become so controversial and gained some national media interest.

Josephine told me that she did not want them to call to her home, but was afraid to offend them as they were her landlords. It was sad to hear the initial happiness and joy of her home was all gone now. She said that she felt tricked by how she had been used by Housing officials in contributing to getting Bríd evicted.

Galway City Council Vs Bríd Cummins: Preparing to Evict

In the Council's own records in the *Report to Councillors*, it shows that Blake and Kenny, Solicitors for the Council wrote to Bríd's solicitor Jarlath McInerney on 13th January 2004. Record number '000168' makes it clear that the Council want Bríd Cummins to attend for a meeting at City Hall, in person.

> Dear Sirs,
>
> We confirm that we have been requested by Ciarán Hayes of Galway City Council to write to you on behalf of your above named client, Bríd Cummins.
>
> We would like at the outset of this letter to make it perfectly clear that this letter is not written in connection with the current Circuit Court Proceedings issued by you against Galway City Council, but is in relation to alleged breaches of your clients Tenancy Agreement and which were to be discussed with your client at a meeting which was arranged for Tuesday 27th November, 2003 at City Hall.
>
> We understand that your client declined to attend this Meeting for the reasons as set out in a letter from your firm to Mr Ciarán Hayes and dated 25th November 2003.
>
> The breaches of your client's Tenancy Agreement as alleged relate to your client's behaviour towards adjoining neighbours, specific details of which will be given at the proposed meeting.

We would point out that the current complaints with regard to the breaches of the Tenancy do not relate to the Circuit Court proceedings and the matter of the meeting is of extreme importance.

We therefore now call upon your client to confirm her availability to attend for a further meeting at City Hall for the purposes of discussing serious complaints received from adjoining neighbours.

In the event that we fail to hear from you within 10 days confirming your client's willingness to attend a meeting, our clients will be left with no alternative but to institute recovery proceedings for an Order for Possession arising from breaches of the Tenancy Agreement.

Yours faithfully,

Blake and Kenny

The Council were not willing to provide Bríd's solicitor with specific details of the alleged anti-social behaviour accusations against her. Council management refused this request and held they would only relate the alleged accusations against her if she attended at City Hall in person.

On 3rd March 2004 Ciarán Hayes signed a Manager's Order under Section 62(1) of the Housing Act 1966 citing the intention of Galway City Council to resume possession of 5a Munster Avenue, Galway, notifying that Blake and Kenny, Solicitors were being instructed to:

'Institute all any legal proceedings deemed necessary for the recovery of vacant possession of the dwelling'.

Council management believed that allegations were a sound enough basis on which to move to evict Bríd Cummins from her home. Using that particular legislation, no evidence needs to be presented to achieve this result.

Local authorities are bound by the legislation of the State. The Local Government Act, 2001 is the main instrument to guide and regulate the operation of local authorities in the Republic of Ireland. This makes it a 'bible' by which local authority Managers and executives are legally bound. This resource enables citizens to access the law of the land to see what the responsibilities of their agencies are.

The City Manager John Tierney had the ultimate powers at this time at his discretion to react and deal with the transfer request of Bríd Cummins. He chose to delegate his executive powers to his Director of Services, Ciarán Hayes. Under Section 2 (3a) of the Act:

> 'The employee shall perform the delegated function under the general direction and control of the manager'.

This is significant, because the manager was directly involved in sourcing a solution in relation to Bríd Cummins, as concerns were being pressed by a number of Councillors. To this end, he called me to his office for suggestions and I identified specific suitable vacant properties which would have brought an immediate and satisfactory remedy. He seemed happy and amenable to the suggestions, after the pros and cons of the properties were discussed. As Manager of the City, and a man who had previously worked as a Housing Officer himself, he chose to defer the ultimate decision down the line to the Director of Services, Ciarán Hayes. Regrettably it appears that Mr Hayes was not amenable to the transfer solutions on offer and insisted on proceeding to evict Bríd Cummins.

Another Court Action Against Bríd

Some months later, when the case was listed for Court, the city manager John Tierney had left to take up a new position as County Manager in Fingal County Council. A director of services, Joe O'Neill, was installed as Acting City Manager until a new appointment was made in January 2005. During the intervening months, under manager Joe O'Neill, Bríd Cummins was taken into Court by the City Council.

On 13th August 2004, a Managers Order 001922 was signed by Mr WM Dunne. This Order approves an application to the Court under Section 3 (2) of the Housing (Miscellaneous Provisions) 1997 that:

'..Proceedings be initiated to obtain an exclusion order against Ms Bríd Cummins 5A Munster Avenue Galway in relation to the property at 5A Munster Avenue and 6 Munster Avenue Galway'.

The Court hearing was set down for 24th August 2004. As the senior engineer in Housing at Galway City Council, Mr Dunne was also aware of the tenancy of Bríd Cummins. He had drafted an earlier report in relation to the condition of her flat, contradicting the identified shortcomings of the property claimed in Brid's independent engineer's report.

Although Ciarán Hayes had signed the earlier Manager's Order invoking the '1966 Housing Act Section 62' (Recovery of possession of dwellings and other buildings) on 3/3/04, the Council decided to invoke a parallel second court action against Bríd Cummins. This second action was invoked using a different piece of legislation known as the Housing (Miscellaneous Provisions) Act, 1997. This legislation was enacted nationally to combat serious criminal acts of anti-social behaviour. In particular, it would deal with situations where

54

gangs and serious criminal families were involved, wherein victims would naturally be terrified of giving evidence against them. This law facilitated local authorities in securing 'Excluding Orders'.

The *'Report to Councillors'* states that Frances Mullarkey (SEO Housing, Galway City Council) has been in contact with a social worker in the Brothers of Charity Services, regarding one of their clients; Mary Walsh. The client is a daughter of the Walsh family, Bríd's next door neighbours. The client lives with a rare condition known as 'Taybi Rubenstein Syndrome', which is typified by a range of severe physical and mental challenges. Ms. Mullarkey sought the provision of a Report from a social worker employed by this charitable organisation. The records show that their communications had been in progress since the previous year.

The social worker reports having conversations with the client and duly furnished Ms Mullarkey with a written report for court. A copy of the reply letter dated 24th August 2004 is furnished in the *Report to Councillors* in response to the request, sent by the Principal Social Worker at Woodlands Centre, Renmore, Galway as follows:

> Dear Frances,
>
> Re Mary Walsh, Renmore House, Home Address 6 Munster Avenue, Galway
>
> As promised, I am enclosing an up-to-date report for the Courts on Wednesday next.
>
> I trust this will cover the situation.
>
> With kind regards,
>
> Yours sincerely,
>
> ...

In the report enclosed with the cover letter, this Principal Social Worker outlines Ms Walsh's condition at that time. She refers to a previous report issued in November 2003 and says that '*Mary has not been at home either for Christmas or for her annual summer holidays this year due to the situation next door*'. The Principal Social Worker refers to her 'deteriorated' health.

In August 2004 an emergency hearing came before Judge Conall Gibbons in Galway District Court. The result of this action was described by Bríd's solicitor:

> He admonished the local authority for bringing this matter during the vacation sittings. He said the 1997 Act should not have been invoked, as this had been brought in for serious matters dealing with drugs. This was nothing more than a neighbourly dispute and he couldn't understand how there was no complaints made to the Guards, but yet they deemed it sufficiently urgent to bring the matter during August. He threw the matter out.

> [Jarlath McInerney, RTE Primetime, broadcast June 7th 2005.]

Back to the Drawing Board

Council management decided to go back into Court again, this time using a 38 year-old law, which required no evidence to be presented. This was the other legal avenue that had been initiated in March of that year, which the Council's advisors were now proceeding with again.

Under Section 26 of the 1966 Housing Act, a local authority can demand that a tenant vacates a property and hand back the keys to the Council. There is not any obligation on a Council to explain why this course of action is being taken. It is a summary procedure, which means the court has no option but to grant it when a council seeks it.

On 29th October 2004, Bríd's solicitor wrote to the Council's solicitor:

Dear Sirs,

We await hearing from you, further to our previous letter. A couple of matters arise.

Firstly, as far as we are concerned, this is a full fight and we will be asking the Judge to fix a date.

Secondly we note the last day in court there appeared to be a Garda witness. A Garda called to our client a couple of weeks ago relating to an alleged complaint. This Guard actually indicated to our client that the matter was coming back into court on the 3rd November. This was before any summons was served.

If a Garda witness is being called, please let us have his name as we wish to contact him. We will be asking him to furnish us with all statements, complaints etc that he may have which may be relevant to this case.

On 2nd November 2004, the Council's solicitors Blake and Kenny responded:

.. The City Council case essentially is that the defendant's anti-social behaviour with regard to her neighbours gave cause for the issue of a Notice to Quit and it is the failure to comply with this Notice that is now before the Courts.

We would point out that we propose to call the following witnesses in connection with this case:

Mr Paddy Walsh or Mrs Nora Walsh who are adjoining neighbours of Ms Cummins and the main witnesses in the case. We confirm that we do not hold any written statement or otherwise for or on behalf of Mr and Mrs Walsh and we understand that their evidence will to be fact that the actions of the Defendant, Bríd Cummins, have resulted in a total loss with regard to the enjoyment of their own dwelling.

Ms Patricia Philpen [sic] of Galway City Council, will give evidence, as to the nature of the complaints received and will also outline the position and the difficulties experienced by the previous occupant of No. 5B.

Dr _____ GP may be called to give evidence as to the medicine prescribed to Nora Walsh with regard to her present nervous condition.

[Named] Social Worker to the daughter of Bríd Cummins. We confirm there has been an involvement of a Sergeant ... of Mill Street, but it is not intended to call him.

(This was a misstatement by the solicitor in the last point – Bríd Cummins did not have any children.)

The Council's solicitor engaged the Brother of Charity's social worker to provide evidence. It is notable that the Council representatives are now referring to 'the defendant's anti-social behaviour' and not as previously referred as 'alleged breaches of your clients Tenancy Agreement' in January 2004.

The Council's records show that they were in regular contact with the Walsh's GP. A record in the Report to Councillors (Manager Order 001885) authorises payment for standby duty for a doctor. This Order was signed by Caroline Phelan (A/Director of Services) to pay for standby duty for the GP for the 14th July, after the council had neglected to inform him that the case had been cancelled for that date and his services were not required, although he had made himself available for attending court. The records show an invoice was presented to the Council for payment and that Ms Mullarkey instructed this to be paid, directing it to be 'charged to Estate Management'. It seems strange that the Council's Housing section took ownership of the expenses for the private citizens' doctor.

It is clear from correspondence in the file that Ms. Patricia Philbin was preparing to take the stand in Galway District Court as a witness for her employers. She was preparing to give evidence based on an off-the-record retrospective opinion, solicited by the Council from another council tenant. In my opinion, this was not a statement. It was an unsigned off-the-record rant, with specific instructions from the former neighbour that her comments were not to be used in any official way.

November 2004: Eviction Order is granted at Galway Courthouse

Judge orders eviction of 'disabled' woman for anti-social conduct

Source: City Tribune Friday, November 05, 2004 (Front Page)

A woman on a disability pension who had nowhere else to go was thrown out of her Council flat for anti-social behaviour, which included firing objects on the roof, disconnecting a neighbour's electricity and alleged assaults.

However, Bríd Cummins of 5A Munster Avenue said it was her neighbours who were causing all the trouble, claiming one of them had left a dead rat outside her door. She had written 25 letters to the Local Authority about an adjoining council tenant, who she complained was making unreasonable noise by sleeping in a creaking bed and wearing high heels.

But Galway City Council housing official Patricia Philbin said this tenant, who did not wish to be named, had lived for 11 years in her flat prior to Cummins' arrival without any problems.

Relations between the two escalated when Cummins allegedly removed fuses which left the upstairs tenant without electricity. After this woman was allegedly assaulted by Cummins, the Council agreed in December 2002 to move the tenant, who was too scared to testify against Cummins.

The flat had been vacant since, Ms. Philbin told Galway District Court.

Up to then Cummins had been on such good terms with her other neighbours, Nora and Paddy Walsh, that she had given them her key in case she was locked out.

However Mrs. Walsh explained she then became "the culprit".

Things soured when Council workers came to redecorate the vacant flat. Cummins locked them out of the building. They asked Mrs. Walsh to speak to Cummins so they could get their tools.

When she did, she saw Cummins "firing cups and saucers all over the place". "I ran like the hammers of hell," Mrs. Walsh told the Court.

On another occasion, sometime in January last year, Cummins invited Mrs. Walsh into her home. Cummins locked three sets of doors before turning and grabbing Mrs. Walsh around the neck.

"She was screaming 'this is what they do, they use it against me'. She turned into another person," Mrs. Walsh said.

Mrs. Walsh said she somehow managed to get out of the flat but was left traumatised. She believed Cummins was sick so she did not complain to the Gardaí or the Local Authority and did not tell her children.

Five months later, her son had just trimmed the hedge between the two properties – as the family had done for 45 years – when he noticed Cummins in the garden "ranting and raving".

Cummins came into their house "very calm", Mrs. Walsh explained. "She then got violent, she started shouting at us and told my son to go out there and pick up the leaves. Before I got her out of the house she made a dive. She shoved me in the left breast. I had a mastectomy. I couldn't take this," Mrs. Walsh said, breaking down in tears.

Besides these two incidents, Cummins routinely fired things on the roof, screamed abuse and would bang on the fence.

"She gave us an awful time. In the end I made a statement to the guards. I couldn't take it anymore. It got so bad during the night I used to ring the guards thinking it was out the park and neighbours told me it was next door," she said.

The Walshes had a severely disabled daughter, Mary, who Mrs. Walsh looked after at home. Her social worker Ann Byrnes said those involved in her care noticed a dramatic change in her behaviour.

"Mary complained about the 'at night'. She said she saw her mother crying and said she was too scared to go home," Ms. Byrnes testified. Since November last year Mary has lived in residential care.

Cummins denied assaulting Mrs. Walsh or any part in anti-social behaviour. She told the court the trouble began when she caught Mrs. Walsh in her flat, having used the key she gave her.

"I was very upset. Nora got completely hysterical, completely aggressive and abusive," Cummins said.

When Judge Mary Fahy asked if she ever became aggressive, she replied: "Not at all, no. I'm very easy going. I'm very quiet. I don't have any parties or anything like that." She admitted asking Mrs. Walsh's son to remove clippings because he had shaved the hedge, which was on her side, right down.

"Nora shot out of her chair and started shouting. She was extremely aggressive to me," Cummins said.

She added: "I was physically afraid. I thought I was going to be physically attacked by Nora."

Judge Fahy expressed surprise at this, noting that Cummins looked very fit and did not look as if she suffered from the back and hand problems which had prevented her from working and for which she was receiving disability payments. Mrs. Walsh on the other hand did not look robust and had undergone a mastectomy.

"A mastectomy 20 years ago," Cummins retorted.

Judge Fahy said she believed this remark, which was delivered "in a bitter, cold voice", showed the defendant's true colours.

Cummins later told the court the Walshes had left a dead rat outside her door. She had also caught them on at least six occasions in her back garden, "banging on my back window, looking through the window, rattling on the door to see if it's open".

Her solicitor Jarlath McInerney said Cummins had nowhere to go if the Council evicted her.

But Judge Fahy said she had no hesitation in granting the order for eviction. She dismissed Cummins' allegations as "unbelievable lies" saying the defendant had tried to exude "a holier than thou attitude" but was in fact "clever and very manipulative".

She had fooled somebody into getting a disability pension and Council house, the Judge believed.

"I find it very difficult to believe that she has to have a personal assistant to carry things for her. She has a Local Authority tenancy when we know there's a crucial, crucial problem in obtaining housing in Galway. In my view she's abused it to such an extent her neighbours who own their property have absolutely no peace," the Judge said.

She added: "She won't be happy until she has everybody gone from the street".

Many questions arise in regard to how management at Galway City Council pursued the eviction of Bríd Cummins. Although the Council did not need any prima facie evidence in order to secure an eviction and take back the keys of the flat, they set about gathering it retrospectively.

It is sad and regrettable that the full facts were withheld by the Council officials from the Court at that time. A picture was painted for the judge that was not accurate. Bríd's full housing file would have exhibited her reported suicidal tendencies in the past, as well as her attendance with Professor Fahy (Consultant Psychiatrist) and comprehensive information on the continuous pain in her back and in her face that she described as 'excruciating' (suffered as a result of an accident in a swimming pool years previously).

I believe that if Judge Fahy had been presented with access to the full housing file for Bríd Cummins, and knew the true facts of her situation, she may have viewed matters somewhat differently. However, her alleged anti-social behaviour involved the participation of two Senior Social Workers. It is difficult to reconcile how somewhere during their professional training and experience, they had failed to learn how to broaden their understanding of a situation, by looking at the causes and effects of both sides of a neighbourly dispute.

It is most regrettable that Patricia Philbin misrepresented the reason why the overhead tenant had been transferred. This was of the issues that I had clarified subsequently in the High Court record.

After this woman was allegedly assaulted by Cummins, the Council agreed in December 2002 to move the tenant, who was too scared to testify against Cummins.

This was an outrageously false piece of evidence. The successful transfer of the upstairs tenant actually came about because she reached the qualifying age to be moved into a complex, built specifically for elderly and disabled people. The former upstairs tenant made it clear that she did not want to get involved in any action. She was a private person and personally did not at all like the idea that the council were seeking to evict Bríd Cummins.

It would have been helpful for the judge to know that 5 Munster Avenue was an ordinary house, where separate flats were created, whilst the tenants of both flats shared a small hallway and a front door. There was not a concrete first floor. Upstairs noise was easily heard and vice versa.

An independent Consulting Engineer commissioned by Bríd, had recorded that Bríd flat was 'living in substandard and potentially very dangerous (electrically) housing conditions.' Could this be a reasonable explanation about why Bríd removed a fuse, as accused of in court?

The actual reason why the flat overhead was not re-let in the interim by the Council was because they had decided to restore the divided house back into its original form as a single property. Whilst they were setting about evicting Bríd, they left the upstairs flat vacant with this in mind. This actually made good housing sense, as there had been many difficulties with tenants who shared that house over the previous years. Two and a half years after Bríd's passing, they had achieved this.

The positive sides of Bríd's personality were not heard in court, such as her gifts for painting, poetry and her previous fund-raising efforts for the Simon Community, where she had compiled and published an anthology of poetry from acclaimed poets, as well as her own poetry publications. Ironically, in her better days, she was a good supporter of homeless charities in Galway. Where were they when she needed them? Every one of them would have been aware of her situation.

Judge Mary Fahy is renowned in Galway for her sound judgements and humanitarian approach, which are often published in local newspapers. In my opinion, it was wrong of the council officials to deny the judge full and reliable information. However, the council wanted their eviction. Her solicitor appealed the decision to the Circuit Court, but was unsuccessful in overturning the original decision of the District Court.

Days later when questioned about her faith in the justice system, Bríd told local radio station Galway Bay FM:

> I lost my faith in the justice system after the first case, and I was very reluctant to go ahead even with the appeal, because I thought it was such a waste of time, we might as well not have even gone in there. You know, we weren't listened to. My case wasn't put at all. I wasn't given a chance to defend myself. And it was really dreadful, it was very intimidating.

Whilst Housing officials were updating Council policy on anti-social behaviour, civil legal action was initiated by Bríd Cummins against the Council. Ciarán Hayes then declared his intention to evict Bríd. The Council's paperwork was rendered tidy in this regard, by having an 'updated antisocial behaviour policy' by the elected members of the council. A special policy was also passed, wherein a tenant who was convicted by a court for anti-social behaviour, could then additionally be denied access to homeless services on the direction of a Senior Executive Officer in Housing. One wonders whether all the elected members really understood the powers they were providing to Council officials by this additional clause. Who did they think was using the homeless services anyway?

"We thought, because we had power, we had wisdom."

Steven Vincent Bennet (1935), 'Litany for Dictatorships'

Social Worker Powers in Galway City Council

Under the national 'Better Local Government' programme, Galway City Council management applied for funding of a new position of a Senior Social Worker and were successful. Gerry Flanagan was selected for the post. This executive was charged with establishing the facts of the Bríd Cummins sexual abuse complaint by the Director of Services, Ciarán Hayes. By any measure, this was a poorly executed task. Key people with tacit knowledge relating to the circumstances were ignored. As the tenant liaison officer, I expected him to extend the scope and remit of the investigation to include all pertinent employees who had interaction with Bríd Cummins.

The new Senior Social Worker came into the Council post with previous experience of dealing with sexual abuse investigations. This was detailed in a legal case of an acquitted ex-Christian Brother, which attracted media attention. This court account was published by the *Galway Advertiser* in 2008.

66

'Ex-Christian Brother acquitted of 35 sex assaults in Galway school'

(Extract) Galway Advertiser 31/7/2008.

Judge says there is 'significant inconsistency' between evidence and statements

An ex-Christian Brother has been acquitted by direction of Judge Tony Hunt of sexually assaulting boys some 40 years ago in a Galway industrial school. Judge Hunt withdrew all 35 charges from the jury on day-11 of the trial at Dublin Circuit Criminal Court. The 72-year-old accused had pleaded not guilty to the 35 counts of indecently assaulting six boys between 1967 and 1973 when they were residents at the school.

Judge Hunt thanked the jury of five men and five women for their patience and attention in the case and told them that there was significant inconsistency between the evidence given by witnesses in the trial and the statements they made to Gardaí, and inconsistencies between some witnesses and documentary evidence. He said he felt that in those circumstances the jury, properly charged by the judge, would not be able to safely convict beyond a reasonable doubt. Judge Hunt said there was "no doubt that many of the men in this case have unhappy lives" but told the jury a case cannot be decided on sympathy.

The jury heard during the trial that a social worker investigating the case had previously worked at the school and was "extremely anticlerical". Judge Hunt called retired Superintendent Jim Sugrue as a witness for the court "in the interests of justice" after it emerged Mr Sugrue had written to the Director of Public Prosecutions outlining his concern that witnesses were being "coached" before they made their statements.

Judge Hunt questioned Mr Sugrue about a letter, written in November 1995, in which Mr Sugrue stated that the social worker, Mr Gerry Flanagan, had worked in the school in the late seventies as a "house parent" but had left "under a cloud." He then left the area and became a social worker with the Western Health Board. He began visiting the school again in 1982 but was soon barred from the property by officials.

Case cannot be decided on sympathy

Mr Sugrue said in the letter Mr Flanagan investigated abuse at the school on behalf of the Health Board and that he and another social worker, [named], "trawled" the country for complainants and were successful in finding several. He said he believed Mr Flanagan had a "fixation" with the school and was "extremely anticlerical", as demonstrated by two letters he wrote to the Irish Press newspaper concerning clerical abuse.

Mr Sugrue also told the DPP he was aware that Mr Flanagan and another social worker, [named], had counselling sessions with all of the complainants before they made their Garda statements. He said on two occasions witnesses came to Gardaí with prepared statements after meeting with them. Mr Sugrue said he warned Mr Flanagan that it was a police investigation and that witnesses should come forward voluntarily.

He said he was very concerned that witnesses were being coached and told Mr Flanagan this several times. In another letter to the DPP, Mr Sugrue said he was concerned about "false memory syndrome", a theory that adults could mistakenly remember instances of child sex abuse in their past. "The power of suggestion cannot be overlooked," he stated in the letter.

Mr Sugrue said Mr Flanagan had been taken off the case by the Health Board in 1995 but had continued to write him letters asking why the investigation was taking so long. This caused Mr Sugrue to reply that Mr Flanagan had no more function in the investigation and his enquiries were "impertinent".

Senior Social Worker Report: Bríd's Neighbours

In the *Report to Councillors*, a report prepared by the senior social worker Mr Gerard Flanagan (not showing any date on it) stated:

> As requested by Ciarán Hayes at the end of May 2004, to link in with Nora Walsh and her husband Paddy in relation to concerns and difficulties they were experiencing with their neighbours.

Mr Flanagan further reported:

> My impression of this meeting would be that the Walsh's are under extreme pressure, both in terms of themselves and their daughter. I asked them had they made any official complaint to the Guards and they said no. I said in terms of the assaults that Ms Cummins had perpetrated on them and they said no. We spoke at length about this in terms of the difficulties for the City Council if they are to go to Court on the basis of anti-social behaviour it is important that we have concrete evidence to sustain this.

69

I also spoke to them and said as far as I would be aware that as this assault had taken place in the previous year, it may be statute barred but I would check it out for them. I said to Nora and Paddy that they should sit down and write down very clearly what had happened instead of trying to remember the issue and I would contact the Guards and have someone come out to them and make a statement.

I told them when I had information from the Guards I would let them know and they thanked me for this.

On the 3rd June 2004, I telephoned Tony O'Donnell in Mill Street. I spoke to him and told him exactly what we were looking for. He told me there may be a problem due to the length of time and that there may a legal problem attached but that he would get a Guard to call and take a statement and they would take it from there. Later on I called Nora Walsh and told her that the Guards would be making contact with her but if she wanted she could call the Guards and make an appointment.

This seems an extraordinary interaction between the council social worker and the private citizens living next door to the council's tenant. In my role as Tenant Liaison Officer, I knew from previous experiences and meetings with the Walsh's that they were resolute in neither wanting to go to court nor to involve the Guards in their dispute with their neighbour. They repeatedly requested that Bríd Cummins be transferred.

In the previous September (2003), I had been instructed by Ciarán Hayes to accompany Paddy Walsh to the Council's firm of Solicitors (Blake & Kenny) where he was being sponsored by the Council to take a civil action against Bríd Cummins. He hastily left that office when the full ramifications of what the Council wanted him to do were eventually explained by the Solicitor, John Carr. The Walsh family

70

simply wanted Bríd Cummins to be transferred to a more suitable property, but the council executives had already decided to evict her.

In his submitted report, Gerry Flanagan stated that Nora Walsh queried him about the discussed Court hearing:

> She asked me if she would be called as a witness and I said more than likely in terms of what her needs were. I also informed her that she had completed her statement and we had received a copy of that and a lot of the evidence would be based on what they are saying is going on down there.

Letter from Gerry Flanagan to Inspector Tony O'Donnell, Mill Street Garda Station

In September 2004, Galway City Council's Senior Social Worker Mr Flanagan, in preparation for the case against Bríd Cummins, wrote to Inspector Tony O'Donnell at Mill Street Garda Station, letter dated 22nd Sept 2004:

> Re: Mrs Nora Walsh, 4 Munster Avenue, Galway
>
> Dear Tony,
>
> I refer to the above named lady who as you are aware has been experiencing a number of difficulties with her neighbour at number 5 Munster Avenue. As you are also aware, Mrs Walsh some months ago gave a statement of complaint to the Gardaí, this statement was taken by Sgt. Willie O'Beirne.
>
> Mrs Walsh reported to me on the 21st Sept 2004 that while returning from the chemist on Thursday 16th September 2004 at 3.45pm, she was confronted by Ms Cummins who allegedly shouted at her 'You are a dirty old woman and I am going to get you'.

Mrs Walsh said that she was extremely traumatised by the remarks and that she had went [sic] to Mill Street on the Friday but there was a substantial queue there. Mrs Walsh is extremely ill at the moment and cannot stand for long periods of time. She rang Mill Street on Friday night and asked for Sgt. Willie O'Beirne but unfortunately Willie was not on shift. She asked me to report this matter to yourselves and she asked that you follow it up with Sgt. O'Beirne.

While possibly these alleged remarks by Ms Cummins in different circumstances would not evoke such a response, what has been going on for Mrs Walsh and her daughter in the family home has caused enormous stress and strain for her and I would be very concerned for her own health and that of her husband's. I would be grateful if you could follow this up.

Yours sincerely,

Gerard Flanagan

Senior Social Worker

CC Mr John Carr, Solicitor Blake & Kenny

Ms Frances Mullarkey, Galway City Council

Questions arise as to why the Council's senior social worker is so active in representing private citizens against the council's own tenant. With all of these 'professional' forces working against her, Bríd Cummins was facing a huge challenge to defend herself. At this point, her complaints have been disregarded by the Council.

The Council's own published records show that senior executives prioritised the bringing of Bríd Cummins before the courts for alleged anti-social behaviour. They were spending an unknown quantum of public monies in pursuit of evicting this single, disabled woman, living on her own, who had never previously come to the attention of the

Gardaí. Having records on her council file that highlighted variances in her mental health, it seems very strange that she was considered so sufficiently dangerous to society; that the Council applied to the courts during the Court holiday period in August for an Excluding Order against Bríd Cummins.

Days of Hope and Despair

The 24th, 25th, 26th of November 2004 were significant days of hope and ultimately despair for Bríd Cummins.

24ᵗʰ November: Appeal of Eviction in Circuit Court

Bríd's appeal to Galway Circuit Court was heard by Judge Harvey Kenny, in relation to the Eviction Order previously given against Bríd in the District Court. The council retained the legal services of Blake and Kenny (principal solicitor Michael Molloy) with prosecuting solicitor John Carr.

During the course of the Circuit Court hearing on 24th November 2004, Bríd's solicitor Jarlath McInerney indicated that his client would leave the flat voluntarily after Christmas 2004. Her barrister Alban Carney pleaded for her to be allowed to stay in her home for the Christmas period. However, Galway City Council refused this request, and indicated their consent to the voluntary surrender of the tenancy, if she left by the 8th December. The case then continued before the Circuit Court judge, who made the order that she was to vacate by noon on the 6th December 2004.

The details of the Court happenings were reported in *The Irish Independent* newspaper during that week:

Woman 'feared for her life' after neighbour put hands to throat

(Source: Irish Independent, Brian McDonald, 25/11/2004)

AN elderly woman fled terrified from a neighbour's apartment after the neighbour put her hands to her neck in an apparent attempt to choke her, a court heard yesterday.

Galway Circuit Court was told that the attack took place after the neighbour had locked all the doors of her apartment. A distressed Nora Walsh (67) of

Munster Avenue, Galway was giving evidence at an appeal hearing before Judge Harvey Kenny.

The appeal was brought by Bríd Cummins (48) of Munster Avenue against a decision of Galway District Court to grant Galway City Council an order to eject Ms Cummins from her apartment.

Mrs Walsh, who is suffering from cancer, said that she and her husband and their 40-year-old handicapped daughter had lived at Munster Avenue for the last 45 years. They had been greatly upset by problems caused by Ms Cummins who lived in the downstairs flat of an adjoining two-flat property owned by the city council.

Because of the difficulties, her daughter had to be placed in residential care. The problems with Ms Cummins had started in January of last year when city council workmen came to her to see if she could help them recover their tools which were in the flat above Ms Cummins' home.

They told her that Ms Cummins would not let them into the building. When Mrs Walsh went to see Ms Cummins, she threw cups and saucers at her. The following day, Ms Cummins apologised and asked to borrow a toilet bag because she had to go to hospital. Mrs Walsh said she wanted to be Christian and went back to Ms Cummins, believing that the previous episode was a once-off.

As she entered Ms Cummins' flat, she put four locks on the doors behind her. "I said jokingly that this place was like Fort Knox. She then put her hands around my neck. She turned into another person. I feared for my life. How I got out of that flat, I don't know," said Mrs Walsh.

On subsequent occasions, Mrs Walsh told Judge Kenny that Ms Cummins had hit her by banging a heavy porch door against her, banged repeatedly on the roof of an extension built for her daughter and screamed at her.

Mrs Walsh, who became weak during her testimony, told Judge Kenny that she was very afraid of Ms Cummins.

"I couldn't continue to live there. My daughter is terrified of her," she said.

The lady in the upstairs flat had to be removed to other accommodation "in her own interest" and was afraid to give evidence against Ms Cummins. She was also concerned that Ms Cummins would discover her new address.

The Acting Administrative Officer of Galway city council's housing department, Patricia Philbin, said that Ms Cummins appeared to turn her attention on Mrs Walsh after the other tenant left.

She stressed that the city council fully accepted that Mrs Walsh's complaints were genuine. In evidence, Bríd Cummins denied the allegations made against her by Mrs Walsh. She had tried to resolve her differences with her but Mrs Walsh had been aggressive to her, she said.

Mr Alban Carney BL, for Ms Cummins, told Judge Kenny that a medical report indicated that his client suffered from depression.

Judge Kenny ordered that Ms Cummins vacate the flat by noon December 6 and that she surrender all keys.

The final order for eviction was now made.

25th November: Council Conference on Homelessness

"To deny people their human rights is to challenge their very humanity."

Nelson Mandela

One day after the Circuit Court upheld the decision of the District court to evict Bríd Cummins, Galway City Council hosted a conference on homelessness. This resulted from an initiative by the Department of the Environment during 2004 to appoint consultants to evaluate the Homeless Action Plans of a number of Local Authorities, and Galway City Council was one of these

Ironically the theme of the 25th November 2004 conference was *'Prevention of Homelessness and Tenancy Sustainment'*. The invited key note speakers addressing the council-sponsored conference were Fr Peter McVerry and Fr. Sean Healy, who are both well known housing and homelessness advocates in the social justice sector.

Fr. Seán Healy gave a presentation on the 'Impact of Social Policies and Procedures on Homelessness'. It seems bizarre in the extreme that a Council-sponsored conference with such insightful speakers in the area of homelessness were in Galway City speaking on these pertinent issues, on the same days the Council management were expending enormous resources to effect the eviction of Bríd Cummins. Where was the *proof* that she was so bad a tenant that she warranted eviction?

In poignant irony, on Friday November 26th, the very next morning after the Council's conference on homelessness, Bríd Cummins was on local radio, describing her situation on foot of losing the Circuit Court appeal of her eviction.

According to Galway City Council's own 2004 Annual Report (published in 2005), it is stated:

> Galway City Council has made provision for the special accommodation needs of homeless people in Galway in co-operation with various voluntary and statutory organisations in the City. The City Council assesses the homeless status of applicants in a sensitive and caring manner, and every effort is made to meet the emergency accommodation requirements as the need arises. (p.9).

> The Homeless Forum met every quarter, where new projects and issues surrounding homelessness were discussed. Issues progressed by the Forum in 2004 included:

> - Rough Sleepers Initiative
>
> - Service Users Involvement
>
> - Projects to address long-term homelessness

> Galway City Council provided emergency accommodation for 424 homeless applicants in 2004. A variety of services are in place throughout the city for the purposes of providing emergency accommodation. The voluntary sector manages a number of facilities in a professional and sensitive manner. They also work closely with the statutory agencies both in individual cases, and through the Homeless Forum. (p.10).

There is no mention in the Council's Annual Report relating to the recently deceased Bríd Cummins, nor any reasons or justification given as to why the homeless services that would normally be available to a person in this position were instructed not to accommodate Bríd should she request assistance. Ciarán Hayes wrote to Cope (published in the subsequent *Report to Councillors*) instructing them not to provide Bríd Cummins with shelter for the night. Where did they expect her to go? I believe that this cruel act was an unnecessary and shocking continuum of the Council management's behaviour.

Ciarán Hayes wrote about the positives of the Homeless Forum in the Council's Annual Report:

> The Homeless Forum has been in operation in Galway City since 1997 and is representative of the statutory and voluntary sector homeless service providers. Since its inception, the forum has evolved whereby inter-agency co-operation and understanding has broadened and deepened. It facilitates a consistent level of awareness among the membership of homeless issues, promotes a shared understanding of the differing organisational perspectives, seeks to eliminate duplication and encourages complementarity of service provision.
>
> (Galway City Council Annual Report, 2004, p9)

COPE is a voluntary organisation of charitable status, which is also contracted by the City Council to provide homeless services. The provision of homeless services is a statutory responsibility of local authorities in Ireland.

79

26th November: Live radio interview with Bríd Cummins

On the 26th November Bríd Cummins contacted the local radio station, *Galway Bay FM* and was interviewed live on air by the CEO of the station and presenter of the morning show, Keith Finnegan.

To the end, Bríd held out some hope that common decency would prevail and humanity would emerge from some quarter to prevent her being evicted. She emphatically proclaimed her innocence.

The following is a verbatim transcript from the audio of that interview during her 8 minutes live on the air across Galway City and County:

Radio Interview: Keith Finnegan (KF), Bríd Cummins (BC)

KF: You are the person who has been told to get out. Two Courts found in the Council's favour.

BC: Yes, very devastating for me. So I will be homeless two weeks before Christmas. I didn't feel like I was given a chance to put my side, it was very one-sided. It was very much in the Council's favour. I think an opinion was formed even before we went into court, and I felt that (you know) I would like to give my side of the story. I felt that I had been victimised and bullied and intimidated because I had a case pending against Galway City Council, and I really feel that that was part of it.

KF: Would it not be fair though to say Bríd that the situation is, if that you feel like that, that that should have been brought out in the District Court and Circuit Court?

BC: Yeah, we did try, but we weren't really given an opportunity to put my side of the story.

KF: But the story doesn't read well Bríd Cummins. The story reads that you have made life allegedly, well sorry, according to the Courts, you have made life difficult

80

and that somebody who is living overhead in an apartment belonging to Galway City Council had also got to move out. So, are the two courts wrong?

BC: Well none of that is because of me. It has been presented now as if it has been my fault, when it was nothing to do with me. I mean the lady from the flat upstairs had been looking for a move for a long long time, and was delighted with the move, and it was when she reached a certain age that she was housed in a certain area which is for people of that age.

KF: But why was the flat left empty then? Why did the City Council say they couldn't put somebody in there? 1500 people on the waiting list and because of your actions Bríd Cummins, they couldn't put somebody in there.

BC: Well it wasn't because of my actions. I mean, I know that the place was shown to two people, who said they wouldn't take it because it was so damp. The house is very very damp, and the roof was in a shocking state, and I mean the council has been told about it and asked to do some repairs. I have water leaks in my flat for five and a half years, which they refuse to repair. The place is damp, it is mouldy. I have an independent engineer's report for my place, and the council refuse to do anything about it - and they are blaming me!

KF: Now, alongside this, your legal team, - you have a case against Galway City Council for this, which takes place on the 23rd of December.

BC: Yes.

KF: But you won't be in the apartment at that stage.

BC: No, but the case just stands, because the damage is done. Because of the effect on my health, and all the doctor's reports are there, because of the way it affected my health over the years, because I suffer from asthma, and my health has deteriorated a *lot* in the years, and my doctor wrote repeated letters to Galway City Council which were ignored. I applied for a transfer on numerous occasions. I had letters from public representatives as well, and they were all ignored.

81

KF: But how do you refute the claim that you've been an unsocial tenant of Galway City Council?

BC: I haven't been unsocial or anti-social or anything. I mean I am very quiet and easy going, and I live my life. I have a part-time job, I live on disability. I have a part-time job in the university and I swim, I do my programme. Because of my disability I have to do swimming and special exercises, and I do that to keep myself going every day.

KF: But the District Court heard a litany of- and I don't want to go into the 'You and Them' situation - but the District Court heard of a situation, and then the Circuit Court upheld the District Court decision when you appealed it there, and yet none of the caring aspect that you are coming across with this morning came out in either case.

BC: No it didn't, we weren't given a chance at all. I might as well not have been there really.

KF: Do you feel let down by the legal system?

BC: Definitely. I lost my faith in the justice system after the first case, and I was very reluctant to go ahead even with the appeal, because I thought it was such a waste of time, we might as well not have even gone in there. You know, we weren't listened to. My case wasn't put at all. I wasn't given a chance to defend myself. And it was really dreadful, it was very intimidating.

KF: Court is intimidating. I mean, you come across this morning, with all due respects Bríd, as a person who - you are making sound sense on the wireless this morning. But there is another side which came out in court, which doesn't seem like the Bríd Cummins that's on the radio today.

BC: Well it's not me. I mean they were painting me to be some kind of monster. I have *never* done any of the things that I was accused of. Absolutely outrageous. They had no evidence; they had no proof, nothing.

KF: Was there a Garda investigation into the claims against you?

BC: There was one guard who called here to me one evening, and asked me had I done something to this lady next door, and I said "no".

KF: Was there a criminal prosecution taken against you by the Gardaí?

BC: Oh not at all. No. I mean, I had made complaints to the Gardaí over the past year and a half, because of the way I was being harassed and bullied and intimidated. I had made *valid* complaints to the Gardaí, so I mean I am the one who has been victimised. But my story wasn't heard, you know, at all.

KF: Are you going to leave the apartment on Munster Avenue on the 6th or are you going to stay in protest?

BC: Oh well I have to go. I mean I have been told that I have to go.

KF: Where will you go?

BC: I have no idea. No idea. I mean I am going to be homeless, I don't have the means to rent privately, and the Council have refused to transfer me. So I am absolutely devastated about the whole thing - I'm sorry.

KF: So, you, so, you feel you have done no wrong at all Bríd?

BC: I have done *no wrong*. I can swear to you absolutely, on my mother's life, I have never done any of the things I was accused of. It was lies and slander, and I was maligned in the Court, with no chance to defend myself.

KF: It says in the report, that 'Bríd Cummins denied the allegations made against her', but Judge Kenny said that he didn't believe you.

BC: He didn't believe me. No he didn't. He believed the Council, and the Council supported the people next door against me. The council were determined to get me out because they wanted to stop me in my case against them.

KF: That's not the way law goes though?

BC: Well it won't stop my case, I mean, you know, if they thought that they could intimate me into giving up my case then it's actually made me more determined,

83

because the lies that were told, were really scary, for people to tell lies under oath is really scary.

KF: But that unfortunately is an allegation that I can't substantiate. The situation is that: *if* what I have read from the Court report happened, and you are telling me today categorically on your mother's life today that it didn't happen?

BC: Oh it definitely didn't happen.

KF: I'm totally confused.

BC: *No, it definitely did not happen*, I mean, I never did any of the things that I was accused of, it was...

KF: Do you think you were a model client for Galway City Council?

BC: Well, I think I have given them a hard time, because I always wrote letters about the state of repair, and trying to get them to do jobs. I got a public representative involved. I always did things through official channels, because I worked in offices for twenty years and I was a civil servant and that's the way I would do it, through official channels, keep copies of everything, and that's why I had four years of correspondence to hand over to the solicitor. Because, Catherine Connolly came down here last year, looked at everything, saw the state of the place, looked through the correspondence, and said 'hand it over to the solicitor; this is absolutely dreadful', and that's what I did, and from then on I was harassed and intimidated and this is what happened down in the court in the past few weeks.

KF: Okay, thanks Bríd for joining us today. Bríd Cummins joining us on the line from her Munster Avenue flat which she must vacate by - you will vacate you said yeah?

BC: Well I'll have to, because I mean I really don't want to have to - I'm not able for all the hassle or any more trouble.

KF: And where are you going to go to?

BC: Well in the meantime now, I was just onto the Western Health Board and they actually told me to go back to Galway City Council and insist on being re-housed.

But, after what's happened in the last few weeks, I really don't think that that would be possible, you know, I'll probably go stay with a friend in the meantime, until I can figure something out, you know. I need to be close to where I work because of my disability, I can't actually travel, I'm not able to drive any more, and I need to be within easy reach of where so that it's manageable for me. I have a PA from the Galway Centre for Independent Living, for so many hours a week, so I have to try and fit my hours around when she, you know, she can pick me up or drive me places.

KF: Alright, Bríd Cummins thanks indeed for joining us this morning. Thought and comments please to the comment line.

[End of radio interview]

It was evident from Bríd's sorrowful tone throughout this interview that she believed there was a last flicker of hope out there in the public arena to help her. Unfortunately this did not materialise. Inaction from various quarters (aside from attempts by Martin O'Connor of COPE) raises questions as to whether the reliance of charitable bodies on council funding restricted their interest or involvement in Bríd's situation.

The Council's senior social worker Gerry Flanagan had been in court giving evidence against Bríd (representing the private citizens who lived next door to her). It was regrettable that the council officials did not furnish the Courts with the full file they held on Bríd, which confirmed the long history of psychiatric illness. It would be normal for both judges to regularly encounter persons engaged in very serious anti-social and criminal behaviour. It would however, be very rare for either of the judges to encounter the Council seeking the eviction of any of those persons, many of whom are council tenants.

It is possible to see in that context, how the judiciary would be convinced by the local authority that this woman's alleged action must be extreme for the Council to have gone to such efforts to have her evicted.

In research for this book, I cannot find any records or evidence to show where previously convicted criminals were ever brought back into court again by Galway City Council seeking an eviction or exclusion order against them. An extraordinary level of intervention and legal resources were used by the Council in this energetic eviction process against Bríd Cummins.

Eviction of Bríd Cummins: Council activities

Whilst the Council-sponsored conference on 'Prevention of Homelessness and Tenancy Sustainment' was in full flow on the 25th November, John G O'Donnell BL wrote to John Carr (Solicitor) at Blake & Kenny, advising of the next steps re Bríd Cummins. These records were released by the City Council in the Report to Councillors file.

> Dear John,
>
> As you know, Judge Kenny made an Order for Possession with stay on the Order until 12 noon on 6th December 2004, and directed that the key be delivered up to Patricia Philbin on or before that time and date and that the Defendant was not to retain a copy of the keys. He adjourned the matter for mention to the 7th December.
>
> If it necessary to bring a Committal/Attachment Notice of motion, please revert to me. I enclose herewith Fee Note and many thanks for briefing me in this case.
>
> Kind regards,
>
> John G O'Donnell

On the week beginning Monday 29th November 2004, a series of letters were written to the Council-sponsored homeless services in Galway City. The letters emanated from the Housing section of Galway City Council, citing a 'Contact Name: Frances Mullarkey' with her extension number, as well as a printed signature citing 'Ciarán Hayes, Director of Services'.

These were addressed respectively to:

- Caroline McDonnell, Manager of Osterley Lodge, Lower Salthill
- Ursula Collis, Coordinator, 2 Upper Dominick Street, Galway

These stated:

> A Chara,
>
> Subsequent to the recent court decision on the 24th November 2004, Galway City Council obtained an eviction order on the above named tenant due to issue of anti-social behaviour.
>
> You are advised not to offer Ms Cummins homeless services prior to or after the 6th December 2004.
>
> Should you have any queries on the above matter, please do not hesitate to contact the housing office.

This seems somewhat at odds with the stated objectives of the homeless services. In Galway City Council's Annual Report, 2004, (p11), the purpose of the Osterley Lodge facility was described as follows:

> A major objective of the Homeless Action Plan was achieved on 6th February 2004 with the official opening of Osterley Lodge Hostel for Homeless Women by Mr. Noel Ahern, Minister of State at the Department of the Environment, Heritage and Local Government. The facility is managed by Cope on behalf of Galway City Council for the provision of emergency accommodation to Homeless Women.

On 30th November 2004, an email was sent from Martin O'Connor of COPE to Gerard Flanagan (Senior Social Worker at GCC) and Helena Martyn (GCC), copying in his boss, CEO Jacquie Horan:

Hi Gerry and Helena,

Further to our conversation on Thursday last, with regard to whether or not homeless services will be available to the City Council tenant currently in the process of being evicted (due to be evicted on Dec 6th 2004 according to the press reports). I am anxious to discuss further the response to be given if she presents for homeless services.

My understanding from our conversation is that City Council are strongly of the view they are not to be provided to this woman and additionally I anticipate that she will have difficulties getting financial support in the form of rent allowance under SWA leaving her without the means to provide for herself in terms of housing and accommodation. Potentially this woman will then be street homeless and may well present to COPE homeless services. I am anxious to have further discussions in advance of this scenario developing and to have clarity in terms of what the response will be. Can we meet later this week – either tomorrow after the Steering Group meeting or on either Thursday afternoon or at any time on Friday?

Martin O'Connor *moconnor@cope.ie*

CC *Jhoran@cope.ie*

On Thursday 2nd December 2004, a number of significant events took place.

A letter was sent from the Housing section of Galway City Council to the Superintendent Welfare Officer in Community Care:

We wish to advise you that following Circuit Court proceedings...eviction order against Bríd Cummins...with effect from 12 noon 6th Dec 2004 for antisocial behaviour, Galway City Council will not be offering her homeless services due to anti-social behaviour.

We are advising you of this occurrence under the terms of the City Council Anti Social Behaviour Policy. Should you have any further queries regarding this matter, please do not hesitate to contact Ms Frances Mullarkey, Senior Executive Officer in the Housing Department.

This letter would have the effect of directly and negatively affecting Bríd's ability to avail of rent allowance. In a case of eviction for anti-social behaviour by a local authority, it may be deemed that the person has made themselves 'purposely homeless', which is a criterion for refusal of rent allowance. This would mean Bríd would not be able to access subsidised private rented accommodation.

On the same day (2nd December), Ciarán Hayes wrote to Bríd Cummins.

Dear Ms Cummins,

Further to the recent court case on Wednesday 24th November 2004 in which you were directed by the Court to vacate your present accommodation and handover the keys of this accommodation to Galway City Council on Monday the 6th December 2004 at 12.00 Noon.

I regret to inform you that Galway City Council will not be in a position to provide housing services to you including emergency homeless accommodation after this date.

Yours sincerely,

Ciarán Hayes

Director of Services, Housing, Planning and Economic Development

The Director of Service for Housing didn't yet know that Bríd would not be upset by this letter, as she would never read it.

On the same day (2nd December), a memo on the *Report to Councillors* was written by 'Hilary' titled 'ATTENDANCE', from the office of Blake and Kenny, stating:

> I spoke to Ciarán Hayes in connection with this matter. He is aware of the terms of the order as per John O'Donnell's letter to us dated 25th November and I have just reiterated that the order for possession was made with a stay on same until 12 noon on 6th December next. I have explained to him and he is aware that it is for mention on the 7th. We will have to attend on the 7th and we should remind John O'Donnell of it in the meantime.
>
> Ciarán Hayes said he will contact us after the 12 noon on 6th December to let us know whether or not she has given back the keys in connection with same.

Bríd Cummins: Report of her final mortal day

On the same day, 2nd December 2004, Bríd was also busy making plans of her own. She contacted the 'Galway Centre for Independent Living', based locally, to seek assistance. It was arranged on the 30th November by the Manager, that Ann, a personal assistant, would visit Bríd Cummins at 5A Munster Avenue to help her pack as she was 'moving'.

According to the deposition given by Ann at the subsequent Coroner's Court, she had worked with Bríd a few times in the previous three weeks. She agreed as a favour to the manager of the centre, to help her pack her belongings, as she was moving house:

Bríd had been phoning the centre a lot to ask for assistance in packing her belongings. I agreed to go to Bríd house on Thursday at 2pm. Bríd let me in as normal, I don't have a set of keys to the house. I would describe her as being in great form and I was surprised that she was in such a high, after all she was leaving her house. I then helped her pack some of her stuff in the hot press, mainly clothes, and I then left them to the Charity Shop for her. I then returned to her house 5A Munster Avenue. On arriving back to the house there was a friend of Bríd's there, I forget her name, she was in her 30's, dark hair. Her friend only stayed for a short period and left again. We then tried to get the NTL Box disconnected, but we couldn't. Bríd then wanted to go the Post office to see about getting her mail re-directed, when we were that far we also went to NTL to see about getting the box disconnected. We then returned back to the house again in 5A Munster Ave. On the way back Bríd went to the shop and got coffee and chocolate. We then went into the house and had coffee and a chat. She was in great form. I then left at 4.50pm on Thursday the 2nd of December 2004 and that was the last time I seen or heard of her until Jim told me the news today 7/12/04. Just to add Bríd had a habit of locking all doors at all times even when I was in the house. The last time I saw her she appeared very happy.

On 3rd December 2004, Martin O'Connor (Assistant Director COPE) wrote an email to Ciarán Hayes setting out a number of questions, querying the rationale behind the instruction by Mr Hayes to deny Bríd Cummins from accessing COPE homeless services, if she appears. Mr O'Connor stated that he was seeking answers in advance of the impending eviction on the 6th December. He wrote:

I wish to register my protest at this instruction. As you are well aware COPE homeless services respond to people who are homeless on a daily basis and do so in accordance with a vision, mission and values of our organisation. Many of your client population have a history of anti-social behaviour, and some have experienced evictions for this reason, but are facilitated to access Homeless Services, where every effort is made to link them in with appropriate support services. We have a comprehensive assessment and admission process in place for our homeless services which we adhere to in respect of all who seek our services. In addition to this, we liaise with Galway City Council in respect of homeless assessments. This instruction appears to by-pass all established policies and practices in respect of people who present as homeless in Galway. Bríd Cummins has not to date presented to COPE homeless services, so we have not had an opportunity to carry out any form of assessment.

I would appreciate a response to the above as soon as possible in light of the impending date of eviction of December 6th. I am also available to meet to discuss the above.

Yours sincerely,

Martin O'Connor. Assistant Director COPE

In the *Report to Councillors*, an email is released (printed 24/2/2005) from Martin O'Connor at COPE to Jacqie Horan, CEO of COPE, evidencing his continuing concern. He updates Ms Horan on the developing situation regarding the homeless referral services (HRS):

'06 December 2004 - 15:35 Subject: Provision for responding to Bríd Cummins'

Hi Jacquie,

I have not had a response to date to my letter to Ciarán. However, in anticipation of this woman possibly presenting to either Osterley or HRS today or tonight I met with Lisa and Ursula today and we agreed the following response initially:

- If she presents HRS will deal with her – Osterley will refer her to HRS if presents directly to Osterley

- If in hours HRS will inform her that we have been instructed not to provide her with services and direct her to attend Galway City Council and present as homeless

- If out of hours provision will be made for her in a Hostel or B&B for that night (to be covered by ourselves) and she will be asked to attend at HRS first thing the following morning

HRS will direct her to present as homeless to Galway City Council

We will reassess the situation at that point to decide what course of action to take next.

I will keep you posted.

Regards,

Martin

The email (released in the *Report to Councillors*) shows that at 16:40, the email is forwarded on to Ciarán Hayes by Martin O'Connor.

At 17:58, Ciarán Hayes replied to Martin O'Connor's email:

Martin,

No problem with the approach.

Separately, we have had no contact from Bríd Cummins yet, despite the passing of the Court's deadline. From my information, I am not aware that she is in the premises.

Regards,

Ciarán

At this time the Senior Social Worker and SEO for Housing were outside the property at 5A Munster Avenue, at the door of Bríd's flat.

Further details on the events at this time are recorded in the subsequent sworn deposition for the inquest at the Coroner's Court on 29th September 2005 by senior executive officer (SEO) Frances Mullarkey:

> Following Court proceeding Miss Bríd Cummins was due to hand in the keys of the property at 5A Munster Avenue by 12pm on 6/12/04. When this didn't happen myself and another official, Gerry Flanagan made enquiries around the area to establish Miss Cummins whereabouts. When we couldn't establish her whereabouts, we visited the property at 5A Munster Ave. We made further contact with the City Council Solicitor and with Miss Cummins Solicitor, this was around five pm on the 6/12/04. Following these enquiries we became concerned for Miss Cummins safety and contacted the Gardaí at Mill Street. At 6.20pm the Gardaí arrived and we explained the situation to them. The Gardaí then took over.

Meanwhile, back at City Hall, the City Councillors were arriving for their regular meeting with the Council officials in the Chamber commencing at 7pm. This proceeded as normal.

After the meeting had concluded, Ciarán Hayes approached the City Mayor, Cllr. Catherine Connolly. She later described this event:

> If I could tell you my own reaction, it was one of shock. I learned it on a Monday night and I have to say I used unparliamentary language when I heard it. On the night that I heard about Bríd Cummins's death, it was a regular meeting. It started at 7:00 o'clock at that time and I chaired that meeting and when it was over sometime after 9:00 o'clock the director approached me directly. There was a long table and I was chairing the meeting, the meeting was over and he said "Bríd Cummins is dead, Mayor."

> [High Court evidence of Cllr Catherine Connolly sworn to Justice Dunne, May 2010]

Finding Bríd's mortal remains

The deposition sworn for the inquest at the Coroner's Court by the attending Garda who attended the scene at 5A Munster Avenue on the night of 6th December, reports receiving the call at 6.10pm.

On arrival at the scene I spoke with Frances Mullarkey who works for the City Council. She informed me that due to a Court Order the resident of 5A Munster Ave was due to vacate the apartment at 12 noon on the 6/12/04. She informed me that the resident's name was Bríd Cummins. Frances then went on to tell me that the keys hadn't been handed in all day, so they went to investigate. When the Council officials arrived to the house, she said that there was no response from the house and that some stuff was still on the windows of the apartment. At this stage they decided to call the Gardaí to gain entry and investigate it. We knocked on the front door and there was no response, I then decided to go around the back, I knocked on the back door and still I got no response. At this I decided to force entry, smashing the back window which led into the kitchen. On entering the kitchen a second door leading into the apartment was also locked. I once again smashed the widow [sic] on this door and entered into the house. I then went towards the front door to let the Gardaí in. I unlocked the first door leading into the small hallway and I then unlocked the front door of the house. We then entered the house again and I looked around. I entered the bedroom of the apartment and I saw a lady lying on her back in the bed, with the quilt pulled up around her. I approached her and felt for her vital signs but there was none. This lady I now know to be Bríd Cummins had no pulse and was not breathing. At this the house was sealed off, the doctor and Priest were contacted, both arriving a short time later. Dr Elsafty pronounced the body dead at 7.25pm. The scene was then examined and sealed off for the night.

In her submission to the Coroner's Court, Frances Mullarkey reported that she had gone to the flat on December 6th with Gerry Flanagan (social worker) as the keys had not been handed in.

Council-released records show that during these hours, Council staff were communicating with their legal firm, Blake and Kenny. Record 000248 on the file prepared for Councillors is a memo from Blake & Kenny's office dated Monday 6th December 2004 (the day Bríd's remains are found at her flat by the Council executives in attendance with Gardaí):

> Patricia at GCC: (rang at 12.25pm) Bríd Cummins has not handed keys over yet as per order for possession with a stay on same until 12 noon on the 6th December.
>
> Said I would contact John O'Donnell and call her back
>
> Rang John O'Donnell he on route to Loughrea, advised Michelle of the above, she will contact John and get back to me
>
> Michelle – Notice of Motion and look for an order abridging time, (was order taken up? Judge want to see order) serve that on Bríd Cummins together with Order (a penal endorsement on the back – if you not complied with order then go to prison). John's devil (apprentice barrister) will going down [sic], his name is Conall.
>
> John said Friday in Loughrea would be a good day.

Bríd's mortal remains were transferred to the City morgue for a post-mortem examination on 7/12/04. The results of this showed the cause of death was 'Due to a lethal Cardiac Arrhythmia with Pulmonary Oedema due to Toxic Effects of a drug to be identified'.

Bríd was laid to rest in her native Clonmel, Co Tipperary.

One Swift Command (by Bríd Cummins)

Poor little lamb

Bleeds all over

My plate

I lap it up

All that blood,

Just as they lap up

My blood

As I bleed all over

This town.

They soak it up

Spew it out.

My blood.

This time I don't

Lap it up.

If I can't swim

Through it,

I'll part it

With one swift command

And

A raised hand.

This vivid poem was written by Bríd Cummins and published in an anthology of poetry called 'Meters' (2007), published by Arlen House. Rita Ann Higgins (Afterword); Catherine Connolly (Foreword)

[Reproduced from 'Meters' (2007), published by Arlen House]

Media Reaction to the Death of Bríd Cummins

There was extensive media coverage after Bríd's body was found, particularly owing to the discovery shortly afterwards of a letter that Ciarán Hayes had written to COPE directing them to deny homeless services to Bríd if she presented as homeless to them.

Eviction tragedy: fury grows over Council's bid to halt rehousing

Bernie Ní Fhlatharta (City Tribune, Friday, 10/12/2004)

The death of a woman about to be evicted from her Local Authority flat on Monday has led to a blazing row between the City Council and COPE, the crisis housing organisation.

Forty eight years old Bríd Cummins was found dead in her bed at her Council flat in 5a Munster Avenue on Monday afternoon — the day she was due to hand over her keys to the Local Authority who had secured a Court order for her eviction.

Ms. Cummins, a clerical worker in the city and a native of Clonmel, had appealed the Galway District Court eviction order made by Judge Mary Fahy and lost her appeal before Judge Harvey Kenny in the Galway Circuit Court, where she was described as the neighbour from hell.

The eviction order was granted to the Council following evidence of her anti-social behaviour towards neighbours, whom she had traumatised with her temper tantrums.

On one occasion she terrorised one of her neighbours in a locked room and verbally abused her. Another neighbour in an upstairs flat had to be transferred elsewhere because she couldn't live with the constant abuse from Ms. Cummins. That flat has been vacant for a number of years as a result.

Judge Fahy made the original order in favour of the Local Authority, which Judge Kenny affirmed in the Circuit Court.

However, the Council's subsequent directive to COPE, who are an independent voluntary organisation, not to offer a homeless service to Ms. Cummins following her eviction has sparked a major controversy.

The Mayor of Galway, Catherine Connolly told the City Tribune yesterday that she was "cross, sickened and very angry" at what had transpired. She said she was saddened by what she described as a "terrible tragedy" and that it was a death that shouldn't have occurred.

"What is most serious is the directive from the Council to COPE not to rehouse her. It is shocking that an official felt he had the power to give that directive.

"Ms. Cummins had put in for a transfer and though I hadn't met her personally, I had written letters on her behalf. There is a policy in place, but it wasn't adhered to in this case. This case should never have gone to Court.

"There were other alternatives that could have been used because she certainly qualified for a transfer to alternative housing on medical and other grounds. She was always unhappy with the level of repairs in the flat. Her battle was with the council."

Mayor Connolly said she would be raising the matter at next Monday's Council meeting and asking questions about how this situation could have led to such a tragedy.

Ms. Cummins was found at her rented flat on Monday evening after neighbours had told Gardaí she hadn't been seen for a number of days. A post mortem was carried out on the body the following day and foul play has been ruled out.

This week, COPE issued a statement saying that it had been asked by the City Council not to house Ms. Cummins - however, she hadn't sought emergency housing and was not known to COPE personnel at all.

Martin O'Connor, Assistant Director at COPE, explained that it had been decided on Monday to provide emergency accommodation to Ms. Cummins if she had presented herself to them as being homeless — she was due to be evicted on Monday.

COPE voiced their objection to the instruction (from the Council) in the case of Bríd Cummins at a steering group meeting of the Galway City Homeless Forum held on December 1. COPE then wrote to Ciarán Hayes, Director of Services for Housing at Galway City Council last Friday putting our objections to the instruction on record and asking answers to a number of questions in respect of this instruction.

COPE, he said was an independent voluntary organisation contracted by Galway City Council and the Western Health Board to provide emergency accommodation services in the city.

"In keeping with the organisation's ethos, it operates independently of these statutory bodies. COPE carries out its own assessments of the needs of those presenting and responds accordingly from its own resources if deemed necessary," he added.

Mayor Connolly said it had also been shocking that the City Council officials were publicly welcoming the Court order to evict Ms. Cummins, while not making alternative arrangements for her, in the same week (last week) as she opened a conference about homelessness in Galway.

Deputy Mayor, Cllr. Pádraic Conneely told the City Tribune yesterday that he was proposing that the Council debate its policy in relation to anti-social behaviour with a view to reviewing it in light of what had happened this week.

Ms. Cummins was in receipt of a disability payment and her medical records showed that she suffered from depression, but she also worked part-time in administration in NUI Galway, according to evidence before the Circuit Court two weeks ago.

The matter of Ciarán Hayes directing COPE to deny homeless services to the soon-to-be evicted tenant was reported in the Galway Advertiser that week.

'Don't help her' letter to Cope was a policy approved by councillors
Report on Cummins' case due before Christmas

(Galway Advertiser, December 16 2004)

The letter sent to Cope by Galway City Council asking them not to help their tenant Bríd Cummins was part of a policy approved by Councillors just five months ago, it has been revealed this week. The announcement has been made in a report on the matter by City Manager Joe O'Neill who said that within the next week City Hall will present a report to Galway's city councillors outlining the actions taken in the case. The council has also said that in light of what has happened it is open to reviewing its policies relating to tenancies.

At Monday's city council meeting Cllr Tom Costello called for a discussion on the matters surrounding the death of Bríd Cummins. Councillors expressed their sympathies to the woman's family and to all connected with the tragic events of last week. The Labour Party called for an independent enquiry into the handling of the case which would have a wide remit and look at all the circumstances surrounding the situation. However a number of councillors criticised views expressed by the Mayor of Galway Cllr Catherine Connolly during an interview on local radio. Many felt she spoke "too freely" and Cllr Michael J Crowe accusing her of "adding fuel to the fire" on an already sensitive matter.

Mayor Connolly defended herself saying she had been reluctant to speak publicity on the subject. She restated her views in the council chamber saying Bríd Cummins' death was a "needless death" and that "there were avenues other than eviction" which could have been explored. She said she was not criticising council staff but was criticising council policy and the manner in which it was enforced. She said she had appealed for Ms Cummins to be given a transfer in both "her interest and in the interest of her neighbours". Finally Mayor Connolly appealed that it was "time to ask questions, time to learn, and time to go forward".

The city manager Joe O'Neill then read out a statement to outline the council's position. He said Ms Cummins' death was "a great tragedy" and he extended the council's sympathies to her family, friends, and the people of Munster Avenue.

Mr O'Neill said it was "regrettable" that the media was used to "publicly criticise the manner in which Ms Cummins' case was handled" by the city council's staff. "In my view, this was grossly unfair and was in breach of the council's Dignity at Work policy," he said. "The criticism caused great distress and hurt to the staff who had acted with great humanity and deserved better." The city manager was also concerned that comments, "however unintentional", could be taken as implying some wrongdoing by council staff and that procedures were not followed. He said staff actions were independently examined by both the district and circuit courts and "were vindicated in both instances". With regard to the correspondence with Cope, Mr O'Neill said the following is the position: The letter was issued in accordance with council policy on anti-social behaviour adopted by the city council "without dissent" in May, having been recommended by the council's Housing SPC and considered by the homeless forum in which Cope participates.

He said Osterley Lodge is not an independent facility but a council facility managed by Cope on contract with the council. He added that Cope's Martin O'Connor had confirmed that Ms Cummins had not approached them but that if she had, Cope was in a position to provide support for her. In conclusion Mr O'Neill said there was "merit in reviewing policies in the light of experience" and if the council consider it appropriate, a review of "our proceedings and policies relating to tenancies can be undertaken". Mr O'Neill promised councillors that within the next 10 days, he will provide them with a report "outlining the actions taken in this case without going into personal details".

In my research for this book, I cannot locate any of the records that Mr Joe O'Neill refers to, that support his statement that:

'Staff actions were independently examined by both the district and circuit courts and were vindicated in both instances'.

The case before the courts was the matter of evicting Bríd Cummins, not the manner or content of staff actions. It was a summary procedure where the judge had no discretion. The outcome was inevitable using that powerful legislation.

Editorial on Death of Bríd Cummins

'Cummins' case — not in our name'

Editorial, Declan Varley, Galway Advertiser, December 16 2004

The tragic death of Bríd Cummins in her Munster Avenue home last week caused reverberations around the city, especially as it occurred on the day she was due to be evicted for what has been described as antisocial behaviour.

There is no doubt that antisocial behaviour is one of the biggest problems that Galway City Council and indeed many county and town councils face in their day to day activities and there is every day pressure on them to exert some control over the properties they operate. At the time of the court case involving Ms Cummins, there was a quiet universal applause for the manner in which the city council was being seen to act in the face of such problems. However, with the news of the tragic end to the case, all of that changed. The heroes became zeroes.

Then last week came the announcement that not only had the council acted in such a manner, but that it had followed it up by asking Cope, the city homeless organisation to ensure that Ms Cummins would not be helped or housed by Cope. It is one thing to put a person down, but to kick her when she is down is seen as behaviour that would not be meted out to an animal, let alone a human being, not withstanding her personal circumstances or past behaviour. Our revelation of this has caused much disquiet to some council staff who understandably felt victimised, but it did happen. Fact.

The letter was signed and sent. In the public's name. What the public now need to know was why such a seemingly heartless approach was taken. If you abandon your pet dog, isn't that bad enough or do you follow it up by asking the GSPCA not to take it in. Or feed it. Questions have been asked all week about why this letter was sent and who had signed it. Councillors climbed over themselves to absolve themselves of any blame and the infighting that is a feature of this new council came into play once again.

At Monday's meeting, the Mayor was roundly savaged by her fellow councillors and city officials for breaking ranks and talking to the media last week, but these attacks were just the latest in the game that has become mayor baiting at city council level. However what had she done apart from express her own views and ask the questions that the people of the city wanted asked and answered? If other councillors had their way perhaps the entire matter would be swept under the carpet. The answers though are not that palatable.

Now it has emerged that not only were councillors aware of this process of writing to Cope, but that Galway City Council were the ones who had actually voted this in less than five months ago. The statement of city manager Joe O'Neill this week made it clear that the letter to Cope was issued in accordance with the council's policy on anti-social behaviour which was adopted "without dissent" by the city council (the previous council that is) when it met on May 17 last.

So it seems that such action is city council policy. Is eviction not enough in the cases of anti-social behaviour? Does the council then have to go out of its way to ensure that further help is not provided? Antisocial behaviour is a living hell for the people who have to put up with it in the city, but surely the swift action of eviction is sufficient. Doing any more seems like being plain bad minded, and it is a policy that most city people would not like to see implemented in their names.

The council has promised a full report on the matter within 10 days. Perhaps when that is published and the full facts of this case are made available to us all, we will be able to see if all this could have been avoided.

Galway City Council Ordinary Meeting – January 2005

After Christmas the first Ordinary Council Meeting was held on Monday 10th January 2005 at 7pm at City Hall, with Mayor Cllr Catherine Connolly presiding. This was the first Galway City Council meeting since the remains of Bríd Cummins were discovered on the evening of the previous meeting. The released minutes of this meeting are reproduced here in full. (Note: SPC= Special Policy Committee)

Presiding: Cllr. Catherine Connolly, Mayor of the City of Galway.

Present: Councillors: Brolcháin N. Ó; D. Callanan; B. Cameron; P. Conneely; Colette Connolly; J. Connolly; T. Costello; M. J. Crowe; M. Leahy; D. Lyons; D. McDonnell; J. Mulholland, T. O'Flaherty and B. Walsh.

In Attendance: Mr. J. O'Neill, City Manager, Mr. C. Hayes, Director of Services, Mr. T. Hernon, Director of Services, Mr. T. Connell, Director of Services, Mr. J. Considine, A/Director of Services, Mr. P J McGovern, Head of Finance, Mr. B. Dunne, Senior Executive Engineer, Ms. F. Mullarkey, Senior Executive Officer, Ms. A. Brett, A/ Senior Executive Officer, Ms. P. Philbin, Senior Staff Officer, Ms. H. Martyn, Administrative Officer, Ms. M. Gibsey, A/Senior Staff Officer

1. REPORT ON TENANCY OF NO. 5(A) MUNSTER AVENUE, GALWAY:

The Mayor welcomed the members of the public to the meeting. She referred to the report of the City Manager dated 23rd December, 2004, already circulated to councillors. She welcomed the report and thanked the Manager for having the report to Councillors within the agreed timeframe. She then invited questions from Councillors on the report.

A lengthy debate followed in which the following were the main questions and concerns raised by Councillors;

- that an independent enquiry should be established to examine all matters prior to the death of Ms Brid Cummins R.I.P.
- whether it would be appropriate for local authority staff to carry out an investigation on its own actions.

- that this was not a witch hunt of officials but that questions needed to be answered.
- that the late Ms. Brid Cummins was an independent woman who had been willing to take on the system and the City Council.
- that there was no evidence in the City Managers Report to substantiate that Ms. Brid Cummins was engaged in anti-social behaviour which led to her eviction from the flat and what documents exist to prove that Ms. Cummins was involved in anti-social behaviour. Reference was made to the legislative definition of anti-social behaviour which did not encompass the type of anti-social behaviour Ms. Cummins was alleged to have engaged in and the need to review such policy, including the appeal process included in the policy and to whom that appeal should be made.
- criticisms of the format of the Report were made with some Councillors stating that they would have preferred a chronological report.
- that the report did not mention the letter dated 2nd December, 2004, issued to Ms. Cummins.
- questions were raised regarding the role of the City Council's Tenant Liaison Officers and the Social Workers and their involvement with the late Ms. Cummins, if any.
- clarification regarding the involvement of other agencies was sought e.g. the Gardaí and the Western Health Board
- The late Ms. Cummin's transfer request was discussed, the rationale behind the City Council's decision to refuse her transfer request, that Ms. Cummins should have been given a transfer of accommodation due to the condition of her flat at 5a Munster Avenue and that it was misleading to claim that Ms. Cummins would not engage with and meet Council officials to discuss her transfer application.

The City Manager stated that a lot of questions had been raised by Councillors but that he took issue with a statement made by a member of the Council which suggested that the City Council had acted in bad faith in this matter. He stated that there was clearly no wrong doing on the part of staff and that this case has had two separate court hearing and has been adjudicated on by the Courts confirming the actions of the Council. He stated that the City Council had no role in interfering with the judicial decision of the courts. He stated that staff of the City Council are accountable but that the comments made by Cllr. B. Cameron were out of order and he asked Cllr. B. Cameron to withdraw his remarks. He further advised that a report in chronological order can be provided to Councillors, and he read from the Housing Act 1997 the definition of antisocial behaviour which does not require that there be a conviction in court before antisocial behaviour can be alleged.

Mr. C. Hayes, Director of Services, then stated that this was his first opportunity to comment publicly on the case. He sympathised with the family and friends of Ms. B. Cummins, and he empathised with neighbours in the broader area of Munster Avenue and with staff members of the City Council who are deeply effected [sic] by this case. He stated that throughout all the media exposure on this case, a number of features are evident and are disappointing and in particular the manner in which Council officials have been publicly criticised for decisions made by the District and Circuit Courts. He also referred to the manner in which public comments and conclusions were made in the absence of the facts without an attempt to consult the officials to ascertain the facts.

The Mayor, Cllr. C. Connolly requested the Director of Services to confine himself to answering the questions raised in the report, and when Mr. Hayes continued with his statement, she threatened to rule him out of order.

Mr. Hayes further stated that staff were exposed to severe public criticism and vilification for carrying out the policy of the Elected Council, i.e. their policy. With regard to anti-social behaviour, he stated that public comment has been made that this was not a serious case, that he disagreed with this comment as did the victims of Ms. Cummins behaviour, the District Court and the Circuit Court. He stated that the both Courts had the benefit of hearing all of the evidence from both sides and both sides were legally represented. He stated that while the Mayor met with Ms. Cummins, he was not aware that other Councillors had met with her, nor was he aware that any Councillor had met with the victims. He therefore could only assume that criticisms, conclusions and judgements were based on hearsay and not the facts. He stated that if there is difficulty with the judgements of the District and Circuit Court in this regard, it is unfair that officials of the City

Council should be publicly criticised and he questioned why those who criticised had been silent on an alternate appropriate sanction in this case.

With regard to the application by Ms. Cummins for a transfer, he stated that the Elected Council decided the policy regarding transfers and the officials implemented that policy; that as a professional in the area of public housing and having regard to all the facts of this case, it is his professional opinion that Ms. Cummins was adequately housed. He stated that she was in accommodation suited to her needs, in an area of her choice, at a rent she could afford, that he was satisfied that she was adequately housed and that the City Manager was similarly satisfied. He advised that the Ombudsman had regard to the complaint made by Ms. Cummins and having examined the Councils policy and the actions of the City Council in this case, closed the file in November, 2002. He stated that the Ombudsman is completely independent and has a remit to enquire into the actions of statutory bodies regarding their decisions. He further stated that it is disappointing that this case was discussed in the media in advance of the burial of Ms. Cummins and in absence of the facts or any effort to obtain the facts and that a declaration be made in the media that the simple solution in this case was to transfer Ms. Cummins; that this declaration was without justification as to how Ms. Cummins qualified for a transfer and how her existing accommodation was deficient as regards her needs, medical or otherwise.

Regarding the maintenance of no. 5A Munster Avenue, Mr. Hayes stated that Ms. Cummins had issues with the maintenance of the premises, that he had the premises inspected by professional housing engineers who reported that it is in compliance with Articles 5(1) and 5(2) of the Housing (Standards for Rented Houses) Regulations 1993, relating to the structural condition of the property. He further advised that the Ombudsman had investigated issues regarding the maintenance of the property and was satisfied in that regard in November, 2002; that he was not aware that any of the Councillors had inspected the property and he questioned therefore how they were in a position to say that the property was deficient as regards maintenance.

With regard to the question of a public enquiry, he stated that the decision in this case was made by the District and Circuit Courts on the basis of direct evidence given in Court, that it is not possible to isolate the actions of the Galway City Council from the decisions of the Court, that both Courts had enquired into the actions of the City Council; that the Courts are independent, that both sides were legally represented with equal opportunity to present their cases and that in any public enquiry, it is difficult to know how the actions of the Courts could be enquired into and whether the enquiry would extend to the legal teams on both sides. He questioned if Councillors had confidence in the Courts and what terms of reference could be set to compel Judges or the Ombudsman to attend.

In summary, he stated that Ms. Cummins had many interactions with Galway City Council including interactions with staff at all levels from Housing Maintenance Staff to the City Manager and that it had proved extremely difficult to resolve the many complaints made by her to her satisfaction. He stated that there was a pattern of behaviour of an anti social nature that ran in tandem with these complaints and that there were many attempts and interactions at many levels with Ms. Cummins to resolve these issues and address the breach of tenancy issues. He stated that; he had enquired into the complaints and was clear that there was a breach of the tenancy agreement; that the City Manager similarly enquired into the matter and agreed with his findings; that the Ombudsman had enquired into the complaints at the request of Ms. Cummins and was satisfied with Galway City Councils position in the matter; that the Courts enquired into this matter and determined that Galway City Council should recover possession of the property and that Ms. Cummins was legally represented throughout. He stated that other than suggesting that Ms. Cummins should be transferred, those who criticised the actions of the City Council have not made any alternative suggestion as to what an appropriate sanction would have been and that in his opinion, the transfer of a tenant that is guilty of anti social behaviour is wrong in that it rewards anti-social behaviour and sends out the wrong message and that those who criticised have been silent as to an alternative appropriate sanction in this case.

Finally, he stated that the staff of the City Council had been subjected to the most serious criticism and vilification, that the only thing they had been guilty of was doing their job, that they had responded to the unfair criticism

110

and vilification with great restraint, professionalism and dignity and that the Elected Council is fortunate to have such staff working on their behalf.

Further debate followed in which Councillors discussed the manner in which the case was handled by the City Council. A number of Councillors took issue with and criticised the manner in which the Mayor, Cllr. C. Connolly had dealt with this issue in the media. Some Councillors criticised the handling of the matter by City Council stating that:

- There was a rush to judgement resulting in a tragedy that should not have happened.
- That it was an effort by officials to take someone down a peg or two.
- That Ms. Cummins had applied for a transfer in January 2000 which had not been granted, while the upstairs tenant was granted a transfer in December 2002.
- That no reference was made to anti social behaviour by Ms. Cummins in the meeting held with the City Manager in May 2003.
- That there is no evidence of contact by the City Council with Ms. Cummins doctor despite her request for a transfer on medical grounds.
- That the motivation in this case resulted from proceedings taken by Ms. Cummins against the City Council.
- That the Courts seem to have no role in actions taken under certain legislation.
- That this case should not have been referred to the courts in the first place.
- That it was necessary to advise if the Health Board had any dealings in this case.
- That there was a serious error of judgement on the part of the City Council.

Some Councillors also further criticised the Managers Report stating that:

- Additional information was being given at the meeting, which was not included in the report.
- The report did not state that the City Manager had inquired into this case as stated by the Director of Services.
- That Councillors were asking questions, not seeking to vilify staff.

- That copies of documents mentioned in the report needed to be supplied to Councillors.
- That the report did not deal with the Ombudsman's report on maintenance and transfer issues.
- That the report does not include copy of the letter to cope and explain why it was sent
- That the report needs to indicate whether files available to the City Council were made available to the Courts.
- That the report needs to clarify why Ms. Cummins behaviour was considered anti social and how it fits with the definition of antisocial behaviour.

Councillors debated the anti social behaviour policy. Some Councillors pointed out that:

- The policy was adopted by the Housing SPC and also by the City Council with input from the voluntary organisations who deal with homelessness.
- That the policy is the policy of the elected council and that implementation is a matter for the officials and that Councillors should stand by their policy.
- That the policy should not reward anti social behaviour by transferring tenants who carry out anti social behaviour.

Other Councillors felt that the policy should be reviewed to ensure that this type of tragedy does not reoccur.

Councillors also debated how this case should be reviewed stating that it was in the interest of the public that questions are asked and some Councillors further supported the idea of having a public inquiry on the case, which would be quick and speedy. Some Councillors took serious issue at the comments made by members of the Council that there was a serious error of judgement on the part of the City Council and that the Council acted in bad faith.

The City Manager advised that he had no notice of the type of questions Councillors may wish to have addressed in the report, that the information provided in his report was factual and that while the City Council is not above criticism, there is nothing to hide in this case. He also stated that no one had raised questions following the outcome of the court case and that he was satisfied that the Council was correct in involving the antisocial behaviour policy in this case. He further stated that the question of a review of the case was a matter for the council and that information requested can be supplied to Councillors.

Mr. C. Hayes, Director of Services, advised that in his opinion Ms. Cummins was adequately housed and that this was the reason she was not transferred; that the vacancy in the upstairs flat at 5B Munster Avenue is due to the difficulties of the Bríd Cummins case; that there was nothing to substantiate the Mayors claim that the transfer application had been put on hold. He also confirmed that the City Council did adhere to policy in this case and he referred to the requests made to Ms. Cummins and her Solicitor to come to City Hall to resolve the issues. He advised that the Threshold document was stamped by the City Council on the morning of the 6th December, 2004.

Following further debate by Councillors on the question of an independent inquiry. Cllr. D. Lyons proposed that;

> " the City Manager would come back to the elected council with answers to the questions raised."

This was seconded by Cllr. T. O'Flaherty.

The City Manager indicated that he could answer the questions raised and would be prepared to bring back a further report.

Cllr. M. Leahy proposed the following amendment;

> "that questions be submitted to the City Manager by Monday 17th January, 2005, to enable the Manager to give a detailed response to questions raised by members."

This was seconded by Cllr. D. McDonnell.

Following further debate in which some Councillors still supported the idea of an independent inquiry, the Mayor called for a vote to be taken on Cllr. Leahys amendment which resulted as follows;

In Favour: 10

Against: 4

Abstention: 1

The Mayor declared the motion carried.

Cllr. T. Costello proposed an amendment to this motion that;

> "an independent inquiry be set up including a review in relation to all events surrounding the tenancy at No. 5 Munster Avenue and that the terms of reference for the inquiry be agreed."

This was seconded by Cllr. Colette Connolly.

In answer to a question raised by Cllr. Brolcháin N. O. the City Manager advised that if a vote on this amendment was defeated that in accordance with Standing Orders a motion to revoke or amend this resolution could only be inserted on the agenda after the expiration of a period of 6 months from the date of its adoption, except with the written assent of not less than one half of the members of the Council.

The Mayor then called for a vote to be taken on the amendment, which resulted as follows;

In Favour: 6

Against: 8

Abstention: 1

The Mayor declared the motion defeated and called for a vote to be taken on Cllr. Leahy's amendment as the substantive motion. This resulted as follows:

In Favour: 10

Against: 4

Abstention: 1

Following debate it was further agreed that the report be presented in chronological order as far as possible and that all correspondence/documents referred to in the original report dated 23rd

December, 2004, and in answers to members questions on the report be provided to Councillors with exception of correspondence subject to issues of confidentiality. It was also agreed that the date for submission of questions be changed to Friday 21st January, 2005, rather than Monday 17th January, 2005, as provided for in Cllr. M. Leahy's amendment. This was agreed unanimously.

Galway City Council Special Meeting – February 2005

The second Manager's report prepared by officials for Councillors officially amassed to 253 records being released under the stewardship of Acting Manager Joe O'Neill. This was officially presented to Councillors by the new incoming Manager Joe McGrath,

This 'Report to Councillors' file has provided many of the primary source records mentioned in this book. It was a bulky file and contained a lot of operational records. The report was formally presented under Item 3 on the Councillors Meeting Agenda. The following are the released minutes:

Minutes of Ordinary Meeting of Galway City Council, held on Monday, 28th February, 2005 at 7.00 p.m., at City Hall, College Road, Galway.

Presiding: Cllr. Catherine Connolly, Mayor of the City of Galway

Present: Councillors: Brolcháin N. Ó; D. Callanan; B. Cameron; P. Conneely; Colette Connolly; J. Connolly; T. Costello; M. J. Crowe; M. Leahy; D. Lyons; D. McDonnell, J. Mulholland, T. O'Flaherty and B. Walsh.

In Attendance: Mr. J. MacGrath, City Manager, Mr. J. O'Neill, Director of Services, Mr. C. Hayes, Director of Services, Mr. T. Hernon, Director of Services, Mr. T. Connell, Director of Services, Mr. P. J. McGovern, Head of Finance, Ms. F. Mullarkey, Senior Executive Officer, Mr. J. Considine, Senior Executive Officer, Mr. L. Blake, Senior Executive Planner, Mr. B. Dunne, Senior Executive Engineer, Ms. P. Philbin, Administrative Officer, Mr. J. Doody, Executive Planner, Ms. M. Gibsey, Assistant Staff Officer.

3. CONSIDERATION OF REPORTS OF OFFICIALS:

Cllr. M. J. Crowe proposed that;

> "Item 3 (e) Manager's Response to Councillors Questions on the Tenancy of 5A Munster Ave., be dealt with as the next item on the Agenda".

This was seconded by Cllr. D. McDonnell who requested that the Part 8 Proposals for Clybaun Road, at Item 5 (c) on the Agenda be also dealt with.

Cllr.Colette Connolly proposed that;

> "Item 3 (e) be deferred and that a separate meeting be held or it be considered at the next Ordinary Meeting of the Council".

This was seconded by Cllr. T. Costello.

Following further debate, the City Manager requested that the Elected Council would deal with Item 3 (e) at this Meeting. He stated that every effort had been made to give the Report to Councillors by the 24th February as agreed and that it had not been given to anyone except Councillors; that it is important that it be considered at this Meeting or otherwise it would be discussed in every other forum in advance of a meeting of the Council. He further advised that he had been requested by the media to comment on the report but that he had declined to comment until it was discussed by the Council.

The Mayor, Cllr. Catherine Connolly then called for a vote to be taken to determine the number of Councillors in favour of dealing with item 3 (e) at this meeting. The vote resulted as follows;

In favour 11

Against 4

The Mayor declared the Motion carried.

(e) Manager's Response to Councillors Questions on the tenancy of 5 (A) Munster Ave.

The City Manager referred to his Report dated 24th February 2005, already circulated to Councillors, and outlined the contents of the Report to the Elected Council. He stated that in line with the resolution passed at the Meeting of 10th January 2004 a total of 210 questions were submitted to him by Councillors and all had been answered in his Report, that there is a willingness to learn from the issues raised and that he hoped that the proposals set out by him may help to facilitate that learning and to move forward with this issue. He then outlined to the Elected Council the three steps being recommended by him in his Report. He pointed out that what he proposes is a review of the policies mentioned rather than a re-writing of them and he guaranteed the co-operation of staff in the process.

A lengthy debate followed in which all Councillors welcomed the Report and the amount of detail supplied to Councillors and complemented staff in this regard, they also debated at length the handling of the case and the need for review of policies as suggested in the City Manager's report.

With regard to the handling of the Bríd Cummins case some Councillors supported the manner in which it was handled. The following were among the sentiments expressed by them in this regard:

- That Ms. Cummins, R.I.P. was adequately housed in an area suited to her needs.

- That they were satisfied that what was done was done in a humane manner recognising difficulties in a number of areas.
- That there was need to take account of the impact of the tenants actions on others.
- That there was no evidence of anyone in the Council operating outside of policy and that officials were implementing policy made by the Council.
- That it was unfair to say that there was a lack of compassion in dealing with the case.
- That we need to examine if Council staff have the necessary skills to deal with this type of case or if it is fair on staff to have to make such decisions.
- That it is not possible to legislate for or foresee with any certainty the outcome of this type of case.

Many Councillors suggested that the Council should have had the assistance of other agencies and professional help in handling this type of case. Councillors also empathised with the staff who had dealt with this case and the considerable pressure on these staff resulting from the outcome of the case. The need for closure on the case in the interests of the friends, family and neighbours of Ms. Cummins was also expressed.

Other Councillors criticised the manner in which the case was handled and in particular raised the following issues;

- Why the Director of Services for Housing is also a Director of C.O.P.E.
- Why Ms. Cummins, a vulnerable person, was not given a transfer despite repeated requests from various people.
- That there was a lack of compassion in dealing with this case.
- That in view of her depression and physical condition and having regard to the praiseworthy psychological report she should have been treated differently and given the help she needed.
- That there was no justification for the eviction decision.
- Why no legal advice was sought in this case as provided for in Policy No. 4 of the Anti-Social Behaviour Policy.

- That an independent file review was necessary by someone from outside the organisation.
- Why the document from Threshold was not given in the correspondence.
- That there appears to be a connection between the case taken by Ms. Cummins against the Council and what occurred thereafter..
- Why a Social Worker visited the alleged victim in this case and not Ms. Cummins.
- That her case was not suited to be dealt with under the Anti-Social Behaviour Policy.

Questions were also raised regarding the e-mails issued on the day of the tragedy, why Ms. Cummins was written to in December when her Solicitor had requested previously that all correspondence be issued to him, why the City Council had taken nine months to answer the Equity Civil Bill issued on Ms. Cummin's behalf.

With regard to the review of policies, Councillors generally welcomed the proposals in the Manager's Report to review the Anti-Social Behaviour and Tenant Transfer Policies. Some Councillors emphasised the need for a strong Policy on Anti-Social Behaviour and reference was made to various representations made by tenants to Councillors when preparing the current policy. The dangers of weakening that policy in any review were highlighted. Some Councillors also suggested that all housing policy should be reviewed including the Housing Strategy while others emphasised that policies such as the Scheme of Letting Priorities for Social & Affordable housing should also be reviewed and compared to other Council's policies. It was also pointed out that policies should take account of sensitive issues and that policy on transfers in particular need to be clear and precise and it was indicated that dialogue regarding transfers between the City & County Councils should commence. Some Councillors, however, did point out that granting a transfer in cases of anti-social behaviour will not solve the problem, that it merely transfers it and may cause others to do likewise.

During the course of the debate Cllr. T . Costello proposed that;

"An Independent Review of the case be carried out by someone from outside the Authority".

This was seconded by Cllr. Colette Connolly.

As the time was now 9.00 p.m. it was proposed by Cllr. D. Lyons, seconded by Cllr. T. Costello and agreed to extend the duration of the Meeting by sufficient time to complete consideration of this item and other urgent items on the Agenda.

The City Manager, in response to the debate and issues raised, acknowledged the emotion generated by this case and referred to the recommendations made by him in his Report in an effort to move forward and he thanked the Mayor and members of the Council for their understanding in allowing him additional time to bring the Report forward.

He stated that every effort had been made to give the maximum information to the Council and that no Independent Review or examination could bring more details to the Council than this Report. He referred to the conclusions made by Councillors and acknowledged that the actions of officials are open to review by the members of the Council. With regard to compassion shown by staff, he advised that while he was only, as yet, getting to know staff in the City Council it is already evident to him that staff do not lack compassion in their day-to-day dealing with the public. He stated that his duty was to examine if the persons who had to make decisions on this case had acted in a reasonable manner and he stated that he believed that they had. He referred to the issues raised particularly relating to transfers and anti-social behaviour policy and he agreed that the transfer policy needs to be reviewed. With regard to the Anti-Social Behaviour Policy he stated that the policy should not be abandoned but should be reviewed and that there was good reason for that policy to be in place in order to balance the rights of tenants on both sides of a dispute. He recommended that the proposals set out in his report be put to a vote of the Elected Council and he assured Councillors that there would be no lack of co-operation in carrying out this review of policies.

Councillors expressed sympathy to all concerned and felt that the case should be brought to a close in the interests of all concerned.

Cllr. Brolcháin N. Ó then proposed the following amendment;

"That the City Council accept the recommendations set out in the City Manager's Report".

This was seconded by Cllr. M. Leahy.

Further debate followed and in answer to questions raised by Councillors the City Manager advised that the question relating to the Director of Housing being a Director of C.O.P.E. is answered in the Report. He explained that prior to staff changes resulting from Better Local Government the Assistant Town Clerk was nominated as Director of C.O.P.E. but since Better Local Government the Director of Housing had been assigned as a Director of C.O.P.E. as the most senior person in housing and reflecting the importance of the position. He also advised that following the request made by Ms. Cummin's Solicitor that correspondence be addressed to his office all correspondence, therefore, had been referred to the Solicitor, with the exception of the one letter in December 2004 which was addressed to Ms. Cummins.

He then suggested to the Elected Council that as a way forward terms of reference for the review of policies should be prepared and he suggested that Councillors submit, in writing to him, what they feel should be included in the review and that he would put the suggestions together and bring them back before a meeting of the Elected Council at the second Meeting in March.

The Mayor, Cllr. Catherine Connolly suggested that an Independent file review be carried out and that Cllr. Costello's Motion be changed to accommodate that wording.

A Debate followed in which a number of Councillors argued that this Motion would be similar to the Motion defeated by 8 votes to 6 and one abstaining at the Meeting held on 10th January 2005 and, therefore, should not come back before Council for a period of six months.

Following further debate the Mayor, Cllr. Catherine Connolly called for a vote to be taken on the amendment proposed by Cllr. Brolcháin N. Ó which resulted as follows:

In favour 10

Against 4

Abstained 1

The Mayor declared the amendment carried and called for a vote to be taken on it as the substantive motion. This resulted as follows;

In favour 10

Against 4

Abstained 1

The Mayor declared the substantive motion carried.

Councillors had voted to accept the new City Manager's report recommendations for a review to be carried out on the Council's Anti-Social Policies, inviting submissions from the Councillors.

However a vote on having an independent file review by someone from outside the Council was rejected by the Councillors, as it was argued that their council meeting procedures precluded them from voting on that proposal for six months, as it was similar to one voted on and rejected at an earlier meeting.

Return to Sender

An internationally acclaimed and well-known Galway poet Rita Ann Higgins wrote a poem to reflect the feelings of many Galway people at the time. A member of Aosdána, Rita Ann Higgins composed the following poem regarding Galway City Council eviction policy, originally published in *'Throw in The Vowels: New and Selected Poems'*, (Bloodaxe Press, 2005).

Return to Sender (by Rita Ann Higgins)

Our acting city manager

Never stops acting.

He never stops playacting.

He's a rule-book carrier.

He letter-of-the-laws it.

He jaw-jaws it.

He praises and praises,

His full of humanity staff,

His staff who gush with kindness,

His staff who sing while they work,

His staff who say, good morning,

How may I help you?

Free from blame all the same,

A councillor said, exonerated,

They are all exonerated,

Staff exonerated he said it again.

Another councillor said policy

Abuse of Power: Because Councils Can

Policy, policy, we have to carry out council policy.

Galway city council policy.

We have to letter-of-the-law it,

We have to jaw-jaw it.

Good staff, lovely staff,

Full of humanity staff,

Gush when we walk staff,

Gust when we talk staff,

Staff exonerated, all exonerated.

Policy policy, letter of the law, all jaw-jaw.

Clever letter-writing member of humanity staff

Writes great letter bereft of hope,

Sends great letter bereft of hope

To emergency housing authority 'Cope'

Telling Cope to spare the hope this Christmas.

Don't re-house her

When we evict her,

The clever letter writer wrote

In a clever letter sent to Cope.

A clever letter bereft of hope.

She answers back.

She calls back.

Abuse of Power: Because Councils Can

She's a trouble maker.

She's riddled with anti-social behaviour,

She claims a back injury,

She's always looking for repairs,

And if it's not repairs it's a transfer.

She's taking legal action against us.

She pisses us off

And us dribbling with humanity.

We gush when we walk.

We gush when we talk.

We are exonerated.

A councillor said so,

Exonerated, staff exonerated,

We were carrying out council policy,

Galway City Council policy.

Our acting city manager,

Our playacting city manager,

Playacts on our behalf.

He has a duty to protect his staff.

He has a duty to protect his back.

He knows how kind we are

All year round

But especially at Christmas.

[Rita Ann Higgins, *Throw in The Vowels: New and Selected Poems* (Bloodaxe, 2005)]

Personal pleas to amend the erroneous 'Report to Councillors'

1. Newly appointed City Manager Joe McGrath

In 2005 I met the newly appointed Manager of Galway City Council Mr Joe Mc Grath, and I wrote to him several times subsequently, beseeching him to correct the erroneous report published to Councillors. He refused to do this. Ms Justice Dunne has since clarified the record in this regard.

2. Previous City Manager John Tierney

After many attempts to contact the former City Manager by telephone, who had since moved on to Fingal County Council, I wrote a letter to John Tierney, seeking his assistance in correcting the misstatements published by Galway City Council, misinforming councillors that the former TLO had not recommended a transfer for Bríd Cummins.

A short time later, I received a typed, signed letter of response from John Tierney, who neither agreed nor disagreed with my comment.

He dismissed my request of him to set the record straight, absolving himself by saying that he had moved on from Galway City Council and any issues arising were the responsibility of the new manager. This was a very disappointing response, because at this point, his intervention could have brought about a simple remedy, as he was the one primary witness in my defence against the misreported details by Council officials to Councillors.

Disappointingly, Mr Tierney did not act positively for his fellow Tipperary native Bríd Cummins. As City Manager, he had the ultimate executive power to rectify her situation. He deferred his powers to Ciarán Hayes, who was not for turning from his decision not to transfer Bríd.

RTE Primetime Programme: Bríd Cummins

On June 7th 2005, RTE's Primetime programme broadcasted a feature on the special powers that local authorities possess in dealing with suspected antisocial behaviour. It featured the "disturbing case" of the eviction of Bríd Cummins in Galway, highlighting it as a case study and posing the questions: "Do these powers go too far" and "are they implemented in a fair and reasonable way"?

The programme asked:

- "A conspicuous tenant and troublesome neighbour possibly, but was Bríd Cummins guilty of a pattern of anti social behaviour as the Council alleges?"

- "In relation to the upstairs tenant, 34/40 of the complaints on the Council's log were made by Bríd Cummins about her neighbour."

During the investigation by the RTE Primetime team, the following contributor opinions were featured on the programme:

1. Jarlath McInerney (Solicitor acting for Bríd Cummins)

"The way the Corporation went after this lady was relentless. They went out to get her. It was corporate bullying as I can see. It was an individual against a Corporation, and she hadn't got a chance."

2. Dr Padraic Kenna (Law Lecturer NUI Galway, author of 'Housing Law and Policy')

"Under the 1966 Act procedures to the Court cannot enquire or take evidence in relation to the tenant. It is a summary procedure. Once the correct papers are served; The Notice to Quit, The Proof of Tenancy, the court has no discretion but to grant the order.

I think it was a shocking case. The whole procedure for taking away somebody's home must compatible with Article 8 and Article 6 of the European Convention on Human Rights Act. This has been in force for over a year in Ireland. If someone is accused of anti-social behaviour, then the judge and jury cannot be local authority officials. There must be a proper process of law to determine that position."

3. Marlene O'Connor, CEO Galway Simon Community

"Evictions will occur. But I think it's important that when or if they do occur, that there is consideration given to the welfare and health of people who have been evicted."

4. Rita Ann Higgins (Poet and friend of late Bríd Cummins)

"She fought the jackboot of bureaucracy, but she lost, because they had the might and the money. She had the disability, the loneliness, the struggle."

128

5. Mayor of Galway (2003-2004): Cllr Catherine Connolly (Barrister-at-law)

"How could someone like Bríd who had a physical problem, a mental health problem, how could somebody like that not get a transfer?

She had received a letter in November of 2003 saying that she wasn't getting a transfer, and to appeal that matter to the Director, Ciarán Hayes, who had already said that she couldn't get a transfer. Now she was advised to appeal that transfer to the man who already had made the decision. I mean there are so many bizarre things in this case, and that one stands out for me."

"I wouldn't use the word anti-social at all in relation to Bríd. It has to be emphasised that in January 2000 when she applied for a transfer, she was the person making complaints about the upstairs tenant, and the word 'anti-social' was never used until the middle of 2003, and retrospectively the word was used. I think that's a very important point."

6. Mayor of Galway (2004-2005): Cllr Brian Walsh (First Citizen at time of the Inquest into Bríd's death)

Comment 1:

"The Council met with Bríd and agreed that they would move the tenant overhead to an alternative location and Bríd was satisfied with that outcome. Once the overhead neighbour had moved, it appears that unfortunately, Bríd's attentions moved to another neighbour in the area and again a pattern of anti-social behaviour emerged."

Comment 2:

"It is clear that Bríd was a very complex individual and she was a highly intelligent person, a sensitive and caring person, but unfortunately there was a side to Bríd's character which caused difficulties for people that lived around her."

Comment 3:

> "The case was taken ultimately by the City Council to evict Bríd because all other avenues they had explored failed, and both a District Court judge and a Circuit Court judge independently of each other and independently of the parties involved in the cases, found that Bríd was involved in anti social behaviour, and found that it was inappropriate [sic] to issue an eviction order."

Cllr Brian Walsh would not have known Bríd or the tenant upstairs. Had he undertaken his own objective research, or indeed reviewed the published Council files closely, he may have had a different evaluation to offer. The upstairs tenant applied for a transfer and was moved on the basis of her age and other qualifying criteria to a purpose-built complex. Bríd Cummins as a neighbour did not feature in that transfer decision whatsoever. It's disappointing that a City Mayor and elected representative could be so careless to go on national television and make personalised statements about someone he did not know, without checking the facts properly.

Subsequently in the course of writing this book, I contacted Deputy Brian Walsh, now a national parliamentarian (T.D., Galway West) furnishing him with the confirmed findings from my High Court action against Galway City Council: (extract)

> For your convenience, I enclose as requested (attached), details of your televised statements to the 'Primetime Investigates' programme aired on RTE on 7th June 2005. In your capacity as City Mayor, you fronted an attempt to achieve a positive spin on the actions of the council.

I asked Brian for his updated comments with the benefit of hindsight in relation to the Bríd Cummins situation. In his email response he said: (extract)

> I was unaware that you were writing a book. I would appreciate if you could provide in writing details of any positive comments that I allegedly made in relation to this subject.
>
> As previously advised, please furnish me with precise details in writing to substantiate the allegations that you are making if you wish me to pursue these matters.
>
> In relation to your question, only in the aftermath of Ms Cummins' sad passing did I become aware of any psychiatric illness.

In my opinion, it is regrettable that an elected member of the national parliament does not feel an obligation to set the record straight publicly nor to apologise to the family of Bríd Cummins for the hurt he caused by misrepresentation of the situation, unwittingly or otherwise.

Coroner's Court: Inquest of Bríd Cummins

In 2005, in the final report to the Coroner, Dr Ciarán McLoughlin, Galway West Coroner identified the critical medical facts surrounding Bríd's demise:

- **Time of death:** 2nd/3rd December 2004
- **Clinical history:** Last seen alive on Thursday 2nd December 2004 at 5pm Past Medical History: Background of severe chronic facial pain due to radiculopathy of her cervical spine noted on nerve conduction studies. Pain located in the face, arms, and shoulder and right leg and possibly related to an accident on a slide in Leisureland ten years previously (whiplash injury). Patient seriously disabled and unable to socialise. Referred to the Pain Clinic – she obtained reasonable pain control with Amitriptyline (25mg nocte) and Neurontin (Gabapentine) (1200mgs daily).

Medication: L-Thyroxine, Zopiclone Zimovane (hypnotic), Neurontin. She also had a history of depression and had been on Gamanil, a tricyclic, in the past.

Histology: Tissues show extensive autolysis

Heart – no evidence of a cardiomyopathy

Lungs – Show pulmonary oedema

Liver – Shows marked autolysis

Coronary arteries – Show minimal atheroma

Cause of Death: The precise cause of death is unclear after a complete autopsy. However it is almost certainly due to a lethal cardiac arrhythmia with acute congestive heart failure due to the toxic effects on the heart on the combination of Amitriptyline and Zopiclone which were found in the blood and urine. The Zopiclone level of 3µg/ml is relatively high, (therapeutic range (0.01 – >0.05 3µg/ml) and is very close to the lethal level of 0.4µg/ml which has been found in deaths from this drug in association with other drugs. The Amitriptyline level is in order of 0.2 µg/ml and is not precise because of post-mortem autolysis due to the long interval of 3-4 days between death and the discovery of the body and subsequent autopsy. It may well have reached a higher level just prior to death.

Signed: Charles Eugene Connolly, Consultant Pathologist

Reporting of Coroner's Court: Death of Bríd Cummins

'Cummins case has not altered council policy bemoans coroner'

Galway Advertiser October 6 2005

Senior housing officials had 'gone to the bother' of going to flat to get keys back, inquest told.

Galway City Council has not made any changes to its housing policies in the ten months since Bríd Cummins' body was found on the day she was to be evicted from her council flat, an inquest into the 48-year-old woman's death heard last week.

Galway West Coroner Dr Ciarán MacLoughlin expressed concern that the local authority had taken no steps in the interim to revise its housing policies in order to avert a similar tragedy occurring again and he called on the council to provide alternative accommodation to anyone it was planning to evict in future.

The death of Ms Cummins from a drug induced heart attack in the council flat at 5a Munster Avenue, Galway city, on December 2 last year - four days before her body was discovered - sent shock waves through Galway city, and not least through the corridors of City Hall, as housing officials who had won a long legal battle to secure her eviction from the flat came to grips with the tragedy.

Hearing that the local authority had made no alternative arrangements to rehouse Ms Cummins, who suffered from physical as well as psychiatric problems, prior to her eviction from the flat, Dr MacLoughlin said that every agency should work together to try to reduce the number of people who take their own lives.

133

Following allegations of ongoing anti-social behaviour involving her neighbours, Galway city council had secured an eviction order against Ms Cummins at Galway District Court early last year. Ms Cummins appealed the decision to the Circuit Court in November but the District Court order was upheld by the higher court and Ms Cummins was ordered to vacate the flat and hand the keys over to Galway City Council by 12 noon on December 6.

Ms Cummins, a native of Clonmel, who suffered from chronic pain in her spine and face due to a spinal injury sustained in a swimming pool slide accident ten years previously, also suffered from depression. She was last seen alive on December 2, but her body was not found until December 6, when Gardaí on the instructions of city council officials, broke into the flat.

Pathologist Dr Charles Connolly said that levels of prescribed antidepressant and sleeping medication were found in Ms Cummins' body, and the toxic combination of both had led to a fatal heart attack. Hearing that proposed changes to the council's housing policies following Ms Cummins' death are still at draft stage, Dr MacLoughlin expressed concern that systems had not been put in place whereby a person who is being evicted would be offered alternative accommodation, "to stop this sort of thing ever happening again".

The coroner asked senior housing executive Frances Mullarkey if the council made alternative accommodation arrangements for Ms Cummins prior to her eviction and was told it did not. Ms Mullarkey said that the council's housing policies were currently under review and new proposals were at draft stage. Dr MacLoughlin asked if the same thing might happen again. "I would be coming from the perspective that if someone dies from circumstances which could be corrected in the future then surely protocols or systems must be put in place to stop it happening again. "Some agency should be asked to intervene to provide some degree of shelter so that a person would not be put out on the road, particularly a person in receipt of social welfare. And this was December," he said.

Ms Mullarkey said it would up to Homeless Services to provide accommodation for a person in such circumstances and would not be up to the local authority. Mr Jarlath McInerney, solicitor for the family, asked that a rider be attached by the jury to its verdict which would indicate that no vulnerable person be evicted from local authority housing in future without alternative accommodation being made available to them. Mr McInerney told the inquest that Ms Cummins' family had concerns about the way their sister was treated by Galway City Council. "Their (council's) heavy handed approach continued right to the bitter end. Senior housing officials had 'gone to the bother' of leaving their desks on December 6 last to go to the flat to get the keys themselves," he said.

Mr McInerney put it to Ms Mullarkey that Ms Cummins had voluntarily sought a transfer from her flat providing alternative accommodation was found. Ms Mullarkey replied that Ms Cummins was deemed unsuitable for transfer. She denied the council had been "heavy-handed" with Ms Cummins and said she had gone to the flat on December 6 with another official out of concern for Ms Cummins' welfare when it was discovered neighbours had not seen her since December 2.

Mrs Angela Harte, a sister of the deceased, said the family was particularly distressed by a letter from the city council to their sister because it outlined to the deceased that she was not going to be rehoused and no emergency housing would be made available to her. "That letter was dated December 2," Mrs Harte pointed out. The coroner suggested to the jury that if it felt a rider was to be attached to the verdict it should state that in the event of a

135

person's tenancy being terminated, alternative arrangements should be put in place so that a person has shelter, heat and food.

Referring to the deceased, the coroner told the jury, "This person was disabled and had difficulty interacting socially because of her medical conditions". The jury returned a verdict in accordance with the medical evidence but declined to add any rider. Dr MacLoughlin said the deceased died on December 2, 2004, and the cause of death was a lethal cardiac arrhythmia due to the toxic effect of antidepressant and sleeping medication. The family of Bríd Cummins have called for an independent inquiry into the local authority's handling of the case. After the inquest, former mayor of Galway, and city councillor, Catherine Connolly said she was horrified at what had come out at the inquest. "It confirms the case was not dealt with properly. I always believed she [Bríd Cummins] should have got a transfer. I can't see why she didn't," Cllr Connolly said.

An uphill struggle all the way for Bríd Cummins

'Up-hill' (by Christina Rossetti (1861))

Does the road wind up-hill all the way?

Yes, to the very end.

Will the day's journey take the whole long day?

From morn to night, my friend.

But is there for the night a resting-place?

A roof for when the slow dark hours begin.

May not the darkness hide it from my face?

You cannot miss that inn.

Shall I meet other wayfarers at night?

Those who have gone before.

Then must I knock, or call when just in sight?

They will not keep you standing at that door.

Shall I find comfort, travel-sore and weak?

Of labour you shall find the sum.

Will there be beds for me and all who seek?

Yea, beds for all who come.

(Reprinted from *Macmillan's Magazine, 1861*)

137

Catherine Connolly, Mayor of Galway (2003-2004)

In 'Meters' (2007), published by Arlen House, Councillor Catherine Connolly wrote a brief summary of her analysis of the Bríd Cummins situation:

Unbelievably one year after the sad and tragic death of Bríd, there has been no enquiry – public or otherwise. What we have are two reports from Galway City Council, together with answers to 210 questions specifically submitted by a small number of City Councillors. One would have expected, or at least certainly hoped, that the two reports and 210 answers would have, in some way, enlightened us as to how decisions were made, including decisions:

- To not to grant Bríd a transfer

- To issue proceedings to evict her

- To issue proceedings to bar her

- To issue instructions to the emergency services not to house her

- To send what can only be described as bizarre e-mails prior to and on the day she was found dead

- To allow a City Council Meeting to proceed at 7pm on the very night she had already been discovered dead in her home unbeknownst to the then Mayor and City Councillors

..to mention only some of the more pertinent and detrimental decisions made.

Rather than enlightenment, however, the language and content of the reports and answers supplied have, in my opinion, served only to obfuscate, to evade, to ignore, to justify, to defer, and most tellingly of all, to exonerate.

Moreover, the absence of senior management officials from Galway City Council and the absence of any representative from any of the homeless organisations in the city at the recent inquest into Bríd's death was in reality, a potent absence."

138

What type of society have we become, when a person's life and death can be treated in such a manner? What are the consequences for the person directly concerned, and for society generally, of the repeated and restrictive use of language and labels to describe that person's behaviour and/or a given problem? What is the value we now place on human life and human discourse? These questions, amongst others, are ones which much be addressed by all of us, given that actions are taken and language is used in our name.

[Foreword to 'Meters' (2007), printed by Arlen House]

Catherine Connolly is an elected Galway City Councillor, a practising Barrister and a qualified Clinical Psychologist. She is a well-respected independent public representative, who promotes social justice through open, accountable and ethical human-rights practices.

Calls for a Public Enquiry

'Michael D Higgins backs call for a public inquiry into Bríd Cummins death'

Michelle McDonagh, Connaught Sentinel (1/11/2005)

Labour Party President and Dáil Deputy for Galway West, Michael D Higgins, has supported calls by the family of the late Bríd Cummins for a public inquiry into her tragic death.

The inquest into Ms Cummins' death in September found that the 48 years old single woman died from a heart attack caused by a combination of prescription antidepressants and sleep medication at 5 A Munster Avenue on December 2, 2004.

The family of the late Ms Cummins reiterated their call for a public inquiry into her death after the inquest.

Deputy Higgins said: "It is absolutely understandable in the light of the terrible event and the many unanswered questions which the family has, that they should request a public inquiry into the distressing nature of Bríd Cummins' passing.

He said he fully supported the family's request and had contacted the Minister for the Environment and Local Government regarding the issue. "This family has suffered greatly over the last year and it is necessary, right and essential that they should be afforded the opportunity to have their questions answered satisfactorily and that, in this way, they might be in a position to try to come to terms with the tragedy which has befallen them," said Deputy Higgins.

'New call made for inquiry into death of council tenant'

Connacht Sentinel Tuesday, 6/12/2005

A new call has been made for a public inquiry into the circumstances surrounding the death last year of Bríd Cummins in her council flat in Munster Avenue in the city.

Speaking at the launch of a book of poems by the late Ms. Cummins in the Bridge Mills last night, Labour city councillor Catherine Connolly said she found it "unbelievable" that there had still been no inquiry — public or otherwise — into the events surrounding Ms. Cummins' death.

The South Ward councillor, who has campaigned from the very start for an investigation into the events early last December, says the launch of the book of Ms. Cummins' poetry one year to the day when she was found dead in her flat was particularly poignant.

"The book allows the opportunity to remember Bríd, to celebrate her life and creativity but also to acknowledge her courage and persistence despite the pain which was so much part of her life.

"The publication of her poetry provides some redress to the appalling one dimensional portrayal of Bríd by some elements of the media and some people in positions of power and influence, both prior to and subsequent to her death," Cllr. Connolly said last night.

Cllr. Connolly then launched another broadside at Galway City Council over the matter of the issuing of eviction proceedings against Ms. Cummins' last year, claiming the local authority was not living up to its responsibilities in the area of human rights.

"The city council has completely failed, and continues to fail, to comply with their obligations under the European Conventions on Human Rights Act 2003.

"There is absolutely no evidence that the city council is even aware of their new obligations under the Act, which is in force since January 2004, despite the tragic death of Bríd Cummins," Cllr. Connolly says.

She says it is a matter of urgency that the Department of Environment and Local Government takes steps to ensure that city council officials are provided with training and education in the new Human Rights Legislation and she will be putting a motion on the city council agenda in this regard.

After the passing of a few years, the property at 5 Munster Avenue was back in the news again in 2010. The Council had restored the house back into an original configuration to suit one family unit.

A complaint arose from the neighbours at 6 Munster Avenue in relation to the neighbour now occupying Bríd's former address. This was heard in Galway District Court:

'Judge dismisses woman's noisy neighbour complaint: City Council had found no evidence of drunkenness or revelry at house'

(Connaught Sentinel, Tuesday, November 16, 2010)

A MOTHER of two, who was accused of playing loud music and with having all night parties, had a neighbour's complaint against her of excessive noise dismissed when the matter came before Galway District Court.

Nora Walsh (73) had brought the case against Eilish McInerney, 5 Munster Avenue, under the Environmental Protection Agency Act 1992.

She claimed that her neighbour moved in next door in July 2007, with what was to be just her two sons, but that other noisy family members frequented the City Council house.

She said that she, and her ill husband and daughter, had to endure screaming, shouting, all night parties, loud music, banging of children's drums, and verbal abuse from Ms McInerney and her guests.

"I'm too old to live like this," she told the court, adding that complaints had been made to the City Council and Gardaí.

Mrs Walsh told solicitor for her neighbour, Patrick Keane, that she had rejected mediation between the parties because Ms McInerney was not a trustworthy person.

The defendant told the court that when she moved into the house that her next door neighbour was quite pleasant, but after six weeks things changed and that Mrs Walsh started harassing her children.

"On May 24, 2008, Gardaí called at 11pm asking was I having a party – I was in the sitting room and my children were in bed," she said.

"I kept a record of all incidents, and contacted the City Council every time. Gardaí called to me on New Year's Eve at 3.30pm asking was I going to have a party (that night)."

Ms McInerney said that this was the final straw, and went to a solicitor about what was happening.

She sought a transfer that same month, but later decided to stay as her children were happy, and she asked the City Council to consider mediation instead.

"I go to college, it's an intensive course, I just don't understand how I managed to do well in my exams and get into a Masters if I'm portrayed as this wild neighbour," she said.

"I don't know why she's lied. She doesn't want anyone to live near her."

Michael Collins, who lives on the other side of Ms McInerney, said that he never had problems with either neighbour.

Therese Carroll, Galway City Council Housing Liaison Officer, told the court that she visited both parties to investigate the complaints, during which she found no evidence of drunkenness or revelry at Ms McInerney's house.

She added that the local authority had decided that the defendant was not in breach of her tenancy agreement.

Judge Aeneas McCarthy offered Mrs Walsh sympathy on account of her domestic circumstances, but said that there was insufficient evidence against the defendant, and he duly dismissed the matter.

The Council took an entirely different approach this time. Although Mrs Walsh details her own poor health and describes her responsibilities as a home carer, it is notable that the Council's social workers are not providing reports to the Court on this occasion.

Working in Galway City Council

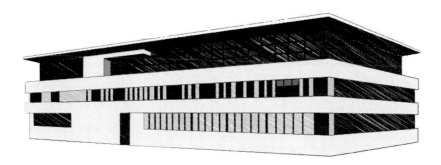

When I first went to work for Galway Corporation, I was initially employed as a revenue collector, which involved working 'out on the ground' around neighbourhoods of Galway City, collecting revenue owed to the Council for rents, housing loans and other monies. It was a tough but enjoyable job. It involved being out in all weathers and engaging with interesting people on a daily basis. Some great stories were shared and I gained huge work satisfaction in this role over the years.

Two days were rarely ever the same. Most tenants and business people were happy to pay up what they owed. They got used to the same person calling regularly, and a bond of trust and friendship built up over the years. My previous experience as a Community Welfare Officer provided me with an in-depth knowledge of the welfare system. Many of the people I met while collecting housing rent were at times dependent on social welfare payments. I was always happy to share my knowledge when it could be of assistance and benefit. Part of my revenue collection duties included tallying a weekly reconciliation of the monies collected and it was my responsibility to ensure that it was banked safely and on time.

Local Authorities are responsible for maintaining a correct and annually-updated Register of Electors. This Register is the list of voters who are legitimately entitled to vote in local, national and European elections and referenda. If your name is not on a Voting Register, you are not issued with a polling card to vote at election times. Council-employed staff covered regions of the city, calling to every housing unit, with a copy of the previous year's Register to establish which qualifying electors are still living at the address, or have moved since the previous year. It is important that this official register is kept as up-to-date as possible.

One story I remember in my early years working on the Register, was of a new housing development where no one was yet living. Yet, at every dwelling listed on the Register, forms had been submitted for named people who claimed to be living there. I marked the names to be removed by the County Registrar at the Electoral Review Court, which is held every autumn. This is an open court session, where any citizen who disagrees with the 'Draft Register' can appear in person to have their circumstances discussed with the County Registrar. I was surprised that particular year by the attendance of a local TD. He demanded to know why I had requested the removal of the block of names from the Register. I explained to the County Registrar that there was no sign of anyone living in any of the houses in the development, and to be sure I called back the day before the Register Court to check again. The red-faced politician ground his teeth and threw an angry look in my direction. He saw nothing whatsoever wrong about his irregular attempt to register non-existent residents.

The rise and fall of the Rahoon Flats

The Rahoon Flats were built in the early 1970's on a similar basis and design as the Dublin Ballymun Flats. They were functional shelter at the time in answer to housing thousands of families. They were transient accommodation, as anyone allocated keys to a Rahoon Flat knew they would eventually be allocated a house by the then Galway Corporation.

In the early years, these flats were much sought-after. Families were very happy to achieve security of tenure and knew they were getting nearer to acquiring their own home. Many former residents of Rahoon Park have fond memories today of starting off domestic life there, many friendships were forged and families were conveniently located to amenities such as schools, hospital, university and Salthill beach, which were all within walking distance. The Westside area was also served with a public bus service to the city centre.

Over the subsequent years, due to a laissez-faire attitude, flat complexes and some housing estates degenerated physically and socially. It was recognised by the authorities that a change of thinking was needed, and a new strategy emerged. It was decided after many meetings between the tenants, the Corporation and public representatives that the flats would be knocked down and new housing estates would be built in the same area.

I remember the official announcement granting many millions of punts being enthusiastically welcomed by the locally-based national parliamentarians. One of these was (now president of Ireland) Michael D Higgins. As a politician he made himself easily accessible in the Westside community and to his neighbours in Rahoon. When it came to representing the underdog or disadvantaged, 'Michael D' was a force to be reckoned with, where he proved to be vocal and articulate in representing his constituents.

His wife Sabina was a willing pair of hands in the community and was a lively supporter to fledgling community groups. She was also the local TD's 'eyes and ears' with women's issues, and demonstrated a genuine compassion and empathy for people suffering with disability and other life challenges. There was an immense cross-political party respect and a wealth of fondness towards them both, as they were ordinary people, speaking in ordinary language. For a man of academic intellect, Michael D exuded humility and interest in people.

The resettlement out of the flats started from 1998 onwards. As they were knocked down tower block after tower block, residents were resettled into adjacent new-build, mixed-design houses. At the time, this was an exciting development for the city, where the flats were coming down after 30 years on the landscape. Tenants were likewise delighted to be moving into brand new housing. They were excited to find out who their lifelong neighbours would be. Tenants could purchase their homes if they wished, under the Tenant Purchase Scheme. As their financial situations improved, tenants could apply to buy-out their homes at a discounted price. Local authority housing in Galway City would never be the same again. The specifications of the homes were as high as any private estate.

Estate Management: A new concept in Social Housing

In line with national policy, the Department of Environment sanctioned creation of the post of 'Tenant Liaison Officer' (TLO) to liaise with communities and engage local residents in becoming more involved in the management and maintenance of their own estates.

During the early years, I worked closely with the resettlement of tenants from the Rahoon flats, moving into houses. I knew many of the tenants from when I collected their rent, and they knew and trusted me. The residents were from diverse backgrounds, and often times did not have local family or friends. I was privileged in that many confidences were shared, and I always respected the trust placed in me. As part of my role, I devised various programmes and implemented these through tenancy training to assist the new home owners. This was an exciting time for everybody concerned.

When tenants signed up for their new homes, they also undertook to comply with all of the conditions of their tenancy agreement. The Council would provide training to everybody to enable full understanding of what this agreement entailed. The Council undertook to enforce all of the conditions and guaranteed residents of the estates that they would not have to endure anti-social behaviour again. Residents were empowered to address issues arising on their estates through estate-management training, which I was directly involved in delivering. Various statutory bodies came on board and partook in several meetings with newly-formed residents associations. A new air of positivity and hope for better lives developed.

The new estates started out very well, as eager Residents Associations wanted the best for their children in amenities and safe and clean environments to grow up in. Community leaders emerged, who organised the establishment of community crèches and a myriad of community services sprung up. It was a pleasure to assist the progression of these applications and to see people pulling together for the common good.

As part of my duties I also dealt with issues of anti-social behaviour and mediated in disputes of newly-forming neighbourhoods where they arose. I designed and published a Tenants Handbook for council tenants, outlining the respective rights and responsibilities of both the tenant and the landlord. This helped to minimise misunderstandings and moved residents towards a new mindset of 'ownership' of their property as well as their neighbourhood.

Residents in one of the council estates flagged up 'slippage' in the early days of resettlement. This was in the form of anti-social behaviour that included criminal activity, as well as gangs taking possession of houses and terrifying residents. This estate was populated by a mixture of young families, single parents and the elderly. There was a common recognition that these were some of the same problems that they had experienced previously in the Rahoon flats.

Residents were fearful of making reports or giving evidence to the Gardaí Siochána. The Residents Association came together and identified a CCTV system as being the best way to deal with this problem. This would provide evidence for the Council (as landlords) to deal with the criminal activities. The Residents Association consulted all the houses in the estate, where although the overwhelming majority of households wanted the CCTV system into the estate, there were also some objectors. At this time the Housing

Officer gave the CCTV initiative his full support. To progress the majority decision, meetings were set up between the residents and the Council, and the Gardaí came on board. It was agreed that the Council would provide the funding for the CCTV infrastructure and cameras, and the Gardaí were going to accept the signal into the Garda station for monitoring.

After many meetings, the Gardaí advised that for logistical and other reasons, this arrangement was not going to be possible. The residents were disappointed, but meanwhile this empowered group researched the alternatives. There was already a similar scheme in operation in Moyross, Co. Limerick, which the residents visited. Having secured the support of the City Council in principle, they discovered that the signal could be housed at an independent location.

The Residents Association approached their local TD Bobby Molloy, who was also the Minister for Environment at that time. He was sympathetic to their cause and encouraged their initiative. Tenders were sought and a state of the art CCTV system was installed by a private security company, who fortunately were in a position to accept the signal into their independent offices. The cameras were located on very high steel poles around the estate. They were designed to encompass all of the public areas. It was agreed that the Council looked after the recording and the signal, and that the Gardaí could access the recordings on request from the Council. This CCTV system worked well. It had an immediate beneficial impact in reducing the criminal activity. The joyriding stopped. It was no longer comfortable for persons involved in nefarious activities to enter the estate undetected. The Gardaí made use of the resource and positive community relations were restored. The CCTV cameras gave a real sense of security to the residents because they were prominently positioned. This project highlighted that when local authorities listen to residents and facilitate their identified needs, positive outcomes can result.

At the same time this was happening, another new resettlement estate that I was working in experienced a different interaction. This was a small estate of approximately twenty houses, where everyone knew each other. Neighbours knew that one family had to move abroad temporarily for medical reasons. The residents wanted to help the young family in any way they could. The newly-formed Residents Association were planning amongst themselves how they would look after this vacant house. They wanted to ensure that the family would return to their home to find it exactly as they left it. Having recently moved into this brand new estate, this would be the first bonding exercise for the residents. They knew that the tenancy agreement specifically stated that no resident could at any time sub let a portion or any part of their home to any third party, and that the Council had undertaken that all of the regulations would be enforced.

One morning, I received an urgent phone call from the Resident's Association secretary to come quickly, as people were moving into the soon-to-be vacant home. I went immediately, and when I got there I was flabbergasted when the door was answered by a woman who told me to "take a hike". She claimed that they had a private arrangement with the legal tenant of the house, and "the Council know about it".

On return to City Hall I went to the Housing Department, where the Housing Officer confirmed that he had indeed given permission to those people to sub let. He indicated that he did not want the other residents to be told! I enquired as to why we were breaching our own regulations and undertakings to the residents - that this would seriously undermine my credibility in the community and that of the Council.

He told me he was "bending the rules" to facilitate a local politician's request. That single action pulled the thread of trust from this estate and gave rise to opportunistic sub-letting. The fledgling trust in the council's commitments to the community was lost in that estate.

Unfortunately, this situation deteriorated further into anti-social behaviour and a brand new house in the same estate was destroyed by anti-social 'visitors' to a tenant. No sanctions were applied by the landlord at this time. As a Council employee working in the community, incidents like these had long lasting repercussions. After the Rahoon Flats experience of anti-social behaviour, it was an immense challenge to restore and build new confidence in the City Council as landlords. This was déjà vu for some residents, as the Rahoon Park flats (being conveniently located to Galway University and the Regional Hospital) saw many sub lets that went unchallenged over the years.

First meeting with Bríd Cummins

It was sometime in the Spring of 2000 when I first encountered Bríd Cummins. A new engineer had started in the Housing section. He was a man with great regard for correct procedures and was always very conscious of his responsibilities. I found him conscientious and correct at all times. This engineer believed that females living alone shouldn't ever be visited on their own by male workmen, and in a meeting, arrangements were made with the Housing Officer Ciarán Hayes, that I would make myself available anytime there was a request from the Maintenance section to accompany on such visits. I was requested to assist on occasions in this regard and would always ensure to be available as required. Regrettably this new procedure was not observed consistently, being casually observed after that engineer moved on to another local authority.

At that time, Bríd was complaining about the delays in carrying out the works in the flat at Munster Avenue. She had been allocated to that flat in 1998. After a request to accompany the foreman to visit her, the first thing I did before going out to visit; was to request to see her Housing file. I remember very well the Housing Officer (as per procedure) handing me a file that was on the desk in his office, with very little information on it. It was scant at best.

I specifically recall one of the Council's female Social Workers being in the proximity of the office as I left with the foreman. The Social Worker asked me what I knew about Bríd Cummins, and I replied "very little". I enquired as to what she could tell me from her position. She shrugged her shoulders and walked away.

Creation of Tenant Liaison Officer (TLO) Position
During my years working in the Housing section for the Council, one project was co-funded by Galway City Partnership under the umbrella of 'Community Development and Estate Management'. At that time, it was seen as a prudent way for the Council of availing of European funds.

The role of TLO in local authorities was a novel one. I was the first TLO in Galway, and based on the positive reaction I was achieving across agencies and from the community, the Council applied in 2000 to the Department to employ two additional TLOs to cover the sprawling areas of Galway City. The three positions were being funded by the Department of Environment.

It was my expectation after pioneering, training for and developing the TLO post, and having performed successfully in the position for a number of years, that my employment would not be at risk when the positions came up for permanency. To all intents and purposes during my years of service, I had been treated as a permanent member of staff, insofar as I regularly carried out duties beyond my job description. At one time, on querying him in relation to the status of my employment position, I was told directly in response by a previous City Manager, that I was "doing a great job" and he assured me that I would be working with the Council "for as long" as I wanted to be. Alas, this proved to be an empty assurance after he moved on to become a manager in another local authority in the south of Ireland.

Career movement in local authorities

Most of the people that I worked with in the Council came into the local authority service at a young age. Over the years, permanent staff members were upgraded to higher levels as vacancies arose. It is a feature of careers in local authorities that staff are typically transferred from one functional section to another. Often, this happens without any specific prior training, overt suitability, or desire to be working in a section.

Where an employee comes into a new area of responsibility, for example, Human Resources, Housing, Environment, Planning or Finance, it can be a daunting experience for them, as well as for members of the public with whom they come into contact.

In my experience working at Galway City Council, I noticed that there was little of more importance to most officials than the progress of their own careers. I have friends in local authorities all around Ireland and they advise of the same scene. In the Housing section that I worked in, many Housing Officers passed through that position as part of their career path, moving through the grades. This feature of local authority employment means the public can encounter anywhere from poor to excellent interactions and service, depending on the knowledge and skills of a post-holder at any given time. This often results in humorous as well as embarrassing events and outcomes.

I was fortunate in already knowing many of the former occupants of the Rahoon Flats, now living in houses. The vast majority of the residents never wanted to again live in what they considered a 'ghetto'. I earned their respect and confidence by honest brokering with them over the years and was a trusted public face of the Council out on the ground. I remember in one of the new estates, where the Residents Committee advised me that one of the new houses was going to be abandoned by a Mr M. His female partner had already taken flight to the UK and his good self would be sailing on the next day.

The residents overheard this couple boasting about owing the council for many months of rent. It had now come to the neighbours' attention that the new kitchen was in the process of being dismantled for suspected resale. I went to the house to investigate and discovered that what I was told seemed to be true. With a bit of arm-twisting, I convinced the man who was relatively new into the role of Housing Officer of his need to call immediately to the house. This gentleman was of middle years, well spoken, with a mild manner. I asked him to come out with me, to see this for himself as it was his responsibility to deal with it. When we got to the front door, he knocked gently and got no response. I urged him to come around to the back door, where it was eventually opened by an assistant of the tenant, holding a screwdriver in his hand, after being disturbed from his work!

Before any words had been exchanged, he ordered us around to the front of the house again. Compliantly, we made our way around and eventually the front door was opened. The Housing Officer introduced himself and suggested gently to the tenant: "we need to talk", and invited him up to visit his office in City Hall the next day. Mr M declined the offer, saying that wouldn't suit him, but offered to come to City Hall the day after that. I was surprised that this was the way the conversation had gone, and the counter-offer was being entertained. As we walked away the hammering and dismantling inside the house continued again. Getting into the car it struck me that the surreal experience of what had just happened was akin to the infamous quote of "Come up and see me some time". If it wasn't so serious, it could have made for a good comedy sketch.

Sure enough, next day, the disappearing act of Mr M and the kitchen had been completed. I believe the repair and refurbishment to this two-year-old house ran into a five figure sum. I felt very sickened for the residents who were working so hard to observe the rules and working with the council in the belief that their efforts would be valued and reciprocated. The woman that had made the initial phone call to me advised me later that she had used a scarce bit of phone credit in making that fruitless call. It is hard sometimes to blame people for losing faith in some public officials.

Selection and Recruitment at Galway City Council

I recall clearly an incident where the council advertised a clerical post externally, where the funding provided was conditional on the post being specifically filled by a person with a disability. Local authorities are obliged under law to positively encourage and provide for the employment of persons with disabilities. Interviews were held in City Hall and carried out by internal staff. It was marvellous to see so many people with physically challenging situations making it in for interview.

Alas, they need not have bothered as the successful candidate had already been selected. The woman was already working inside City Hall on a back-to-work scheme. Prior to the interview, she was advised by a member of the Human Resources staff "You must come first Mary, call up to the office first." She was indeed successful. I don't know what her physical disability was but a short time after the interview; I saw her carrying a heavy 8 foot by 4 foot sheet of chipboard with a male member of staff for a display being organised.

One of the most popular outdoor workers in the Housing Dept held down a full-time position with the Council for decades. At the same time he also held down a job with another state agency, and he also did some part-time security work. All of this was achieved by travelling on foot, as he neither cycled a bicycle nor drove a car. He was lucky that his City Council salary attracted a travel allowance as a significant percentage of his salary. This was the cause of much mirth and more than a little envy around City Hall for many years.

In the context of extremely controversial happenings in Galway City Council during 2003/04, wherein senior officials were seeking to evict Bríd Cummins, I was preparing for a job interview to secure

158

permanency in my role. The three housing liaison officer positions were being filled in March 2004, and there were some anxieties amongst the post-holders about what the management were aiming to achieve during a rare 'Open Recruitment'. It is often believed in local authority circles that external interview boards are selected and brought in to achieve 'desired results' of the management.

This would prove to be the outcome in my situation where I was ranked 7th by the panel for suitability for the post that I had pioneered and developed, had the longest experience in, was uniquely qualified, and according to the Council I had an unblemished work record. Ironically, my primary referee, who provided a glowing reference, temporarily moved into the position of Acting City Manager for the days of the recruitment process. Strangely, he accepted the recommendation of the strangers (to me) who met me for approximately 30 minutes and marked me at approximately half scores.

In the aftermath of what I experienced as a sham interview process, I challenged the City Council in the High Court, and I sincerely thank the honourable Justices Mr Daniel Herbert and Ms Elizabeth Dunne for acknowledging the "ungentlemanly" actions of the interview panel chairman, a Director of Services in Limerick Council, as well as the animus directed at me by some officials from Galway City Council.

During my years of service working in the local authority, I enjoyed a positive and active working relationship with Councillors, where I had regular interaction with many of them in my role as tenant liaison officer, as well as encountering them with community groups around the city. I regularly networked professionally with other statutory and voluntary organisations to resolve problems of poverty and domestic abuse. I believe in always affording the highest levels of dignity to people, regardless of their situation or difficulty. I was often impressed by the genuinely altruistic nature of some of the city councillors in helping people, who they certainly knew would never vote for anybody, let alone themselves.

In the weeks after the humiliating episode of the interview, I received a lot of kind wishes from friends and some former colleagues who were stunned when they heard what had happened to me.

A number of Councillors cross-party thanked me officially for the service I had given over the years, in particular to the communities.

High Court Case: Challenging the City Council

Day 1: Grace (Plaintiff) Vs Galway City Council (Defendant)

On the first morning of the High Court action, I met with my solicitor Mike Ward at Distillery buildings on Church Street, located adjacent to the Four Courts complex in Dublin. We had an appointment to attend with the barrister, Gerard Hogan (Senior Counsel) for a briefing in advance of the case commencing.

At the office, Mr Hogan's secretary apologised for his delay, explaining that his return flight from Britain the day before had been cancelled due to the high profile 'Volcanic Ash' incident. He was making his way to Dublin by train and ferry that morning.

Word was coming through from the Courts that sitting cases were running over their expected duration, and it seemed likely that our case would be called for hearing in the mid afternoon, at the earliest. While we were waiting in the chambers, the junior counsel, Ms Siobhán Phelan arrived. At midday Gerard arrived at his office. He apologised for his lateness and explained about his long travels home from London. He confessed that he was feeling less than his full self but anticipated that he would 'liven up' as the day went on. Mr Hogan alerted that it was *possible* that the case might not actually be heard until the next day. At this point I was not overly concerned, thinking that it would actually help to reduce my nerves while I became acquainted with the intimidating surroundings.

We arranged to reconvene over at the Court buildings. The President of the High Court would be assigning notice of the available court room and sitting judge. We walked the short distance over to the High Court complex, pulling our documents in wheeled suitcases. As we approached the gates, photographers got their picture, and we went through the security room, which scanned all our coats and bags through an x-ray machine, such as used at the airport.

We made our way down the long corridors to the main Rotunda of the Four Courts. This is an impressive building, with a large open circular foyer, where each of the entrance doors to the four courts are at opposing ends. Clients and their representatives were congregated in clusters around the rotunda in hushed conversations. We moved into a vacant spot and waited for the arrival of the Counsel. I spotted the group from Galway City Council and a team of their representatives around the centre of the foyer. They seemed to be enjoying their time away from the office, back slapping and laughing. I was aware that I was entering into the proverbial lion's den. I knew that I had not done anything wrong. Their mood and numbers were in grave contrast to mine. I was there with one of my sons and my solicitor.

A number of hours went by waiting around. It was stressful beyond belief, as the longer it took waiting to find out what was happening I

162

was finding it harder and harder to stomach the laughing and giggling going on amongst the men and women of the other side. I didn't recognise some of the persons in the group at that time, but they all seemed to be well acquainted.

At approximately 4pm, it was advised the case was set down for hearing on following morning at 11am in Court 5. At this early stage, already the defendants were seeking to have the case struck out, claiming that there was 'no show' by Gerard Hogan at the 10:30am call over that morning. Thankfully, the President of the High Court was having none of it and said he was satisfied with the apologies that were offered at the time due to the volcanic ash episode. We had a brief discussion about the format of the day to follow and arranged to meet back in the Rotunda on next morning at 1030. It was already one long day over.

Day 2: Grace Vs Galway City Council

I feel overwhelmed by the circumstances for why I am here this morning, but I absolutely have to confirm my good name. There is a woman dead and all of the facts were never clarified about why this happened. I steel myself for what is to come, and censure myself for letting any negative thoughts invade my head. I feel assured knowing that I have arguably one of the best legal teams in the country representing me. The Junior Counsel is Siobhán Phelan BL, a woman renowned for her dedication to law. The Senior Counsel is Mr Gerard Hogan, a very well renowned barrister and eminent legal academic at Trinity College Dublin (TCD). For all of his due eminence, he is a pleasant and unassuming man. They are instructed by solicitors Staunton & Co., Sea Road, Galway, represented today by Mike Ward. I believe that I can put my faith and trust in his diligence in this case, and have great confidence in his honesty and integrity towards achieving the best result for his client.

Galway City Council's legal team compromises of Junior Counsel John O'Donnell BL, a fellow Galwegian who often acts for the City Council, and they have retained Senior Counsel John Gallagher SC, a tall, mature and imposing-looking man wearing the traditional legal wig. He came to national prominence years previously when appointed to represent the Gardaí in the Stardust Tribunal and again featured as the barrister declined by the Stardust survivors when his services were being offered to them by the then Taoiseach Bertie Ahern.

The Council's solicitors in this case are Blake & Kenny, who are represented in court today by solicitor Gregory McLucas. The principal solicitor of the firm is Michael Molloy, a brother of the former government minister Bobby Molloy. I am initially perplexed that they are being instructed in this case to represent the Council, as I have specifically named them in my Statement of Claim as being part of the action that I am alleging against the Council.

The most important mortal in the room from my perspective today is the assigned judge, Ms. Justice Elizabeth Dunne. I am advised by the legal team that this formidable lady has a reputation for being an excellent listener. Bracing myself for her to appear any minute, there is another woman on my mind now. If she was physically here today, she would be of similar age to the Judge. I reflect on the circumstances surrounding her last days, where some of the people sitting in the courtroom today ensured that she had spent what turned out to be the last days of her life in courtrooms facing the same firm of solicitors for the Council. She was subsequently found dead in her bed by council officials when they called to collect the keys.

I am alleging here today in this court room that council executives abused public resources at their disposal to ensure that Bríd could no longer continue to live in a council home. When I would not join in the cruel campaign to evict her, I was accused of being '*argumentative, belligerent and not of much assistance*' in the eviction process.

I am placing all of my faith and trust in Justice Dunne today. I pray that she will indeed listen, and hear my testimony to establish the facts as they were. The one factor known to me is that Galway City Council will attempt to use any and every tactic to extinguish my action. Only days earlier, I received a telephone call from the Revenue Commissioners in Galway. There were concerned that the human resources department in the Council had contacted them directly, seeking information over the telephone, seeking access to personal information about my financial affairs (despite having ceased employment with them years previously.)

The Judge arrives in brisquely, and assumes her seat. There is a stenographer in situ to record a typed verbatim account of what is said during the course of this case. The Court's tipstaff sits to the side in the courtroom. I take a deep breath and compose myself to stay calm. I have waited for this day for a long time.

Opening of the case

Mr Hogan SC addresses the court, introducing the legal team. He states that there is a bound booklet made available to the court containing the paperwork, which explains the basis for the case. He outlines that this is an action "essentially for wrongful dismissal", but that it is an action for wrongful dismissal with a difference, because it is claimed it was done by mala fides (latin: bad faith) of the defendant. He goes on to describe the history of my employment with Galway City Council between 1993 and 2004. He cites that I am claiming a lack of independent objective basis after I was terminated by reason of what amounted to mala fides in the legal sense of the term on the part of the defendant, by way of a 'sham interview'. Mr Hogan outlines a chronicle of my work history, leading up to the 'interview' where I was judged by three strangers, brought in from other local authorities to make up an external interview panel.

Mr Hogan summarised the case to the Court:

Galway City Council obtained funding from the Department for three .. posts. Now, the new posts were very similar to the position which she then held, indeed she had a role in specifying the advertisement that went out. And she had every expectation that if she applied for the post, that she would be one of the three individuals selected. Now, as it happens, the interviews took place in March 2004, and you will hear about those interviews in due course from the plaintiff. But essentially the plaintiff was not appointed to this permanent position. She was ranked seventh in the interview process. She maintains that at least two of the people who were point appointed were either unqualified in one instance, or manifestly less suitable than her. And when I say one of the persons was unqualified, unqualified in the sense that there was a requirement that the person, the appointee, hold a full, clean driving licence. We contend that one of the persons that was so appointed, Ms. Carroll did not hold a full, clean driving licence. But another person who was ranked ahead of her, actually ranked fourth, .. had no .. particular qualifications and certainly was manifestly less suitable than the plaintiff. Indeed the plaintiff will give evidence that she assisted him in terms of making his application for the post. But at all events, the plaintiff was not so appointed and the plaintiff was absolutely shocked at this and fundamentally dismayed at this. And indeed she contends that her health and reputation suffered, and continues to suffer, as a result.

The judge interrupted Mr Hogan to makes some notes. He then continued to outline the case in more detail, quoting from the affidavit before the court.

In December 2003 Galway City Council advertised for 3 posts of Housing Liaison Officers. The advertisement provided, inter alia, that all applicants must hold a full driving licence. I applied for the post, having previously been employed as Tenant Liaison Officer for in excess of four years. Pursuant to the said advertisement I, this deponent, did apply to the Respondent for the position of Tenant Liaison Officer, I beg to refer to a copy of the said advertisement, upon which I have marked the letter 'A' and signed my name prior to the swearing hereof.

The interview took place on the 15th of March 2004. The panel consisted of two females and one male, the Chairman. The Chairman was openly hostile to me for no apparent reason and the questions which were put to me in the course of the interview had no relevance to the position which I was being interviewed for, namely Housing Liaison Officer and constituted a personal attack on me. To cite an example, the Chairman cited a scenario where there would be friction between the Council and the Community and asked me directly where my allegiance would lie in that situation. When I responded that my allegiance would always lie with my employer, it was clear from his demeanour that he did not accept my assurance in this regard. He also asked me "if my Director of Services was happy with the way I was doing my job?" and went on to repeat himself saying "is he? Is he? How do you know? How? How?" At the conclusion of the interview I queried as to when I would know the result of the interview and the Chairman replied in a sarcastic tone "you will know in five or six weeks". One of the other interviewers retracted this comment immediately and informed me that they were finishing interviews the following day and that the results would be known soon after.

Whilst I was attempting to answer questions in the course of the interview the Chairman interjected on many occasions with supplementary questions and comments. In the course of the interview he accused me of having very strong opinions and suggested that I must have difficulty with bureaucracy. He queried where my allegiance would lie in dealings between the Council and the Community. He forcefully suggested that I would not give my full allegiance to Galway City Council were I offered the job of Housing Liaison Officer, I was extremely shocked by this comment.

I say that the interview failed to comply with the criteria laid down in the Recruitment Procedures in the Local Authorities which provide, inter alia, that all candidates should be treated fairly, and all questions asked at interview should be directed towards assessing the suitability of candidates for the job and should be asked equally of all candidates. No questions of a personal nature should be asked. I beg to refer to a copy of The Recruitment Procedures for Local Authorities upon which marked with the letter 'B' I have signed my name prior to the swearing hereof.

I say that on the 18 of March 2004 I was informed by Eileen Ruane SEO by telephone that I was not successful at the interview. I was eventually provided with a copy of the marking system applied to my interview. I was marked as follows: **65 out of 100 for Education, 130 out of 200 for Experience, 111 out of 200 for Suitability, Total Marks: 305 out of 500**

I challenged the marks for Experience and Suitability. I verbally sought information from the City Manager on the 19th March, 2004 in relation to the weighting applied in the marking and asked him to explain the scientific basis for the analysis. The City Manager verbally informed me that there was no scientific basis. The position of Tenant Liaison Officer is a relatively new post and the job description for this post is based on the work I was doing for almost six years, I had been breaking new ground in carrying out the work of a de facto Tenant Liaison Officer and when Galway City Council was drawing up a job description in 2000, it was actually based on the work being done by me in the co-founded project between Galway Corporation and Galway City Partnership in the years 1997 to 1999 in attempting to involve Local Authority Tenants in the management of their own Estates. The Reference Manual provided to all new Members of Staff in the Housing Section of Galway City Council was researched and compiled by me in 1999. I say and believe that other Local Authorities have used this Manual as a prototype in the design of their own working Manuals.

At that time, I challenged the marks assigned by the interview panel directly with the City Manager John Tierney at City Hall in the days after the interview, once he had returned from his St Patrick's Day period of absence. I queried him in relation to the weighting applied in the marking and asked him to explain the scientific basis for the analysis. I asked him if this was the person he knew me to be? Mr Tierney admitted there was 'no scientific basis' to the process. I beseeched him to reject the recommendations of the interview board in my favour bearing in mind my years of unblemished dutiful service in many roles for the Council. I suggested to him that if I was truly the person reflected in the interview findings, should I not have been sacked years before for incompetence? He said that he sympathised with my position but that he wasn't sure of his own future employment at that point either. Despite his full executive discretionary powers as City Manager, and his known considerations for other employees in the past, he chose not to accommodate my appeal against the interview panel's rankings, despite his knowledge of my unblemished work record. He said the decision had been made by the Acting City Manager Ciarán Hayes during his days of absence on 18th March.

Mr Hogan presented a copy of the job advertisement to the Court, which the Council had published in local newspapers seeking applications for the three posts:

> Firstly, I can hand up the advertisement, and you will see that it's headed: 'Galway City Council Vacancy, Housing Estate Liaison Officer, 3 posts. Applications are invited by suitably qualified persons for the permanent position the Housing Estate Liaison Officer for Galway City Council. The candidates should have a good standard of education, satisfactory knowledge and experience in working with community groups'.

The judge confirmed to the court that she had read it. Mr Hogan continued to read the job advertisement to highlight the essential requirements sought for the post: to hold a full, clean driving licence, and to have access to his/her own car.

Interactions with Bríd Cummins (Galway City Council Tenant)

After what seemed like a very long time reading out detailed documents for the Court, Mr Hogan outlined one of the strands of my action – that of my interactions with the late Bríd Cummins, RIP.

> Now, the other matter that I just should deal with immediately is the question of the Bríd Cummins' affair. I suppose it's a sort of shorthand in the statement of claim as the Bríd Cummins' affair, and it's essentially this: The late Ms. Cummins was a poet who resided in a local authority house. And I am sure there are different views in respect of this, but essentially the complaint made against Ms. Cummins was this: She was a lady with rather singular views and a somewhat unusual character disposition, whereby

effectively by reason of, it is alleged, playing music at very loud volumes, complaining incessantly about the neighbours..

The judge interrupted to query if there was a complaint made to the local authority about this lady. Mr Hogan confirmed that.

Yes, there was. That the immediate neighbours of Ms. Cummins, it was an elderly gentleman, found it extremely difficult. And ultimately the question was this: How to deal with Ms. Cummins? What should be done? And the evidence will be from the plaintiff that a suggestion was made, indeed a direction was given to the plaintiff, that she should facilitate a situation in which using the public resources of the council, that the elderly neighbour should be encouraged to take what amounted to nuisance proceedings against Ms. Cummins, or some type of injunctive/abatement proceedings against Ms. Cummins. The details of this don't greatly matter, but what does matter is this: That the suggestion was made that my client should facilitate and effectively inveigle the elderly neighbouring tenant to take proceedings in his own right using the services of Galway City Council in using public monies for this, and indeed their solicitors, and using public monies for this purpose. This, of course, was something which the elderly tenant didn't want to do, because as far as his attitude was concerned, was that his life was being made a misery by Ms. Cummins and he wanted the council to do something about it. But he didn't want, for understandable reasons of his own right, to have a situation whereby he was the person who would be required to initiate legal proceedings against what he perceived as a very difficult next-door neighbour.

Now, my client didn't go along with that, and she will give evidence herself in relation to this matter, because she considered that it was inappropriate that public monies should be used in this surreptitious manner to inveigle the elderly tenant to take proceedings, the nature of which, perhaps, he didn't fully understand, against Ms. Cummins. Whereas the most appropriate step was that Ms. Cummins should be moved. And that indeed is what the plaintiff recommended.

Now, in the end, the whole affair had a sad outcome, because after ultimately eviction proceedings were taken against Ms. Cummins, Ms. Cummins died shortly thereafter, and it is believed that she didn't die as a result of natural causes. And this was a matter of some local controversy at the time in Galway. But the whole issue in relation to Ms. Cummins appears to have clouded the relations between the plaintiff and the council. The plaintiff will give evidence essentially to the effect that from that point onwards, when she was unwilling to go along with what had been proposed by officialdom in relation to this, that views against her hardened.

The judge queried when precisely this occurred. Mr Hogan confirmed that it had taken place in the autumn of 2003.

And at that point, as I say, the views against her hardened and therefore she says that she was never fairly considered on the merits for the interview process, and that as a result, all of this culminated in a state of affairs whereby she was removed wrongly. Not to put a tooth in it, her evidence will be that from that point onwards, that the council determined, or the relevant officials determined, that she should be removed from office and that the entire interview process was -- again I regret to have to say this, Judge -- a contrivance. She was not fairly marked on the matter. One might, perhaps, have quibbled about whether her precise ranking was one, two or three, but the fact that she was ranked seventh is, I respectfully say, extraordinary and I invite the Court to draw its own inferences from that sequence of events.

It's essentially against that background that the plaintiff moves this Court for damages for wrongful dismissal. A wrongful dismissal which we say was unlawful and in breach of contract in its own right, but which a

172

wrongfulness of which is aggravated and tainted by reason of the determined and arch attitude of the council whereby they had resolved privately to ensure that she was removed from office.

Mr Hogan told the court how the Council officials had decided to deal with this tenant. As Liaison Officer, I was directed to facilitate a situation (using the public resources of the council) that an elderly neighbour should be encouraged to take proceedings against Ms. Cummins. My task was to support and encourage the elderly neighbour to take proceedings in his own right, using the services of Galway City Council's solicitors, at no cost to himself. This was something which Bríd Cummins's neighbour didn't want to do. He felt that his life was being affected by the council's tenant, and it was up to them to deal with that. He did not want to engage in any legal proceedings against what he perceived as a difficult next-door neighbour.

Mr Hogan explained to that Court that I believed it was inappropriate that public monies should be used in this surreptitious manner for the elderly man to take proceedings against Ms. Cummins, the nature of which he didn't fully understand. The neighbouring man believed the most appropriate step was that Ms. Cummins should be transferred to other accommodation. That is also what I recommended to the City Manager. Mr Hogan explained that when I refused to go along with what had been proposed by officialdom, that certain officials' views against me hardened. This was in the context of the upcoming interview.

Mr Hogan then sought permission from the judge to open the plenary summons in the case, to be read into the court record. This involved reading out a detailed account about the particulars of the case, details about my work achievements, and details about how the council had ultimately engineered my removal from employment aged 52. The judge then invited him to read all of the Statement of Claim, to open the notice for particulars, as well as the replies to these.

These documents had been exchanged between both sides over the previous years, where a blanket defence of denial was issued by the Council in relation to all of the elements of claim I had cited. Detailed questions were set out by them in writing, whereon replies were supplied for these in advance of court.

Justice Dunne stated that she had read through all of the particulars and the replies to these.

Mr Hogan then went on to read out the Contract of Employments I had been working under, and the nature of the duties involved in the post of Housing Estate Liaison Officer.

After this exhaustive account, Mr Hogan proceeded to read out the defence documents tendered to the Court by Galway City Council. This is essentially a retort and denial in counter statement to rebut each and every aspect of the case set out by the Plaintiff. There was no admission to any of my claims in their defence.

During this interchange, Ms Justice Dunne challenged Mr Hogan on the issue of the wrongful dismissal claim in the case.

> Judge Dunne: I think it is not difficult to see that, Mr. Hogan, and you can disagree with me on this particular point, but I am taking it that this is a case about wrongful dismissal in the sense of not having been successful in the interview for the permanent position.

> Mr Hogan: And subsequently being dismissed.

Judge Dunne: Well, that follows from the fact that three permanent positions had been created. I mean, taking a common sense approach about the matter, here we have clearly three temporary people employed permanently as tenant liaison officers, is that the case?

Mr. Hogan: That's correct.

Judge Dunne: Funding is obtained for permanent positions, therefore once the three permanent positions are properly funded, the other ones cease. So in that sense the redundancy follows as a matter of course.

Mr. Hogan: In that sense, yes.

Judge Dunne: That is pure logic, pure common sense, there is no issue on that. We are talking about a wrongful interview situation and the consequent non-appointment really, rather than dismissal in the strict sense of the word.

Mr. Hogan: I take the Court's point. The Court is quite correct in that sense, and in that sense only there was a redundancy.

Judge Dunne: I don't see how else it could be described.

After Mr Hogan is finished reading the Defence into the court record, line by line, the judge affirms that she has read the defence, describing it in legal terms as a comprehensive denial of all of the allegations I am making against the Council as follows:

Judge Dunne: In effect is a traverse, apart from about one positive assertion, or two, during the course of the defence, but they were very far and few between. Paragraph 38 contains a positive averment, but in practical terms I think it is a straightforward traverse; isn't that so?

Mr. Hogan: Exactly.

175

Judge Dunne: Mr. Gallagher, would you disagree with that, that it is a straightforward traverse?

Mr. Gallagher: That is what the defence is at the moment.

Mr. Hogan: In perfect fairness to the Defendant, they have denied in emphatic terms, as might be expected, or as could be expected in legal proceedings, that they are guilty of the wrongdoing alleged, and I fully accept that to that extent -- sorry, I take that back. I fully accept the Defendant amounts to an emphatic denial of these allegations, and that's why we are before the Court. Judge, I think the Court has got a thumbnail sketch of the matters in controversy between the parties. I will be addressing the Court presently when the evidence is concluded in terms of the legal issues that arise, but with the Court's leave I propose to go to evidence at this stage.

The Council's position as highlighted by Justice Dunne was to 'deny' all of the allegations. Mr Gallagher agreed that this was their position 'at the moment'. What a strange logic for the truth to reside within. To their benefit and comfort, they had an endless supply of public time and public money to spend.

Mr Hogan outlined to Justice Dunne, how I was 'effectively pushed out' of the TLO position because of the 'Bríd Cummin's Affair'. Neighbours alleged that she was violent, abusive, loud and threatening. She alleged much the same against them. After many desperate attempts to remedy her housing situation, she initiated civil litigation against the council to improve her dwelling. Galway City Council officials decided that the easiest way to deal with Ms. Cummins was to evict her and frustrated her legal efforts until they succeeded in evicting her, after which she would have no entitlement to take a case against them

Ruffled feathers

In December 2003, as part of my job as Tenant Liaison Officer, it became necessary for me to intervene with Housing allocations staff to dissuade them from allocating a property being offered to a family who were transferring from a smaller property on the other side of the city. The property being offered was adjacent to a tenant that had previously suffered a protracted negative experience with a family who had been engaging in serious anti-social behaviour. The neighbour had been assured personally by the Council's Housing Officer Ciarán Hayes that when the abandoned house was being reallocated, it would not be given to a family with an anti-social record. An attempt was made by the allocations staff to effect the allocation without my knowledge, who as a key worker in the area would ordinarily have been updated on upcoming allocations to an area I worked in. I only became aware of the plan when the existing tenant advised me of his shock when he saw who was moving in. This was a failure to comply with the assurances previously given to him.

Following my intervention on behalf of the in-situ tenant, it emerged that the original records had gone missing from the housing file. This was strange, since there had been a specifically noted history in respect of the particular family to whom it was being offered to. The allocation was proceeding on the basis of incomplete information, since the original report had gone missing from the file.

The tenant in the adjacent property had been given a firm undertaking by the Housing Officer, after he had initiated court proceedings against his neighbours, on foot of acts of gross indecency and the council's failure to respond to his complaints. The court found in his favour. It seemed very wrong that once more this man was being subjected to new neighbours with known anti-social history and convictions for criminal behaviours. The Housing Officer at the time, Ciarán Hayes, told him to link in with me as Liaison Officer and he would ensure that this man and his family would not have to endure such persons as his immediate neighbours again.

Despite my requests, I got no heed from the Allocations Officer who stated there was no record of anti social behaviour 'on file', and the allocation *was* going to proceed. I knew Mr Hayes was the one person who would remember the personal undertaking previously given, and when I called to his office he confirmed that he did remember it.

> Mr. Hogan: As a consequence of this intervention by the Plaintiff which required her- reporting the matter to the Director of Services when the Allocations Officer would not accept the Plaintiff's report in the matter, the particular proposed allocation did not proceed but the Plaintiff was accosted by a servant or agent of the Defendant, one Frances Mullarkey who advised her that she had "ruffled feathers here but you won't do it again". Ms. Mullarkey accused the Plaintiff of going over her head in relation to the allocation.

I glanced down to the body of the court and saw Council officials smirking, which was what I expected, knowing the personalities. I steeled myself not to look in their direction too often, and not to get upset in Court.

Mr Hogan described how I had ranked seventh in the interview process for the job, where people ranked ahead did not have either the requisite qualifications nor experience that the Council had advertised for. He highlighted that one of the requirements needed to apply for the post in the first instance, was to possess 'a full, clean driving licence', and he reiterated that one of the successful external candidates, Ms Carroll, did not hold such a licence.

Mr Hogan questioned me about the profile of the successful candidates and what I knew about any of them. I gave evidence that I first became aware of Ms Carroll when I was contacted in 2003 by a mutual acquaintance who was a friend and neighbour of Ms Carroll, asking me how this friend of hers could access social housing accommodation, and what her rights would be in this regard. I agreed to meet Ms Carroll to explain the various housing options. Ms Carroll's friend and neighbour advised me some time later that Ms Carroll wouldn't need to meet me as she had since been 'fixed-up', and had accessed the rent allowance I had advised that she would probably be entitled to.

Subsequently, I was contacted by Ms Carroll herself, who telephoned me at the desk in City Hall. She was seeking a profile of the residents of Currach Buí estate in Rahoon. She said this was necessary for her as part of a project she was doing. I advised her that it was entirely inappropriate that she should seek this type of confidential information from me, and said that if she was doing a project on any estate, she firstly needed to contact each household, seek their permission, and take it from there

The next time Ms Carroll contacted me was in early 2004, when she again contacted me at work, seeking a copy of the Tenant Handbook which she seemed to know that I had compiled, and pressed me for copies. I explained that it was out of print at that time, and it was outside of my remit to order more copies. I advised her to contact more appropriate senior personnel, since I had also been seeking reprints for some time. She said that she had already been referred down the line to me in this regard

Senior Counsel then went to explain the context of steps I had taken after the sham interview process, to seek some legal remedy in finding out why I was being expelled from the organisation, after having exhausted every possible avenue internally appealing for information. Going to court was the last thing I wanted to do, as in all my years in the Council working in different roles, a situation with tenant never came to the point of going to court. My life experience as a trained mediator told me that a mediated resolution is always possible, on the condition that both parties are willing to participate. In this situation, the Council management were not willing to explain their actions.

It was outlined to the Court how I realised the reason for getting rid of me was manifested in my refusal to perjure myself on behalf of the Council who were engaged in a bitter dispute with a Council tenant, Bríd Cummins (RIP) who had been challenging the Housing officials of the council through a civil action in relation to their treatment of her. I would not participate in their heavy-handed approach which other officials were happy to do.

The Bríd Cummins' Affair became very public after she went on local radio when the Council had secured an eviction order against her. There was further intense and protracted media interest surrounding the events of Ms Cummins' sudden death. It was obvious that Ms. Cummins' difficulty would have been resolved by a transfer of accommodation by Galway City Council. The fact that I was wrongly accused of not recommending such a transfer misrepresented my professional judgment and gave a false and misleading account of my actions. I believed that it damaged my reputation and caused stigma to attach to me. This was why I had to go to Court.

Judicial Review attempt of the 'interview' process

Mr Hogan outlined to the Court the basis and result of the judicial review that I had previously sought from the High Court in September after the interviews. A review had been refused by the judge at the time, because the application was made too late in his opinion. Human Resources in Galway City Council had delayed me by withholding documentation which was needed to initiate legal action. The learned judge Justice Herbert commented that having examined the documents, the chairman of the panel enlisted by the council for interview, Pat Dowling of Limerick Council, 'acted in an ungentlemanly fashion'. This comment was reported in national newspapers at that time.

At this point, Mr Gallagher for the Council jumped to his feet alleging that the application for the judicial review was brought on any entirely different basis to the basis on which the current application is brought. He was attempting to show the judge that I was somehow changing my position now from what was claimed in the judicial review proceedings.

Justice Dunne asserted to him that there no issue here – as it was regular that judicial review proceedings are different in nature. Mr Gallagher continued to argue that the claims made at both times were different and still wanted them heard. Mr Hogan said that he had no difficulty with that, since the council would have had full knowledge of this previously and the examination of that previous legal application could be read out forthwith.

I believed the introduction of this historical factor by the Council's legal team was going to add to the Court's time and accumulate additional legal costs. The case had initially been listed to take three days, and I was aware that it was going to take somewhat longer.

Introducing the Statement of Claim

The Statement of Claim sets out the framework for the legal arguments, because the evidence presented in court must be framed around the details set out in that Statement of Claim. The other side are given sufficient time to examine, reflect and address the issues highlighted, and to prepare their planned defence before going to court. The defence submitted by the Council's representatives was a blanket reply to each section that simply responded a 'deny; deny; deny' response to each allegation.

It was uppermost in my mind that if they succeeded in squashing me, that I would go down for their legal costs as well as my own. These would be astronomical and we would be risking our family home. I did know that regardless of what facts came out of this case; regardless of what wrong doings were shown to have been done by the council officials. The only assured outcome for them in the Irish local government system, was that it would not hamper any of their careers. There would not be any professional sanction on them and no legal cost (win or lose) would accrue to them personally. The death of the unfortunate tenant they forced through the court system to criminalise her for alleged anti-social behaviour was on my mind.

Mr Hogan read the Statement of Claim into the court record and also opened the plenary summons, which outlined the history of the problem before the judge. He read aloud the replies given by the other side before the court sitting.

Extract from Particulars:

5. ...It was a term of the Plaintiff's contract of employment that the Defendant, its servants or agents, should not conduct themselves in a manner calculated or likely to destroy or seriously damage the relationship of trust and confidence between employer and employee. It was further a term of the Plaintiff's contract of employment and a necessary corollary of the above term that the Defendant was and would remain an honest public body conducting and recording its affairs with sincerity, integrity and propriety.

Had everything been above board at interview, this was the manner in which the Council should have conducted its business. My experience was the opposite.

Replies to Particulars

A. The Plaintiff was aware that the Director of Services had discussed the position with third parties prior to interview. The Plaintiff was advised by [*name redacted*] (who was not aware at the time that the Plaintiff's position was in jeopardy believing her to be permanent) that she was supporting the application of an employee of [*organisation redacted*] and had made representation to the Director of Services in this regard. The said person was offered one of the posts despite not holding a full driving licence as required by the job description. Further, the Director of Services was heard to speak with Pat Dowling who was the Chairman of the interview committee about the interview process in advance of the interview.

B. In the lead up to the interview, the Plaintiff was excluded from events that she would normally and routinely have participated in. An attempt was made to exclude her from a resident's meeting where she would normally have been in attendance and she was permitted to attend only at the insistence of the residents. In the week prior to the job interviews, the

Plaintiff's participation in a Social Housing Conference in Westport was cancelled and she was advised by Frances Mullarkey "you've been pulled off that housing conference. You're not going".

C. The Plaintiff was also approached by another applicant for the position who had little experience in the area for assistance in interview preparation given her work in the area. The Plaintiff provided assistance and was subsequently advised by the individual that he performed very poorly at interview. He was shocked and dismayed to discover that he had been ranked ahead of the Plaintiff".

When Mr Hogan was finished, he declared that he was going into evidence, and I was called from my position at the back of the courtroom, to take the stand. My evidence was going to be heard firstly on questioning from Mr Hogan.

Called to the stand: Examination by Gerard Hogan SC

I leave my seat at the back of the court, where I am sitting with my son. I reach the witness stand and climb a number of steps into a wooden seat. I look up and to my right towards the Judge.

Looking down from my left are rows of seats that make up the body of the court. The legal teams from both sides occupy the front rows and further down behind them are rows of public servants on behalf of Galway City Council. This cohort includes executive officials of Galway City Council and representatives of two further local authorities.

Whilst the legal people are arranging their papers, I have a few moments to reflect. My emotions are very mixed. I think of my husband at home. I did not want him subjected to this sight here today. He is a decent hard working person who has been entirely honest all of his life, providing a good living for the family down the years. He built a nice home for us to see out our final days and I am risking all of this today. I am momentarily anxious in fear of the unknown; about what outcome could be in store for my family after this case is over.

As I glance down at the two well-populated seats of executives, their continuing jocular demeanours have not changed from yesterday. One would be forgiven for thinking that they were preparing for a night out on the town. Looking down at them reminds me that my conscience and respect for the truth has compelled me to bring them here today.

I was sworn in by the Court official, and my evidence commenced.

Q. Mr Hogan: Now, Ms. Grace, take a seat and I am sure some water can be provided for you.

A. Thank you.

Q. Now, Ms. Grace, can I just ask you at the outset, can you tell the Court your present position and why you have taken these proceedings?

A. My present position is that I am 58 ... Since I have been removed from the employment of the council six years ago, I have been only able to obtain four months' temporary work. I am unable and cannot find employment because of perceptions that abound in relation to me. I am unable to contribute to a pension. There is a public perception that I did something wrong and that the council had to remove me from their employ. There is a belief, and it is a published belief, that I am somehow accountable for the death of a council tenant whom I had been involved in that area, and that is a very difficult one.

Q. Mr Hogan: Now, Ms. Grace, I appreciate that you clearly feel very strongly about this matter, and we will be coming back to this in due course.

But could I just ask you as a prelude to all of that, firstly, to tell the Court briefly your occupational history prior to employment with the council in the first instance, and then we will go on to the council.

I gave detailed evidence on my work history with the council over the ten-year period. Mr Hogan then took me through some of the specifics of my work for official record for the Court. He continued questioning me about the job interview process.

Q. And what was the position or what did you understand your position to be with the council pending the filling of those posts?

A. I knew the council were recruiting for more permanent staff. They had got the funding from the Department of Environment. I believed, and it was expected by me, that from my experience, which was like ten years at this point, in the role working with the community and having all the qualifications necessary, that I would be considered for the post, and I had no fear in that regard. As a matter of fact, I discussed that with the director of services, Ciarán Hayes, in relation to where the salaries were being pitched, and I made the comparison that I felt that maybe some local authorities were using analogous with a grade six for this post. He said, 'with your experience you can naturally expect to come in at the top end of the salary', recognising the amount of work that I had done and, in fairness to him, appreciating that.

Q. Can you say whether you had any role whatever as far as the advertisement was concerned?

A. Yes, I was directly involved in assisting the compilation of duties that was advertised for that post. I was specifically asked if there were any functions that, in a document that was presented to me, were absent from it and I identified one or two, certainly a few items.

Q. Now, the interviews were held on 15th March 2004; isn't that correct?

A. That's correct.

Q. Now, can you, firstly, tell the Court formally whether you were appointed and, if not, what your ranking was?

A. The findings of the interview board were that I was placed seventh on the panel.

Q. And do you know the identity of the persons who were appointed or who were subsequently appointed to the position?

I then outlined the specific details requested in relation to who was appointed to the three positions.

Q. Now, you have suggested in your pleadings that you have superior qualifications to at least two of these individuals?

A. Yes.

Q. And could we just -- I will come to the interview in one moment, but just to deal with this matter. I take it you bear no animus towards those two individuals but you just simply say that you were objectively better qualified?

A. Absolutely. I have no difficulty with those people. In fact, Michael Forde was a fellow candidate for the post, and sometime before the interview he asked if he could meet me and if I could help him to go through the job description and what the role was, and I did that, very willingly.

Q. Now, one of the requirements, we know, was that the candidate would have a full, clean driving licence.

A. That's correct, that was a prerequisite to even apply for the job.

Q. Did you have a full, clean driving licence?

A. I have a full, clean driving licence for very many years.

Q. Can you tell the Court -- again, this is not intended to be a reflection on Ms. Carroll -- can you tell the Court your understanding as to whether Ms. Carroll satisfied that condition, and if not, if you consider she didn't satisfy that condition how you know this or how you believe it?

A. Well, after the interviews, this mutual acquaintance, who contacted me in the first instance, told me she was absolutely amazed that this particular girl who she had looked for help for was after getting the job that I was doing and that she was delighted with herself, and she is now going to buy a car and start driving.

Q. And did you ever see Ms. Carroll thereafter? Driving, that is.

A. As it happened, I was going out to the garden centre in Moycullen one evening when I noticed a car. There was a car driving slowly in the middle of road and when I got to the centre I discovered it was Ms. Carroll from the car that had been described to me that she had purchased.

Q. Was there anything unusual on the car from this perspective?

A. Yes, there was an 'L' plate on the car.

Q. And what inference did you draw from that?

A. That it was somebody who was learning to drive, and the driving style would indicate that.

Q. Just going back to Mr. Kennedy for a moment, did you have any discussions with Mr. Kennedy before or after the interview?

Judge Dunne: Sorry, Mr...

Q. Mr Hogan: Sorry, Mr. Forde.

A. After the interview results became known, which was straightaway, the day after Saint Patrick's day, when actually Ciarán Hayes was acting manager on the day, the interview results became known. Michael Forde sympathised with me and felt so sorry for me, that I was now going to be out of a job. I found Michael Forde a very nice man, he worked in environment, we had a good working relationship. He said, 'you know, Julie, had you come fourth and I had come third I would have swapped positions so you wouldn't be losing your job'.

Q. Did you have any discussions with Mr. Forde before the interview?

A. Yes, I met Michael, on his request, prior to the interview and I had gone through the various elements of the job I was doing and the bounds of the Tenancy Agreement, how I handled different operational matters in relation to tenants, and the daily matters.

Q. Did you form any view as to his competence or suitability for the post in question?

A. I gave him the information that I had. I would not have been in a judging position, but Michael did say to me after the interview that he was shocked that had he come ahead of me and he thanked me sincerely for the assistance that I gave him because he was unable to prepare for the interview due to the death of his granny.

Q. And did he say anything as to how he had performed at the interview?

A. He felt he had done very poorly and he just couldn't understand how he could have performed ahead of me and so well. And again thanked me for the information I gave him, there was no hostility between Michael Forde or I at any time.

Q. Now, Ms. Grace, it's just coming to the luncheon adjournment, but I will ask you one further question and we will continue at 2:00 o'clock. Can you tell the Court what was your reaction on being informed that you hadn't been appointed and was ranked seventh?

A. When I got the telephone call at about 9:20 in the morning I was absolutely shocked. I couldn't believe it. I was dismayed and I asked what was all this about. I was likewise disappointed in the HR person who phoned me and told me on the phone. As a woman, I was likewise disappointed that her understanding of somebody who had worked for ten years, was now going to be out of work. I had very little interaction with Eileen Ruane at any time before that, because I wouldn't normally have. But as I was driving along, I recalled, just a few months before that when another colleague who was in a temporary position and was going to be interviewed for a post, in actual fact I think Eileen herself was on the interview board, she invited her, within my hearing, to call to her office, saying 'you must come first, Mary'. And I thought why that deference to somebody -- I didn't want that deference from anybody, but I did expect fair play and I did expect a little bit more civility.

Mr Hogan: Judge, I see it's just gone 1:00 o'clock.

The court was adjourned for lunch. I left the Court complex with my son as we did every day of the Court sessions, for a light sandwich and cup of tea in a local cafe. On return for 2pm, Senior Counsel Mr Hogan called me back to the stand to continue with questioning.

190

Q. Mr Hogan: Now, Ms. Grace, I just propose to continue. Just before lunch you had spoken about the position in relation to Michael Forde, and I am just going to ask to you continue the narrative until you ceased employment and I will go back and ask you about the actual interview itself and then the whole question of the Bríd Cummins' affair and related matters. Now, we will come back to the interview, of course, but you have described the events of 15th March and its immediate aftermath. Can you then tell the Court what next happened relevant to these proceedings, after about 18th March?

A. Yes, on the morning of 18th March, when I was told verbally of my position, I went and immediately and made an appointment of the director of services and housing, Ciarán Hayes, he was acting city manager on that day. He accommodated me and saw me straightaway. I asked him what had happened. I mean, what had I had been failing to do that would rank me seventh at an interview for the job that I had initiated in 1997, was always told had been completed with diligence, many accolades, even from councillors. It was publicly recognised that I was doing an excellent job. And suddenly I was being removed from the area of where I had expertise, knowledge and interest. He said he had nothing to do with the interview board, and to speak to HR. I then went to Joe Considine in the HR section, who was acting director of services, from what I remember, on that day. He said he had nothing to do with directing the interview board and ask Ciarán Hayes.

Q. Just identify that person for me, please?

A. Sorry, Joe Considine was the man who I believe was acting director of services for HR on 18th March, as my recollection serves me best, that was his function. He was certainly a senior person in HR on that morning. I asked Joe what happened and how did this come about. I said, 'am I the person you know from coming seventh in this interview'? And he said, 'hang

191

on, I will get you your interview marks', which I had already asked Eileen Ruane for when she gave me the result. However, I didn't get them that day, I had to wait until the next day to get those marks. The atmosphere was strained and strange. My colleagues were rather strange. I suppose it was a difficult time. Frances Mullarkey came to the shared office where the three of us worked, I am sure it was that 18th or 19th, and she said, 'I am sure you are disappointed you weren't successful, but the interview board were bowled over by the Whiz kids'. I felt that was a direct reference to me being one of the older people there. However, I didn't pursue that matter.

Q. Can you just identify what role Ms. Mullarkey had in the council at the time?

A. Ms. Mullarkey was a senior executive officer in housing at the time, and was actively interested in the interview. And in the interview directly after I was interviewed, Ms. Mullarkey was very interested in the questions that were asked. Because of her hostile nature prior to the interview to me, I was concerned in relation to the questions she was asking me.

Q. Now, again, I will come back to the interview presently, Ms. Grace, but that was the immediate aftermath of the 18th and 19th March. Can you say whether you were asked to attend if there were any court proceedings at the time?

A. Yes. On the 19th I met with the manager, and that's another matter. On the Monday morning, after I had been told I was now being removed from my post, I got a call, once again on the mobile phone, on my way to work, and with respect, Judge, they were hands free sets, so I wasn't breaking the law. She told me to make my way immediately to Galway Courthouse and I said, 'what for, Frances'? And she said, 'we are in court today with so-and-so', they were residents of an estate that I was working in and that normally I would be au fait with the proceedings, but I realised that there was

192

something happening there, that was confirming to me that I was being frozen out of the communications in relation to that area.

She said, 'Julie, you have to go down and give evidence today'. And I said, 'Frances, I am not au fait with the evidence. Are you ordering me'? She was quite insistent and she said, 'yes, I am ordering you as your superior. Get down there, we want to win this case'. So I went to the courthouse and I waited for Frances to come in with John Carr, solicitor for the council, plus another employee. So when Mr. Carr came in I explained to him my position, that I had been asked to give evidence, I had absolutely no recent knowledge or information on the matter, and neither did I know the exact content of the application to the court. Mr. Carr discharged me straightaway and said, 'Julie, I will not be using you to give evidence. You may leave the court'.

Q. And what inference do you draw from that event?

A. I found that it was a strange matter to be ordered by your superior to go into court, to say something or other under oath that was going to win this case for the council. I also found it strange that while was I was working effectively in that area, information was being kept from me, and it was confirmed to me that I was being excluded from day-to-day events and operational systems inside the council.

Q. Now, again, just to complete the narrative before we go back, after that what happened to you?

A. I felt extremely ill at that point and I went straight to my GP, who diagnosed acute stress and my blood pressure had been elevated. He advised rest immediately, he signed me off as unfit for work at that time, and that continued for some months.

Q. It said in the pleadings on behalf of the council that you didn't turn up for a debriefing session on 1st April 2004, and that you were the only one of the non-appointed interested candidates not to turn up.

A. That is correct. I was incapacitated to the extent I was not able to engage. I was both in shock and I was highly stressed and my blood pressure had been elevated.

Letter of Termination

In pursuit of a formal written notification of my employment position with Galway City Council, I telephoned the HR department and spoke with Eileen Ruane (Senior Executive Officer). She claimed that she had already written to me advising of my discontinuing employment status. Then, some six weeks after the interview, Ms Ruane wrote to me enclosing a formal 'Notice of Termination of Employment'.

I wish to inform you that today, 10th May 2004, offers of employment have issued to the three successful candidates for the Housing/Estate Liaison Officer posts. I will be in further contact with you regarding your contract of employment, once I have the start dates to hand...

This was the first written notification of my position that enabled me to explore the legal avenues open to me. Subsequently Ms. Ruane wrote 'apologising' for allegedly misdirecting post to me. She enclosed a 'copy' of a letter that the Council purportedly posted to me previously dated 5th April, now claiming they had failed to address it correctly. I never received any such letter and do not accept that the Council ever sent it.

Mr Hogan Q. Now, you say this condition continued for a number of months. Can you say whether you received any correspondence in relation to your employment from the council around May of 2004?

194

A. Yes, I was reflecting on the matters that had taken place, and as best I could I was going to seek advice. I needed confirmation in writing and I phoned the council for my position in writing, what my situation actually was. I again spoke with Eileen Ruane, who told me she had posted me a letter explaining what happened, and I said, 'I didn't get a letter'. She said, 'of course you got a letter'. I said, 'no, I didn't get a letter'. She was insistent that I got one and was quite derogatory in my asking for one. She subsequently wrote a few days later and apologised and said she wasn't sure where the letter went to. And the letter that she sent me, it was difficult to know where the letter had been sent, but Grace is a very uncommon name in the area that I live in, and literally anything with J. Grace, County Galway, almost gets to me. So I would query as to whether that letter was ever posted. And as well as that, any post emanating from Galway City Council is franked, so I would have expected that in the normal course of events any letter that wasn't delivered would have gone back into that office.

Q. And in all events, did you receive any letter in relation to your employment?

A. Yes, I then received a letter telling me that my employment with Galway City Council was being terminated on 4th June.

Q. So with effect from 4th June 2004?

A. Yes.

Q. And there is was a manager's order to that effect?

A. Yes.

Q. Now, before we just go back, to complete the sequential narrative, did you endeavour to take any legal proceedings in respect of the actual appointments at the time?

A. Yes, I did. I immediately consulted a firm of solicitors in Dublin ... on the basis that it would be difficult to get someone in Galway City to represent you against the council, because there are interactions all the time. That was my advice at the time. And that company wrote and asked the council to desist from filling the post until further consideration.

Q. That was 2nd June 2004, I think.

A. I think so. My recollections on the dates are not that good.

Q. And was an attempt made on your behalf to apply for leave to apply for judicial review in September of 2004?

A. Yes. After that, I consulted a firm of solicitors in County Galway who felt quite sure that they would be successful in procuring an application for a judicial review. What I really wanted was judicial review of the interview proceedings. At this time, Judge, was to flush out what happened in the council. I needed an answer to know why I was got rid of, and I felt that by way of a judicial review of the interview proceedings and a discovery of documents, it would show me what I needed to know. Because when I spoke with the manager on the Friday after, that was John Tierney, I asked him to please tell me what went wrong, that effectively he should have sacked me for under-performance. According to the interview findings I was operating at about 55 per cent, and I did say to him that I should have been sacked for inefficiency. I asked him what the scientific basis was for the computation of the interview marks for me, and I also asked him at that time for the remarks and notes from the interview board, and he said, 'I don't think there are any'. I again asked him if he would consider making me extranumerary, as had been done in a previous situation with another person who had worked in a same situation that wasn't successful in obtaining the permanent post when the interviews had been had for the job she was doing. And he did that for her. I asked him would he consider doing that for me. He said no. I asked him would he consider marrying my personnel file with the interview results, as the interview board that I had met for a very short time, and I did explain I wasn't terribly happy with what went on. He also refused to do that and he cited the situation that, 'oh, sure in a couple of months I will be looking around for a job myself. I am not sure where I will be in a couple of years either'. I expressed to Mr. Tierney my extreme disappointment after giving ten years' sterling service, acting in many different roles, acting away above and beyond what was in my contract. So much so that if somebody was missing from a housing section on a day, I would very willingly fill in for them. I am not a pedantic person and I was always willing to help.

Q. Now, at all events, that application was refused by Mr. Justice Herbert on 17th September 2004?

A. Yes.

Q. Were you present in court on that day?

A. No. And the affidavit was done the night before. And with all due respect to the firm that were doing it, they were working under pressure, they obliged me at the time. Their normal barrister, who is here today, was not available because he was normally the barrister for the city council. So opinion was sought from somebody else. So that's the picture. But anyway, it was difficult because it was coming into the summer season and advice was hard to get, and the application was hurried because I was two months after the interview without getting my position in writing. So I believed, because I had indicated that was going to seek judicial review, I was being frustrated by the council. They did not give me the information in writing that I needed in order to proceed.

Q. And can you say what your understanding as to the reason given as to why the leave was refused?

A. In layman's terms, it was that the people in the post were too long there and didn't act on time, but that it had merit. And Judge Herbert did recognise that there were elements to the interview that he described as ungentlemanly.

Q. But the council, in fairness, had not been heard in those proceedings.

A. No, and neither had I.

Q. And that was the sequence of events and you ceased employment in June 2004?

A. That's correct.

Q. And we are about to get back to the detail in a moment, but can you just say, again to complete the picture, whether you have succeeded in obtaining any employment since the events of June 2004?

A. I set about applying for any position I felt that I may be qualified for or considered for. I obtained four months' contract work in 2006. After the end of 2004, Bríd Cummins, a council tenant, had died. The whole thing became very public, there was much media interest both locally and nationally, and even Prime Time did a feature on it. I was identified as the liaison officer who was working in that area. I had made a recommendation for a transfer, which the media were saying -- trial by media, whatever -- but there were many other agencies with interests in poverty and exclusion and in mental health who would have recognised that a transfer would have at least alleviated the problem at the time. I did make a recommendation for a transfer but the council chose to deny that.

Q. And we will come to Bríd Cummins in a moment. But you have endeavoured to get employment?

A. Yes. And at every interview, when they look at my CV, and I have spent -- having had so long service with the council, I am asked invariably, 'so what happened'? On one occasion, one of the interview board said to me directly, 'what did you do wrong'?

Q. And this has obviously had very considerable effects on your life?

A. It has had enormous effects on my life. I am 58, I have to accept that I will never be employed again. It is a frightening prospect.

Q. Had this had any effects on your health?

A. Yes, my blood pressure has increased significantly. I feel socially excluded, I have no social life, I am embarrassed, there is a perception that the council had to sack me for something that I did. I can't even go into Tesco and do a little bit of shopping. It only happened to me at Easter time that a former tenant met me and said, 'Julie, why did they sack you that time'? I have had so many of those requests, and that is the reason that I asked to have this case brought here today.

Q. Now, can we go back to September 2003, Ms. Grace, and I am going to ask you about the Bríd Cummins affair and a number of other matters in the lead up to the actual interview itself. Now, in September 2003 you first -- well, you had an encounter in relation to the late Ms. Cummins; is that right?

A. I would have encountered Bríd Cummins on a regular basis, she was well known to me. I thought I knew her very well and I always felt that there was a little bit more to the situation than I found on the file and I incessantly asked for that. And I am sorry to say today that I was quite right about that.

Q. Can you just say, she was a council tenant?

A. She was a council tenant. She lived in an apartment in 5 Munster Avenue. And for the purpose of clarification, this was an old house built in the '40s and it was divided in two. So she lived in the bottom and there would have been another tenant on top.

199

Q. And could you just identify the tenant on top?

A. The previous tenant on top was a Ms. Josephine _____.

Q. And the tenant in September 2003 that was on top was?

A. There was nobody there. Ms. _____ qualified for a transfer to another area.

Q. But who was the immediate neighbour?

A. The neighbours next door were Mr. and Mrs. Walsh. And just for the purpose of clarification, at that time they were home owners, they were not council tenants. All of that avenue at one stage was council owned and people bought out the properties as the years went by. So at that point, a couple of years before that, the Mr. and Mrs. Walsh would have finished buying out their house. They effectively own their house and they were private residents.

Q. And they were living immediately adjacent to Ms. Cummins?

A. Yes.

Q. Can you describe the Walshes in terms of age and so forth?

A. Yes. I got to know the Walshes when I was collecting annuities for the council. They are an elderly couple and they look after their handicapped daughter.

Q. And can you say something about Ms. Cummins?

A. Ms. Cummins lived next door in the bottom half of the apartment, known as 5A Munster Avenue. The Walshes would have been excellent neighbours to any of the people who would have lived in that house over the years. It was divided some years before that, and the Walshes would have lived there for a very long time. And at different times there were tenants there who would have had difficulties, and Mrs. Walsh would contact the council. I

200

know the previous two tenants she had contacted the council in relation to, and they were reallocated to different properties.

Q. Can you describe, without getting in the merits of who was right and wrong, but can you describe the nature of the alleged activities of Ms. Cummins that gave rise to difficulties?

A. Ms. Cummins was accused of making a lot of noise and she would complain about the inadequacy of her dwelling, and the tenant upstairs would make very similar exchanges about the level of noise there as well. But bearing in mind that it was an old '40's house, and you literally couldn't walk upstairs without every footstep being heard downstairs. When either of them played their radio or television loudly, of course it caused distress between the two of them.

Q. And what was the attitude of Mr. and Mrs. Walsh vis-a-vis Ms. Cummins?

A. Mr. and Mrs. Walsh begged for Bríd Cummins to be transferred. Mrs. Walsh, as I said, is a long time resident of Munster Avenue, would be an astute woman, would understand a lot about the human psyche, and felt that Ms. Cummins needed a larger place to live, with a little bit more distance from her neighbours. Ms. Cummins wasn't happy where she was and Mrs. Walsh saw it as an immediate and effective solution to the problem.

Seeking 'the preferred outcome'

Mr Hogan Q. Now, can you say whether matters came to a head, as far as you were concerned, in September 2003?

A. Yes. There was much interest in -- the Walshes are on old Galway family, they know a lot of the councillors, they made a lot of representations, and they felt that at this point they were making a lot of applications for this transfer to take place. I can go back a little bit further and say that Mrs. Walsh came to meet Ciarán Hayes and she asked that I be present and that happened at her request again.

201

In September 2003, I was called by Ciarán Hayes and I was told that he had made an appointment with Blake and Kenny Solicitors that Mr. Walsh was going to avail of the services of the council's solicitors for the purpose of seeking an injunction against Bríd Cummins. He told me to liaise between the solicitor, John Carr, and Paddy Walsh, for a suitable time. It was the preferred way for the council to go about this bit of business, and I was to -- I think the very words were to encourage and support Paddy Walsh on his venture. I contacted Paddy and I contacted John Carr and got a suitable time and we went there, I believe on or about the 14th or 15th September. Sorry, I am wrong about that date now. I think it was 17th September actually.

Q. In all events, in September...

A. There is a relevance. But I did that. When we got to the office, Paddy Walsh was very nervous, he didn't know where Blake and Kenny were, which alerted me because it is right across from the Franciscan Abbey and all Galway people know where Blake and Kenny are. He was very nervous. We met at Moloney's Corner, went into the office, and he sat down and I introduced him to Mr. Carr and Mr. Carr began to talk to him about his experience with Bríd Cummins, and Mr. Walsh related all his complaints and the type of person she was and about his state of health and his wife's state of health and his daughter's state of health. So Mr. Carr was very sympathetic and he took the names and the ages for a profile. I said to John Carr, 'will you explain exactly what is going on, what is happening'? And he said, 'yes, Mr. Walsh you are taking an injunction against Ms. Cummins and no expense will accrue to you'.

Mr Gallagher: I am sorry. If you wouldn't mind speaking up.

A. Basically what he told Paddy Walsh was that he was taking an injunction against Bríd Cummins, and the city council were paying for it. And I asked him to explain it clearly to him in layman's language, which he did. And

Paddy Walsh said, 'no, I am only here to give evidence for the corporation'. And it was significant that he said corporation, because he wouldn't have known -- he is an elderly man, it was always the corporation to him. He said, 'I have only come here to give evidence to the corporation. We are not able for any court case. Let me out the door'. And that's what happened. So afterwards, Ciarán Hayes met with me and said that he was disappointed with the outcome of the meeting with Blake and Kenny and that he was disappointed, it was not the preferred outcome. I realised there was a very palpable difference in Ciarán Hayes' attitude to me after that.

Mr Hogan Q. And why do you think there was such an attitude, change in attitude?

A. I suppose I will have to go back a little bit and say I was shocked, that Ciarán Hayes was a very intelligent perceptive man, was using the council's resources, publicly funded, giving them to a private citizen to take a court action against a vulnerable tenant without resources. While Mr. Walsh is a lovely man, he is an elderly man; he would not be au fait with the rudiments of the law. His hearing is slightly -- he was not at that point in very good health, and I certainly, from my perspective, would not be willing to facilitate such a misrepresentation and misappropriation of public funding.

Q. And as far as you are aware, did Mr. Walsh have any forewarning that he was to be a potential plaintiff in the injunction proceedings?

A. Mr. Walsh would have met -- I now know that Mr. Walsh had met with the manager and Ciarán Hayes prior to that. In fairness, he told me that that day, but I didn't totally understand the significance. He was at sea as to what was going on. His wife was the person who would normally look after those type of matters, she is a younger woman and she did say to me, when I made the appointment with Blake and Kenny, 'for God's sake, Julie, make sure that Paddy hears what is being said. He is not as clued in as me'. And I believed that I did that.

203

Q. And you say then the attitude from Mr. Hayes changed towards you as a result of those events on that day?

A. I have to say that that is true, to the point that my father died in middle of December, and Ciarán Hayes and Frances Mullarkey attended his funeral and I thanked them and said I was rather surprised because I certainly didn't feel that their relationship was civil to me that they would be bothered attending my father's funeral.

Q. And can you then describe what the relationship between Mr. Hayes and Ms. Mullarkey was toward you from September 2003 onwards?

A. I have to say that Ciarán Hayes' attitude was professional but distant. He didn't interfere with me. He wasn't disparaging at any time. And I will say that he had, in my opinion, always been a very honourable person and I was shocked that he would be even thinking about misappropriating the services of the council's solicitor. That came as a major shock to me. Ms. Mullarkey was openly hostile, but I overlooked her lack of professionalism on many counts, and that's the way it was.

Q. And just continuing with the Bríd Cummins' issue for a moment, and we will just continue with that until -- what happened with regard to Ms. Cummins after September 2003?

A. After September 2003, I was called one morning by John Tierney, the manager, in early December. Again, there was a lot of representation, and he asked me to bring up the Bríd Cummins' file.

Judge Dunne: Sorry, I didn't hear that.

A: John Tierney, the manager, in early December, asked me to come to his office and to bring the file of Bríd Cummins from 5A Munster Avenue with me. I did that, and he said to me, 'Julie, do you see any way at all of resolving this problem? There is an awful lot of representation from various quarters. Is there any easy way around this'? And I said, 'yes, I believe there

204

is', and that a transfer from that property would provide an immediate solution. He asked me if I knew of any properties that were available, and I did and I identified two properties. One was a property at Saint Anthony's Terrace, it was vacant. The person who had been offered it eight or nine months before hadn't taken up the tenancy, but the house was in perfect condition. It was outside my area of responsibility, that particular area, I worked the west side. And he said, 'oh, would Bríd take that'? And I said, 'I think she would, it is a nice little bungalow'. We discussed who her neighbour would be, and her neighbour would be Annie _____, who is now deceased, so, with respect, Judge, I feel that we can talk about Annie _____.

So John Tierney said to me, 'is Annie still alive'? And I can remember the conversation so vividly. I said, 'yes, Annie is not as old as you think'. She was a lot of time in the unit in Merlin Park and I recalled being in that unit a very short time before that, meeting her there when she was sitting inside the foyer and she was inveigling the nurse to give me a hot whiskey. She was a character. He said, 'how would Annie and Bríd get on'? I said 'they would get on great because Bríd would spend her whole life trying to sort out Annie and nobody has been successful yet'. So he then said, 'I feel this woman could be a violent person', Bríd Cummins, he said, 'it mightn't be safe putting her in there'. I then said, 'in that case, there is a new estate built out in Fána Burca, which is the other side of the town in Knocknacarra, and it's being populated at the moment and I know there is a ground floor apartment available'. Because Ms. Cummins suffered from some disabilities and a property with a stairs would not be a good option. He then discussed the person who was overhead. Judge, there was some sort of matters in relation to the person overhead, but suffice to say there had been previous criminal charges proven against them, and I don't feel, with respect, that I should go into the details of the person overhead. But suffice to say that it was a person who was very well able to look after themselves in the event of the belief that Bríd Cummins was a dangerous person.

205

Q. Mr Hogan: But at all events, you recommended a transfer?

A. Yes.

Q. When was this?

A. That was in early December. And a few days later I met John Tierney on a corridor and he said, 'Julie, Ciarán Hayes wouldn't agree with a transfer of Bríd Cummins', and I said, 'that's a pity, it would make everyone's life a lot easier'.

Mr Hogan moved on to question me about the attitude of senior personnel in the city council towards me at this time.

A. At the time the attitude to me was difficult because I was working in the community and there had been a situation where an allocation was being made sometime previously, that the neighbour of -- the number is gone from me now, but there was an estate called Droim Chaoin and a particular resident there had difficulty with a neighbour next door, there was extreme anti-social behaviour. The man took them to court, it got resolved, the people abandoned the house and it was now vacant and being re-let. But after that man had taken this case to court, he came to meet Ciarán Hayes and I was also present at the meeting, on invitation, and Ciarán Hayes assured him that he would never again have to deal with neighbours that were involved in anti-social behaviour, and that the next time that property was being let, I would liaise with him and would ensure that he didn't have to suffer like this again.

So around that time that you are asking in relation to, Judge, I was working on the estate, when I was approached by the same man, who said to me, 'God almighty, you were supposed to come back to me and liaise with me about the allocation next door'. And I said, 'yes, there is no one'. He said, 'yes, I have observed people there last night that I know to be involved in anti-social behaviour, and I am not happy with it and I am disappointed with both yourself and Ciarán Hayes that you didn't honour the commitment'. And I said, 'I will look into it for you. I am sure there is some mistake. I will come back to you'. So I went into City Hall and discovered that an allocation had being made and that an offer was going out to this particular person who had been involved in anti-social behaviour. I said it to the person doing the allocations, the senior person, and I reminded her of the guarantees that were given by Ciarán Hayes. She said, 'there is no anti-social behaviour in relation to the people that we are allocating'. I said 'yes, there is. I am so sure of it'. Because there was a report on the file, and, Judge, I am so sure about the report on the file because I did it in 2000 and it was one of the first reports I did on anti-social behaviour. And Ciarán Hayes was housing officer at the time and he countersigned it and we actually did a house visit to that particular household where there was proven, and continues to be, anti-social behaviour. So I was alerted because the report was missing off the file. The person I was speaking to wouldn't entertain me. I went to Ciarán Hayes and I relayed to him what had happened, and he was very supportive and said, 'oh, God, we can't make an allocation like that, that's not fair. Tell them to bring me up the file'.

So a couple of days later, I was coming in to City Hall from working outside, and Frances Mullarkey was standing at the back door smoking a cigarette, and she said, 'I want to see you in my office, Julie', in a broad, hostile tone. And I said, 'that sounds ominous, Frances', and she said, 'it is'. I said, 'whenever suits you', and she said, 'can you come up'? So she finished the cigarette and I went up.

When I went into the office she said to me, 'you went over our heads to Ciarán Hayes about an allocation, you shouldn't have done that'. I said, 'for God's sake, Frances, this is a public service, we are all working to the same end. We are doing the best job we can'. And I felt I had to do it because promises were given and my reputation was on the line, and also it was

Ciarán Hayes' reputation on the line because he had given the assurances. She said, 'well, you have ruffled feathers but you won't do it again'.

Q. When was this?

A. This was, I believe, around December 2003.

Q. And what inference do you draw from that particular exchange between yourself and Ms. Mullarkey?

A. That I was not going to be much longer in the employ of Galway City Council.

Q. Why do you say that?

A. Because I have been proved right. Judge, I am a middle-aged woman, I am able to read the signals.

Q. Now, can we just continue with the narrative with regard to Ms. Cummins. We have seen where you say that the Walshes were inveigled, or somebody was endeavouring to inveigle them to take these proceedings, and that didn't happen. Now, what next happened of note with regard to Ms. Cummins?

A. The situation in Munster Avenue continued with difficulty from time to time. The same stories and complaints came in, either side complaining. And in February, on or about 24th February, Patricia Philbin who was a housing officer at the time...

Q. Again, just for the sake of record, February of what year?

A. February 2004. She told me to drop up to the office, which I did. She referred to the situation that was now referred to as "the situation in Munster Avenue". She told me that the management had decided they were going to evict Bríd Cummins because it was the preferred way to deal with the situation. However, there were difficulties, because the solicitor, John Carr, for the council was not happy with seeking a eviction where there were no written statements and no conviction against Bríd Cummins. She told me she needed to get signed statements for John Carr. I remember distinctly discussing with her the difficulty about signed statements from any of the people they were discussing because I felt they were all equally vulnerable and maybe not the most reliable of witnesses for a document for a court application. Patricia said, "talk to Josephine _____". I said, "I will and I will ask her if she is willing to make the statement". So I did visit Josephine _____, I know I visited her on the 24th.

Q. And Ms. _____ is the former tenant of...

A. Yes. Ms. _____ was gone for about a year-and-a-half from the property she was in. I had known her for many years from a previous life. She was very welcoming, and I said, "Josephine, look, the council are looking for you to make a statement that they can use in court because they are having difficulties with Bríd Cummins and they want to proceed further with it". And she said, "no, I am not getting involved". And I said, 'look, Josephine, will you at least talk to the housing officer and tell her that'? I wasn't leading her in any way, shape or form. She discussed a lot of personal issues that she had overcome and that I and assisted her in overcoming, and her situation was now very good. So I asked if she would meet the next day and she did.

So Patricia Philbin and I went to meet Josephine _____. At the outset Josephine _____ said, "okay, I will talk to you. Julie is here. I promised". So she relayed some of the difficulties she had with Bríd Cummins, and they were, more or less views, the usual housekeeping difficulties that people have living involuntarily in close proximity. So she said, "I won't sign anything, I am not going to court, I won't do it. Don't write anything down". So Patricia Philbin covertly recorded the conversation in shorthand, and at one stage Ms. _____ interjected and said, "you are not supposed to be writing anything", and then looked at me and said, "I trust you, Julie". And Patricia said she was not writing anything and she still looked at her and said, "I won't sign anything". She was very definite about what she wouldn't do.

Grand, back to City Hall, and a short time later, maybe an hour, Patricia Philbin came in to the office I was in downstairs, with a typed up version of this off the record statement. Ms. _____ insisted it was off the record. And Patricia said to me, "Julie, will you sign that there, that's what happened today"? And I said, "it was off the record, Patricia". She said, "but we need it for the court case, we have to get it. Frances wants you to sign it". And I said, "no, I won't, that is not right, I won't do that". So she was disappointed, but she came back again maybe 20 minutes later and said, "Ciarán Hayes wants you to sign it too". And I said, "no, Patricia, I won't do it".

Q. And what was the upshot of your refusal to sign it?

A. I was totally frozen out of any communication from any office onwards. The interview then took place a few weeks later. I was not kept in any loop in relation to any work that was going on.

Q. We will come to the interview separately, but just to pause there. By the end of February, I think you have already given this evidence, but can you say what you understood or what inferences you drew from the attitude of your superiors as a result of your dealings in relation to the Bríd Cummins' matter?

A. Well, I have to say, with some regret, because I had a good working relationship with the council before that, I enjoyed my job, but I have to say that because I refused to facilitate misfeasance and misrepresentation of public office, I would not commit a perjury to suit their desired outcomes, I was got rid of and it cost me a job. I am sorry to have to say it, Judge, but I see it as a fact.

Q. Now, again we will come back to the interview in a moment. But just to continue, after those exchanges with Ms. Philbin at the end of February

2004, can you say whether you had any other dealings in relation to Ms. Cummins, personally?

A. No. And I have to say that Ms. Philbin was not at any time hostile to me, and I appreciate that Patricia Philbin is a fundamentally decent person and that she was working under instructions. It was not, in the main, her idea.

Q. You already told the Court -- and we will come back to the interviews as we know -- the outcome of the interviews, and we know that you ceased employment on or about 4th June 2004. But can you say what in the end happened with regard to Ms. Cummins and why does a t have a bearing on your attitude to these present proceedings?

A. Sometime during 2004 the council continued and they succeeded in getting the eviction order against Ms. Cummins. When they went for repossession to collect the keys of the house, or they expected her to deliver them, whatever way it was meant to be, she hadn't handed them in and they were going back into court the week before Christmas to recover their property.

Q. Now this was December when?

A. December 2004. But when they went there, there was no response and the property was broken into. They gained access and they found Ms. Cummins dead.

Q. And again, without dwelling on this at any length, Ms. Grace, what do you infer were the circumstances which led..

Judge Dunne: I don't think she can answer that. Either there is an inquiry or not. How in God's name is a witness to be able to infer that?

Mr Hogan: Well, it is, I think, a matter of public record.

Judge Dunne: If it is, then produce the public record. But this witness isn't in a position to infer what happened. With the greatest of respect, Mr. Hogan, how could that possibly be?

Mr Hogan: I will leave the matter.

Q. Ms. Grace, Ms. Cummins died, was found dead. Was there any event involving the council thereafter concerning this death?

A. Yes. This generated enormous public interest. The councillors requested a lot of information. There was much interest on the local radio and every other radio and interest groups saying, "if this woman had been transferred this would have not happened and she wouldn't be forced into the situation". Anyway, by way of responses to the councillors' questions, the council management produced a document whereby they gave a chronological account of the whole history of Ms. Cummins' housing history with them, from her application onwards. The councillors are allowed to ask questions. And at the time I asked two different councillors to please make sure that the facts were told and that my input in my recommending a transfer for Ms. Cummins were relayed publicly. The council published the records and denied that I had made a recommendation. I did absolutely everything I could to have that report amended. I met with the new city manager. I wrote to the old city manager, not the old city manager, but the outgoing city manager, John Tierney, reminding him of my input. I wanted that recorded for posterity that, yes, I did make a recommendation, and that, yes, my judgment was not flawed, and that, yes, I was not listened to.

Q. And again, what inference do you draw from that?

A. With respect, Judge, it's not even an inference, it's a reality that I know...

Mr Gallagher: This is an event that occurred some six months after the employment terminated. And as far as it relates to wrongful dismissal, I don't see what inference can be drawn that might have an impact or relate to why the dismissal occurred. Sorry, why the termination occurred. When I say dismissal, I don't...

Judge Dunne: Well the only difficulty about this inference, this is an inference that she is supposed to draw from particular facts and circumstances. That is something she can do. It is another way of saying what was her state of mind in relation to the matter, and she can certainly say what that is.

Mr Hogan: Judge, I will be addressing the Court in due course as to the relevance of all of this.

Q. Now, Ms. Grace, what inference do you draw from that?

A. The inference I draw is that the council are unwilling to amend the records to restore my good name, to restore the level of integrity that I worked with, that my judgment was not flawed, and that I was not culpable in any way for the tragic circumstances that led to Ms. Cummins' death. I have begged various authorities to amend that report to reflect the truth, and it hasn't happened.

Examination evidence: The 'interview' process

Q. Mr Hogan: Now, if we go back to the interview of 15th March 2004, the actual interview itself. Can you just say, firstly, who was on the panel, can you recollect?

A. There was a gentleman, who I believe his name was Pat Dowling, and there were two females. I will not refer to that encounter, in fairness, as a proper interview. I myself have been on interview boards....

Q. We will come to that in one moment. Can you recollect who the two female interviewers were?

A. I didn't know their names then and they were unfamiliar to me.

Judge Dunne: Could you just start again by telling me what was the name of the man?

A. Pat Dowling.

Q. Mr Hogan: And did you know Mr. Dowling before this?

A. No.

Q. And do you know what position he then held?

A. I understood him to be working in the housing section of Limerick City Council.

Q. Now, you say when you entered -- firstly, how long was the interview?

A. I believe it was less than a half an hour. The person before me wasn't on time, so I am not absolutely certain. If I was a half an hour at that interview, it is the most.

Q. Can you describe what happened, first of all?

A. The interview to me was not as I would normally understand an interview to be. I would expect the interview to be an eliciting session, to be referring to how I was doing, bearing in mind that I was already doing this job. I would expect, that I would have been asked for my successes in the area, how I actually did something, how I brought about.., that type of thing. But there were a lot of examples of hypothetical situations.

Q. Can you describe for us the attitude, as you perceived it, of the interview panel?

A. I perceived it to be a very strange attitude. I found Mr. Dowling's attitude to me to be certainly not that of a gentleman. It was quite aggressive. He was very aggressive in his tone. He was accusatory. I was all the time trying to defend my actions and he was making a lot of personal -- he was asking demanding questions in relation to my personality.

Q. When you say what was accusatory, what was he accusing you of, do you recollect?

A. He was accusing me of having very strong opinions, "I would say you have a difficulty with bureaucracy". He cited a situation where if there was a difficulty between a community group and the council, as to how I would react to it and if the community group didn't want such and such a thing to happen, "how would you do that? Where would your allegiance lie"? It was said in such a way that it was an insinuation that I would not be loyal to the council, and I pointed out I had always been loyal to the council, for ten years. He couldn't understand the relationship between the Galway City Partnership and the council, couldn't understand why the council wouldn't just -- or the partnership wouldn't just give the funding to the council and let them run their own show. He felt that I must have had an easy time with the Partnership, which was absolutely untrue, because I worked very hard, I was serving both agencies. He was disparaging, he made me feel very uncomfortable. And at the end of the interview, when I was asked "any questions"? He said, "you will know in five or six weeks", in a tone that said, yes, I would know something in five or six weeks that he now knew and it was not going to be something advantageous to me. However, one of the female members saw this going on and she immediately pulled it back and said, 'we are interviewing tomorrow as well and you will know shortly after that'.

Q. And when you say he was asking you personal questions, what do you understand by that?

A. What I suppose personal in relation to my personality. They were accusatory and I was defending my personality. I am not an aggressive person, I am not a hostile person, but I am a direct person.

Q. And can you just convey to the Court the sense of the questions that were put you to you in relation to your personality?

215

A. He said, "is your director happy with you"? And I said, "well, I take it that he is". He said, "how would you know? How would you know"? He made me feel -- it looked like he was trying to rile me into saying something, to respond to him and his tone, which I didn't do because it's not my style. He kept interjecting with half a question. In fairness, one of the female interviewers was so nervous I saw her having difficulty formulating a question.

Q. And you say in your pleadings that this was a sham interview?

A. Yes, Judge.

Q. Why do you say that?

A. I believe an interview for a position to be an eliciting session, it was not an eliciting session. It was a situation where I was being verbally attacked and I was trying to respond in the best possible way, without, at the same time, aggravating the interview board, whom I believed I was dependant on in recommending me or not for a position. So I was under extreme duress.

Q. And why do you think, or can you say, why the male interviewer, Mr. Dowling, was so hostile to you.

Mr Gallagher: To suggest that he was hostile to her is an improper suggestion.

Judge Dunne: Well, it is very much a leading question, apart from anything else.

Mr Gallagher: Indeed.

Mr Hogan: Judge, with respect, it's not a leading question, because, in my respectful submission, the witness has already said that Mr. Dowling was hostile towards her. I have asked her questions about that and then I have asked her to say why did she understand that he was hostile?

216

Judge Dunne: Sorry, it is not a leading question. You are quite right. What is your problem with the question, Mr. Gallagher, please?

Mr Gallagher: The suggestion is that the Chairman was hostile to this witness, and I suggested that what the witness said, that he was asking difficult questions and was interrupting and wasn't behaving in what...

Judge Dunne: Well, no, she has gone further than that, far, far further, because he has been described as "accusatory", "disparaging", "interjecting", "not gentlemanly". So add them all up, perhaps it does amount to hostile.

Mr Gallagher: Well, I am in the Court's hands, except that...

Judge Dunne: "Aggressive". I am just looking at the various adjectives used.

Mr Gallagher: I accept that this is what has been said. But essentially Mr. Hogan has drawn a conclusion that there was a hostility there that manifested itself in those questions.

Judge Dunne: Perhaps Mr. Hogan should ask the question first as to whether it did amount to hostility and then go on and ask the next question.

Mr Hogan: I am happy to do that, Judge, and I will do beg the Court's and Mr. Gallagher's indulgence. I thought that the witness had actually used that word, but perhaps I misheard.

Judge Dunne: I have taken down a lot of things, Mr. Hogan, but as you will appreciate, I am not taking a shorthand note and an exact note, but they are the words that I have just recorded as a matter of practicality.

Mr Hogan: It may have been an oversight on my part.

Q. Ms. Grace, could you describe the attitude, as you saw it, of the male interviewer during the course of the interview?

A. I wish to confirm that I have said that I did find the attitude of the Chairman of the interview board hostile. I wish to confirm that, and I now wish to further answer your question, with respect.

Q. If I may then formally ask you what inferences or why do you believe that he was hostile to you?

A. That is the very reason, Judge, that I applied to have a judicial review of the interview proceedings, that I might have elicited the reason why and what his instructions were, to behave in such a manner, which to me, as a professional interviewer myself, was operating outside of the normal boundaries in such a situation.

Judge Dunne: That is not really an answer to the question, with the greatest respect. The question that was asked is why do you believe he was hostile, and then you said that you wanted to do the judicial review proceedings in order to elicit the reason. Is the answer that you don't know or that you do know or that you just came to that conclusion because of his conduct at the interview?

A. I don't know why he did it.

Q. Mr Hogan: Now, at all events, we know the outcome of the interview and you have already given that evidence this morning. We know that your employment came to an end in June 2004, and you have said in year pleadings, Ms. Grace, that this was -- I am not asking any legal questions -- but you have said that this was effectively on the bad faith on the part of the council.

A. Yes.

Q. Why do you say that?

A. Because in normal circumstances, the council would meet with the interview board, who have -- in fairness, I don't think they have any statutory responsibility, they are basically obliging the council, I am not sure about that. But my understanding of it is that normally the interview board would be met with and they would be shown the criteria and the type of person that they were looking for to fill the post. Can you refresh me what you are asking me?

Q. Can you say why you consider that you were not appointed to this position in March 2004?

A. My personal belief, the reason I was not appointed to the position is that I was not -- my style did not, for some reason, suit the management, particularly the housing section, of Galway City Council, that I would not perform duties that, to me, were inappropriate, misappropriate, and I most certainly would not commit perjury.

Judge Dunne: Can you repeat the three matters that you just mentioned? I would not?

A. Engage in something that was a misappropriation, or I would not commit perjury.

Q. Mr Hogan: And when you say a misappropriation, what does that refer to?

A. That refers, from my interpretation of it, to the services of the council's legal firm, who are Blake and Kenny, being given to a private citizen named Paddy Walsh. My understanding of a situation like that is that I couldn't accept or believe that it is within the gift of any council official to give funding to a private citizen for a private purpose.

Q. And when you referred to perjury, to what did you have in mind?

A. I specifically refer to the document.. to an off the record account of a person's opinions of a previous tenant, who specifically stated that they were not willing to sign anything, would have nothing to do with a court action and did not want to be involved. Understanding and being told that this particular document was going to be used as evidence in a court of law, where an eviction was being sought.

Q. And that relates to?

A. That relates to the Bríd Cummins' affair and that relates to what happened on 25th February 2004, when I made that refusal in full knowledge of what I was doing and despite the pressure being exerted on me.

Q. And again, I think you have already answered this question, but just for the sake of record, can you say why you consider that you haven't been more successful in obtaining employment in this type of social housing and related sectors?

A. The availability of jobs in the social housing sector are very scarce. It's a very small pool, and as well as that, my position now, as it stands, is that I am tarnished goods, I have done something wrong. And while Clúid found me marvellous for four months, they were not interested in offering me a permanent contract, and that was the acid test. There is a perception, it is more than a perception, there is a belief that there is something enormously wrong that I did while I was in the employ of the city council.

Q. Ms. Grace, perhaps you would be good enough to answer any questions Mr. Gallagher has for you.

Cross examination of Plaintiff by John Gallagher SC

It was mid-afternoon of the third day when cross examination of me by the Council's senior counsel commenced. He was an imposing presence, standing in his position, close to the witness box. He spoke with a loud, projecting voice. He started by emphasising the agreed 'excellent reference' that I received from Ciarán Hayes, Director of Services sometime after ceasing employment.

He laboured over how positive it was, and then questioned me about whether I had ever presented it and he asked about the level of happiness I would have about presenting it. I replied that I believed it was a true reflection of the work that I did. However, it is common knowledge that written references generally require the writer to stand over them in person when contacted by a prospective employer.

I pointed out that there was something not quite right here. Whilst the Manager John Tierney was out of town, Ciarán Hayes knew in advance that he would be the 'Acting Manager' of Galway City Council during that period in March, when the 'interview results' were being accepted by Council management. A colleague had witnessed Mr Hayes being in conversation with Pat Dowling at a Housing Conference in Westport days previous to the interviews. Coincidentally I had been withdrawn from attending that same conference by my line manager Frances Mullarkey, at the last minute.

Mr Dowling let me know during the interview, that it would be "five or six weeks" before I would realise my position. And so it proved to be. I told the judge that I would have been very happy to present the reference, but unfortunately it didn't marry with the council's own actions and I believed it would not have been supported. At this point in the proceedings, Mr Hayes stood up in the court room and whispered directly to Mr Gallagher who was on his feet. Mr Gallagher then advised the court that he wanted to reassure me that Mr Hayes would personally stand over the reference.

I thought this was strange behaviour, considering the circumstances of where we all were at this time. Quite simply, the reference provided by Mr Hayes and that he is now reaffirming, is a direct contradiction of the findings of the interview board, which he immediately ratified whilst he was temporarily acting manager.

Mr Gallagher continued on his theme of asking about jobs that I had applied for and how often I presented the 'excellent reference'. I outlined how the stigma of being a former Galway City Council employee, being indirectly tainted by the death of a vulnerable tenant around the same time as the cessation of employment was causing an unfair interference and disadvantage to me.

It seemed to me that he was filibustering around details and locations of job applications that I had made, endeavouring to show the benevolence bestowed on me by the so-called 'excellent reference'. I found it a somewhat exasperating experience answering the SC. I believed that he was drawing out seemingly irrelevant details in a laborious fashion. Simultaneously he accented great emphasis and intonation by his references to local government officials of a particularly high grade.

Mr Gallagher spent the rest of that afternoon questioning me for the Court in exhaustive fashion about the details of all my previous work contracts; the start dates and finish dates of each contract; the details of who signed off and who the housing officer at the time was; producing photocopies of signed contracts; whilst explaining the hierarchical structure of all of the officials and executives' grades in the Council, and so on.

> Mr Gallagher: Q. Now, would you accept from me that in 2003 there was a structure in the housing department? In other words, there were a number of people employed in the housing department at different grades.
>
> A. That is the norm, yes.
>
> Q. And we know that the manager, the city manager, was Mr. Tierney at one stage and others at different stages. And then there was Mr. Ciarán Hayes, the director of services from May 2001.
>
> A. Those are the dates you tell me, so I accept that. I am not challenging that.
>
> Q. I just want to establish it.

This was very tiresome and mentally tedious detail, which was stressful when being cautious to recount correct dates, times and people who were in place years previously, without any assisting records to hand. I was under immense pressure in not being pushed into giving a fast answer for the sake of it, in either agreement or disagreement, for fear of making any misstatements.

This cross-examination continued until the close of evidence for that afternoon.

Mr Gallagher omitted to explain how the cities of Galway, Limerick and the motor taxation office in Dublin City Council, were managing to operate without these important executives, missing from their posts while attending for six working days in the High Court. When I subsequently spoke with the (Acting) Manager in Limerick Council, he told me that he was not aware of Mr Dowling having been missing from his post and said he knew "nothing" about his involvement in the Court action. I asked him if his Director of Service Pat Dowling was under any sanction in relation to his participation on interview boards. He said he was not. One could have thought by listening to Mr Gallagher emphasising their executive importance; that Limerick must have been suffering greatly by this man's temporary absence.

At the close of the first day of cross examination, Mr Gallagher was still highlighting the career progression of Ciarán Hayes through the local authority grades. He intonated the job title 'Director of Services' with great emphasis. However, he did not acknowledge or extend any gratitude to the tax-paying citizens who were underwriting the Council in defending this expensive outing.

Day 3: Grace Vs Galway City Council

On the following morning the hearing commenced at 11am. This time, there was a familiarity about the surroundings in Court room number 5. I noticed on this morning that Mr Hayes had seated himself further away from the other local government officials, nearer to the legal people. Otherwise everybody seemed to be in the same seating positions.

Mr Gallagher recommenced the dialogue with some gusto. He started off in again describing the hierarchical structures of positions, grades and personnel employed in the City Council. He again reemphasised the seniority and responsibilities and reinforced the considerable status of the officials.

Mr Gallagher then explored some details about my former TLO colleagues (who had no hand, act or part in this legal case). After questioning about their personal profiles and desk locations, he moved on to question me about how the filing systems operated at City Hall. This went on for quite some time, as he explored the procedures for accessing and returning files to the filing system for tenant's files. I found myself in the strange position of having to defend the council's methods of storing files, containing personal and sensitive private information on housing tenants.

Mr Gallagher cross examined my recollections of the interview panel and the interview itself.

Q. And you attended for interview on the Monday the 15th and Tuesday, 16th March 2004?

A. I attended for interview on Monday, 15th March.

Q. Sorry, the interviews were held on the 15th and 16th, you attended on the 15th?

A. That's right.

Q. And you were interviewed by a panel of three individuals?

A. That's correct.

Q. Did you know any of those individuals beforehand?

A. I never met them before or since. I see them in the court now. I never saw them before.

Q. Did you know who they were?

A. No.

Q. Had you established where they came from or what their background or experience was?

A. No.

Q. Have you established it since?

A. I am not quite sure. No, I don't know those people, if that's the question.

Q. But do you know who they are and where they came from?

A. I know that the Chairman -- I believe that the Chairman came from Limerick City Council, I think. I don't know the other two. I do think maybe one girl came from Kilkenny. Am I right?

Q. Mr. Dowling is the Director of Services, he was the Chairman, this gentleman there.

A. I met the man over half an hour. I wouldn't remember his face again. Sorry, Mr. Dowling, if that is offensive but I don't remember your face.

Q. That's Mr. Pat Dowling, who was the Chairman of the interview board that you were so critical about. And beside him is Josephine Coughlan, who is now director of services with Limerick County Council, was at that time employed with Clare County Council in a senior position. And beside her, the lady with the glasses, is Rose Kenny, who is the executive manager of the motor tax office in Dublin at present, and had a senior position at that time with Kilkenny County Council.

A. Oh, she would have worked within Ciarán in Kilkenny I take it.

Q. Pardon?

A. Sorry, it is an aside. Thank you very much, Mr. Gallagher. I don't know those people and I accept what Mr. Gallagher is saying. I don't understand the relevance.

Q. Okay. Now you attended for interview and you were questioned, were you questioned by all three?

A. Yes.

Q. Do you have any complaint about any of the questions that were asked by Ms. Coughlan?

A. No more than myself, some of the ladies have changed their hair colour since. I am not sure which one is which.

Q. All right. Do you have any complaint about any of the questions you were asked by either of the two ladies?

A. No.

Q. So your complaint is solely directed at the behaviour of the Chairman, you say?

A. Yes.

Q. And you say that you found his attitude hostile?

A. I do.

Q. Tell me, did you speak to anybody after the interview?

A. Yes, I spoke -- sorry, may have I have clarification?

Q. Did you speak to any colleagues after the interview?

A. Yes, the interview was discussed with my two colleagues after the interview.

Q. Which two colleagues?

A. The two that applied for the post, they were in the office with me, *[names redacted]*.

Q. And did you tell them how you got on and the type of questions you were asked?

A. That was said openly because Frances Mullarkey went in and she supervised that interview process. After my interview she supervised the question time, where she asked me what I was asked for the benefit of my two colleagues as well. So the information was shared at that time.

Q. Did you make any complaint to Frances Mullarkey at that time that the Chairman was hostile?

A. I did not discuss my feelings from the interview with anybody.

Q. I am not asking about your feelings, I am asking you did you complain to Frances Mullarkey that the Chairman had behaved in an inappropriate manner and was hostile to you?

A. The whole situation regarding the discussion in relation to the interview, with respect, was hostile towards me. I came out from an interview that I felt was not an interview but a sham. I was then visited in a very hostile fashion by the said Ms. Mullarkey, demanding to know what I was asked. I was rather taken aback by the lack of professionalism, because at that point the other two people had not been interviewed. I felt it was very unfair to ask me what I was asked and what I thought for the benefit of, at this point, opposition. We were all vying for this post. And I felt it was totally unprofessional. And rather than be longwinded, why would I make a complaint to somebody who didn't understand the boundaries herself?

Q. Do I take it from that answer that you did not complain to Frances Mullarkey or you did not advise Frances Mullarkey by way of comment in the course of discussion, that the Chairman had been hostile and had behaved in an inappropriate way and had used a sarcastic tone, as you subsequently swore?

A. I do not make comments about other people to a third person.

Q. I take it from the answer that you did not complain of comments to Frances Mullarkey immediately after the interview, about the interview process or about the behaviour of the Chairman?

A. Correct. And I did not complain about her own behaviour either to her or to anybody else at that time.

Q. You have alleged that the interview panel, three senior local government officials here, engaged in a sham interview?

A. Yes.

Q. Do you think that that is an attack on their integrity?

A. It is stating my position and what I believed was my experience.

Q. You believe that these three individuals engaged in a sham interview process with you?

A. I do.

Q. And was that your view immediately following the interview?

A. Absolutely.

Q. Why did you not tell your immediate superior, or one of your superiors, that this was a sham interview process?

A. I was not aware of who I should make that complaint to. I waited for the outcome and I did address it and I did immediately address it. I did not address it on the 15th, I waited until I got the results of the interview, which is what I had to do on the 18th and I immediately addressed it.

Q. And when did you first describe it as a sham interview process?

A. On the morning of 18th March when Eileen Ruane phoned me, I told her it was absolutely out of order.

Q. Well, Eileen Ruane will deny that you said any such thing?

A. I have no control over that.

Q. I see.

A. At that particular time with Eileen Ruane, I discussed it with Joe Considine, I discussed it with Ciarán Hayes, I asked for my interview remarks on the Thursday, I wasn't provided with them until the Friday. I discussed it with the city manager on the Friday. I asked for the scientific basis for the calculation of those marks, he told me there was no scientific basis. I asked for the interview records, he said he didn't have any. I progressed it right through by meeting the city manager on the Friday. But I didn't act in haste, I waited. I gave a fair chance to the interview board, I waited.

Q. Now, did you discuss it with Mr. Michael Forde? Who is here, I understand.

A. I discussed the outcome.

Q. The outcome.

A. Yes.

230

Q. Did you tell him that you regarded the process as a sham process?

A. No. With respect, I am very careful about what I say about anyone else. I would not say anything like that publicly or to a third person. I did not say that.

Q. But you think that there is no difficulty in saying that three senior local government officials, who had no connection with you or Galway City, engaged in a sham interview process?

A. I understand that the Chairman of the interview board at the time took responsibility for the interview. I also understand that they were temporary agents of Galway City Council to whom I addressed the matter. I did not hold it against the interview board. I came to the city manager, because in line with the proper procurement procedures, it was his duty to ensure that the findings were regular.

Q. Did you raise the issue with Therese Carroll whom you have also subpoenaed here to give evidence?

A. No, not at all.

Q. Just as a matter of interest, you say that Therese Carroll didn't have a driving licence?

A. I was told by a mutual acquaintance that she didn't.

Q. Sorry?

A. So I was told. I am saying that I was told that.

Q. Who told you that?

A. A mutual acquaintance. A neighbour and friend of Therese Carroll.

Q. I see. Did you make any specific enquiries in relation to Therese Carroll or in relation to anybody else who might have been interviewed or carried out the interview?

A. I spoke in relation to the interview, after the interview with my two colleagues, and when they were finished their own interviews.

Q. Pardon?

A. After my two colleagues had been finished with their interviews they came back into the office and they discussed their interviews. I did not talk to other people. Except I will say that one person from the outside world, a woman, had phoned me asking me for details on how I did my job...

Q. And did you complain to either of your two colleagues who went for interview that it was a sham interview?

A. No, I did not make any complaint to my two colleagues. I felt it would be inappropriate.

Q. Pardon?

A. No, I did not.

Q. But you spoke to them about the interview?

A. We discussed the interview.

Q. And you spoke to them about the interview before they went to be interviewed?

A. Only on the supervision of Frances Mullarkey, who demanded to know what I had been asked. With respect, Judge, I am not so naive as to come out from an interview and to tell somebody else what I was asked. I would not be comfortable with relaying this information. I would certainly not be reducing my own odds.

Q. Why would you not be comfortable with that?

A. I would not be reducing my own odds. I am not a fool.

Q. I see. You have had a limited number of colleagues who have been mentioned in the course of these proceedings. You have three interviewers, you have made complaints about them.

A. May I set the record straight? I do not believe that the three interviewers -- I would not describe the three interviewers as colleagues.

Q. Sorry. Well, local government colleagues in the local Government service at the time.

A. I would not agree.

Q. You have made complaints against three interviewers; isn't that right?

A. No, I have made a complaint against one interviewer.

Q. But you have said that the interview process, they engaged in a sham process.

A. The interview was controlled by the Chairman, and the women did not engage in his actions.

Q. You said that: "The interview panel were not open to the appointment of the Plaintiff..."That's you. "To a position which, for reasons which were extraneous to the position and the applicable criteria for appointment to the position". That's what you are say in the statement of claim.

A. And that is exactly what I am saying. When this was discussed and being broken down for the purpose of clarification, the Chairman on the day took responsibility for the interview board and he dictated the pace of the interview, he controlled the interview, and the women spoke at his request.

Q. They spoke at his request?

A. Yes.

Q. I suggest to you that they were three independent individuals, who had much experience of interviewing and conducted this interview, yours and every other interview, with the utmost propriety.

A. I would answer that the Chairman of the interview board took control of the proceedings of the interview.

Q. Well, would you not expect a Chairman to be a chairperson, to be the person who would indicate who would ask questions in the first instance and who might perform what you might call a sweeping up role, perhaps?

A. That's what I am saying.

Q. And did he do that?

A. He took control most definitely.

Q. And would you expect the Chairman to take control?

A. Yes, in a professional manner. Of course I would.

Q. And what was wrong with the manner in which he took control?

A. It was dictatorial, antagonistic, hostile and unprofessional.

Q. Now, his two colleagues who were on that board will disagree with you, and too will disagree that that was the situation?

A. I have no control over their opinion.

Mr Gallagher went on with other minor details, coming onto the topic of an alleged complaint being made about Ciarán Hayes.

Q. So you are critical of him in that respect?

A. I am critical of his actions.

Q. You are critical of his actions. And you were critical of him, for the first time in this court, for seeking to use public funds in order to subsidise or to

pay for civil proceedings to be taken by Mr. Walsh against his neighbour; is
that right?

**Mr Hogan interjected at this point to debate a point of phraseology
with Mr Gallagher, and Justice Dunne put them at ease. It was clear
that she was listening intently.**

Q: You have suggested in this court that Mr. Hayes was annoyed in
circumstances where what he had required or wanted achieved, involved, in
your view, a misappropriation of public funds; isn't that right?

A. That's right.

Q. And you have complained, have you not, about Frances Mullarkey? The
lady whom you met immediately after the interview and who was your
superior.

A. That's right.

Q. Have you made any complaint about Patricia Philbin?

A. No.

Q. Have you anything to say about her in the performance of her duty? How
did you find her?

A. I found Patricia Philbin very professional, easy to work with, and was
surprised when she asked me to sign -- to comply with something that was
going to really be perjurous, that was a false document for the purpose of
using in court. I was surprised. And I say straightaway she told me that she
was asked to do it by Frances Mullarkey, it was not her own decision.

Q. Did you find her a truthful person?

A. Absolutely.

Q. Do you remember meeting Patricia Philbin after the interview?

A. No, I don't have a recollection of that.

Q. Patricia Philbin has a recollection of meeting you after the interview and you talking about the interview, this was on the day of the interview, as I understand it, on Monday. You told her, conveyed to her, that you had done a very good interview.

A. I certainly have no recollection of that.

Q. Well, she will give evidence here to that effect.

A. I accept that. I have no control over that. It's whatever somebody else says, I accept whatever she says.

Q. She will say you made no complaint whatever about the interview or the Chairman's attitude or his behaviour in the course of the interview.

A. Like I said, I waited and I made the complaint in relation to the interview to the appropriate authorities when I had the evidence that I required. I do not go around talking disparagingly about people, with respect.

Q. Tell me, of all the officials in the housing department who were senior to you, who would you regard as the most friendly or the one you would be friendliest with?

A. I would have a normal professional relationship with people that I worked with. My socialising didn't revolve around anybody that I worked with. I was in a position where I worked externally quite a bit, out on the ground, and I wouldn't say I am personally friendly with anybody in the housing section.

Q. Did you ever visit Patricia Philbin in her home?

A. After being sick I visited her once.

Q. Did you have any comment to make in relation to any other members of the staff at that time?

A. I don't recall.

Q. Do you recall inviting her to stay out on ... she had broken her wrist; isn't that right?

A. Yes, I remember Patricia breaking her wrist. She fell in the car park.

Q. And you went to see her in her home?

A. Yes.

Q. A social visit, to visit a friend; is that right?

A. That's right.

Q. It wasn't official or business?

A. Not at all.

Q. You were visiting a friend?

A. Purely human. The girl lives over the road from me.

Q. Yes. And did you invite her to remain out sick as long as she could?

A. God, no, that wouldn't be my advice to anybody. I am not in a position to advise anybody. I would most certainly not have said anything like that.

Q. Did you tell her that she should remain out for as long as she could, because the longer she stayed out the more likely another official would fall flat on their face, or words to that effect?

A. No, I have no recollection of saying that, and that would not be my line of conversation. I called to the girl because she had fallen, she lived over the road. And I would not make disparaging comments about other people.

Q. I put it to you that you did, in fact.

A. I deny that.

Q. Ms. Philbin will say that you accompanied her, or she accompanied you, to visit Ms. _____, who had been moved to a home for the elderly.

A. That is not correct, Ms. _____ was actually a council tenant. Ms. _____ had been relocated to a new apartment.

Q. Was that accommodation for the elderly?

A. No, not specifically for the elderly, the elderly and disabled. For the purpose of clarification, it was not a nursing home or supported accommodation.

Q. But you draw a distinction between a home for the elderly and disabled?

A. I do. It was independent living, non-supported.

Q. In any event, Ms. _____ had been moved there because of the problems that she, as an elderly lady, had experienced with the tenant downstairs, Ms. Cummins; isn't that right?

A. Ms. _____ was entitled to a transfer on the basis of her age and to a ground floor accommodation. Ms. _____ is now an elderly lady, she was living in upstairs accommodation, she rightfully applied for a transfer on the basis of her age, and that would be the independent and overriding factor in her transfer, and in her allocation.

Q. Wasn't there an ongoing and serious problem between Ms. _____ and the late Ms. Cummins?

A. There was.

Q. And weren't there allegations and counter-allegations being made over a long period?

A. That's right.

Q. And wasn't it in order to eliminate that and because of her age and because she qualified for a transfer that Ms. _____ was transferred?

A. Ms. _____ qualified for a transfer, and it would be good estate management to have her transferred. So yes, that's right, that reflects the position exactly.

Q. And isn't it the position that the upstairs apartment was left vacant after that?

A. The upstairs apartment was offered, I understand, to one person after that, and I do believe that the person...

Q. Sorry, if you just deal with that fact. Did it remain vacant after that?

A. Yes.

Q. And was it after Ms. _____ was moved that complaints started in relation to the Walsh family?

A. I don't have the complete file with me now and...

Q. I am not going to tie you to a date, but generally speaking.

A. There were three strands to the complaints. There was Bríd Cummins downstairs, there was Josephine _____ upstairs, there were the Walshes next door. The complaints could be going simultaneously between the three of them. As the liaison person I would have listened to a lot of that.

Learning About the Interview Results

Mr Gallagher: Q. Now, you learned of the fact that you hadn't been appointed by telephone call from Ms. Ruane on 18th March, and I suggest to you that whilst you would have been understandably upset and disappointed at not being appointed, you did not complain about the interview process at that stage?

A. With respect, I responded immediately and said that the whole thing stank and it was red rotten.

Q. Now, you then had given evidence in relation to...

Judge Dunne: Sorry, just before you move on from that, if you said the whole thing stank, to whom did you say that?

A. To Eileen Ruane when she phoned me.

Q. Mr Gallagher: You told her that the whole thing stank?

A. Yes, and I was quite irate, I will admit that.

Q. Ms. Ruane will deny that you said anything like that.

A. I have no control over what Ms. Ruane says.

Mr Gallagher then went on to discuss a detailed account of correspondence between my former colleagues and the city council. I felt this was unfair, as they had paid for their own legal representatives, and I was not involved with their particular grievance. Having worked for many years than they did, and having trained them into the positions, I was taking a different legal route, for different reasons. Mr Gallagher seemed intent on using much oxygen on this topic, which was irrelevant to my case.

The see-saw of questioning continued on a similar vein of seemingly innocuous questions, until Mr Gallagher arrived at the matter of how HR failed to send me the letter of termination of employment. They knew that I needed this written confirmation in order to proceed with a legal action of some kind. They deprived me of the benefit of time in this regard.

Mr Gallagher went onto another topic: deciding to read the supporting reference written by Ciarán Hayes.

Q: Ms. Grace, I am sorry to go back on something I dealt with yesterday, but it was the reference which was furnished to you on your leaving employment with Galway City Council, and you didn't have a copy and I have since

240

obtained a copy, and for the record you might confirm that is a copy of the reference that you obtained. It's dated 17th September 2004, it's addressed to you:

"To whom it may concern, this is to certify that I have known Ms. Julie Grace since 1993 when she worked as a revenue collector and enumerator for Galway City Council. I have always found her to be efficient and diligent in her dealings.

"Since 1998, however, I worked closely with Julie in her capacity as tenant liaison officer, a post jointly funded by Galway City Council and Galway City Partnership. This was a new post and a new departure for the city council in its efforts to develop an estate management function.

I was fortunate to be able to rely on Julie's advice and support in this matter and would credit her with a number of initiatives, including the design and delivery of a tenant training program and a tenant handbook. Indeed some of the initiatives and duties undertaken were beyond what was required of a tenant liaison officer, and were fulfilled willingly and completely.

In addition to her support and advice, I found her to be thorough in her research and have good report writing and communication skills. Accordingly I would have no hesitation in recommending her for employment.

Signed Ciarán Hayes, Director of Services, Housing Planning and Economic Development".

Q: Is that the reference you received from Galway City Council on leaving their employment?

A. It is.

Q. I take it you have no complaint with anything that was said about you in that?

A. No.

Q. Would you describe it as a very good reference?

A. I said I would describe it as a positive reference and recognising the work that I did.

Ironically, the marks awarded by the interview panel rated me at approximately 55% overall, where at the time Mr Hayes was Acting Manager for John Tierney who was on leave for a few days. In this temporary capacity, he immediately accepted the findings of the interview board and hastily ratified their recommendation for acceptance. When I spoke with him on the morning that I got the result, he would not entertain debate on the matter.

Mr Gallagher then moved to another topic, some specifics of when I was being directed by my line manager Frances Mullarkey to give evidence in the District Court for the Council in relation to a barking dog upsetting a neighbour. There was much analysis of memos, where complaints were telephoned into City hall, and records were made of calls and passed up the line. Owing to legal reasons, and to protect the tenants involved, I am precluded from giving more details about this here.

Next Mr Gallagher returned to the details about the judicial review taken years previously, cross-examining me on detail after detail. This took up a significant section of the court's time, whilst he read through each of the elements in the affidavit once again.

He then reverted back to discuss the incident of where I accused Patricia Philbin of covertly recording shorthand notes of a tenant's off the record account, gained retrospectively, on alleged incidents from years previously, whilst living in the flat over Bríd Cummins on Munster Avenue. This cross-examination was teasing out minutiae of evidence. It seemed to be taking up a lot of time.

With fifteen minutes remaining in today's session, Mr Hogan proposed to the court, that a main witness who was subpoenaed to the court, Ms Therese Carroll, might be facilitated in giving evidence today, as she was anxious to get back to Galway. The judge permitted this and Therese Carroll was called to the stand.

Examination of subpoenaed witness by Gerard Hogan SC

Mr Hogan: I am very grateful to the Court. It is in ease of Ms. Therese Carroll, who has to go back to Galway. Ms. Therese Carroll.

Q. Mr Hogan: Now, thank you very much. Can you tell the Court your present position?

A. Housing estate liaison officer with the Galway City council.

Q. And when did you apply for that position?

A. The beginning of 2003, I think. [sic]

(Note: the posts were first advertised in December 2003.)

Q. And this was one of positions which is the subject matter of the controversy in the proceedings.

A. That's correct.

Q. And can you tell the Court whether you were appointed to that position immediately?

243

A. Not immediately, no. I was appointed to it at the time others were appointed to it.

Q. In March 2004?

A. Yes.

Q. You were one of the first three ranked applicants; is that right?

A. Yes, that's correct.

Q. And can you tell the Court whether, at that time, in 2003 to March 2004, you held a full driving licence?

A. No, I held a provisional driving licence. I submitted a copy of it with my application.

Q. And just one other thing, did you speak with Ms. Grace before you applied for the post?

A. I spoke with Ms. Grace in 2003, before I was aware of any job ever, before I was aware or had any inkling that I would ever be working for a local authority. I was doing a degree in housing social policy with UCD. Part of the degree in the first semester, one of the prerequisites to advancing to the next stage was to carry out an estate profile. So I identified the key people in the area of the west side where I was conducting the profile. Firstly, I phoned City Hall Housing Section, and sought a statement of policy, I think, a statement of policy on tenant participation in estate management. That was furnished to me by Frances Mullarkey. Then I sought the key people to conduct the estate profile. One of people I was told by the housing section that I should hook up with was Julie Grace, another was John Middleton. I went to the resource centre, I went to numerous people whose names I can't remember now. Now, in that regard I left one or two messages for Julie Grace, and I can't remember if I got a call back from her or I contacted her back again, I was persistent, and we had a brief conversation. I had no idea what per position title was, I had no idea who she was. And I sought information, quantitative stats on Currach Bui. I was doing the qualitative stuff myself, with John Middleton, and that's why I contacted her. It was nothing to do with any job because there was no job ever known to me.

Q. No, I wasn't suggesting for a moment there was. But did you speak with Ms. Grace?

A. I spoke with the person who is Ms. Grace, I had no idea who she was.

Q. And did you seek a copy of the tenant handbook?

A. Perhaps I could have. I had numerous tenant handbooks from around. In the degree course I was doing there were a number of people from all around the nation, from Dublin, Sligo, Wexford, they were all from grade 6 up to grade 8, participating in the degree course that I was in. And from all of them I would have made a collection of handbooks, reference points, start a reference section. And I perhaps did, I don't know, it could have been an automatic part of my research to ask for a tenant handbook.

Q. And finally, Ms. Carroll, how would you describe the ambience and the attitude of the interviewers if you can recollect that?

A. For the position?

Q. Yes.

A. I can actually recollect. Well, I will stand corrected but I do recall a lot. As I was in here on Monday waiting, where I saw no one, in the afternoon the three people who interviewed me walked in and I remembered exactly each one, where they sat, what emphasis they had on each point and what area they covered in the line of questioning. And I actually remember the number of the questions.

Q. And I asked you...

A. The ambience. I loved it. I sat there and spoke, I think, probably non-stop, well, with interjections and questions, for about 40 minutes. I found it -- I just found it a forum for me to totally unleash everything I had, I was very gung ho to get the position.

Q. And no question of any hostility?

A. I wouldn't interpret anything as hostility. I found it very encouraging.

Q. Thank you very much, Ms. Carroll.

This concluded the direct examination of Ms. Therese Carroll by Mr. Hogan. She was then cross-examined by Mr. Gallagher:

Q. Mr Gallagher: Ms. Carroll, where did you come in the placing, do you know?

A. I believe number one

Q. And you were asked about your driving licence.

Judge Dunne: She said she had a provisional driving licence.

Q. Mr Gallagher: From March 2003 to March 2004?

A. Yes.

Q. When did you acquire a full driving licence?

A. Early 2007, I think.

Q. I see. And you were employed by the council and you still are employed by the council. I haven't spoken to you or spoken to ..

A. That's correct.

Q. Tell me, you went to the interview, you said that you found that the ambience was lovely, it was a forum to ...I can't read my own writing.

A. That is the word I used.

Q. Were you asked any questions that you found offensive?

A. Not at all.

Q. Were you asked any questions that related to how you might deal with a potential conflict between, say, a community and the council?

A. Yes, I was, that was one of the questions.

Q. Who asked that question?

A. Sorry.

Q. The Chairman?

A. Yes. I remember the question.

Q. What did he ask you?

A. He posed a scenario and said, if you, for example, had a situation where you had to house a particular troublesome family, it was actually a member of the Travelling community, if you had to facilitate their allocation of a house in one of your estates where you had a relationship with the residents of that estate, and the residents were in pretty much opposition to this happening, how would I deal with it. From what I recall I said that it's hard to hypothesise the relationship I would have, but I would hope and assume for the purposes of this that I would have a very strong and sincere relationship with all the residents in the estate, and I would have a different relationship with each one. I would impart, as instructed, the information that there was a new allocation, because people in estates very often approach you when you enter the estate, if there is a house vacant, to ascertain who is the person going in, or the family going in. So in this hypothetical scenario I said I would slowly approach the residents in various evening meetings. I would impart to them that there was a family of the Travelling community going to be allocated the house, and in their objections I would listen, I would tease out and discuss. But I would also

247

point out to them that, A, there is equality legislation to cater to things like that, and the local authority have a duty to house people. And that if they start picking out particular families that they have decided as a group can't go in, you can't condone that sort of thing because another group could isolate one of them for whatever reason, and that couldn't be supported by the council or legislation or by policy. And ultimately my final thrust to win over would be that I am loyal to legislation, to policy, and ultimately to the council. That was my answer as far as I can recall.

Q. And do you have any other question that you can recall that was put to you?

A. Yes.

Q. Short.

A. Sorry. I am speaking too quickly.

Judge Dunne: I have given up trying to take a note.

A. Okay. I remember when I entered, the first question by the Chairman, he had my CV and said, 'right, you have been in France, you have been in the UK, you have worked in theatre, what have you got to offer an organisation like this?' And I actually welcomed the challenge of marketing and selling myself and convincing him that I would. And because I didn't come from a local authority background, having done a lot of years when I was about 18, in the local authority. I was coming in very fresh from the outside, and it was a challenge to convince him, and I think I did so. I went through my entire CV and traced to where I was. But I took it as his way of identifying the person's specification, the person who was pushing themselves for this job, to get an idea, because it is very much a person related position. Apart from knowing the position, you have to have a way of communicating yourself with people, and I reckon he was identifying my person specification and my qualities and characteristics.

Q. Had you known any of the interviewers beforehand?

A. No, I didn't know very many people in the whole of Galway.

Q. But you didn't know any of the three?

A. No.

Q. Did you have any problem or any concern or any complaint in relation to the manner in which you were questioned, or the behaviour of the panel or any one of them?

A. Not at all. I came out of the interview feeling very good.

Q. I see. Obviously you did well. Thank you very much:

Judge: Can I just ask you one question? I didn't quite hear, did you say UCD or UCG?

A. UCD for that one.

Judge: Okay, thank you. Mr. Hogan?

Mr Hogan: No further questions, Judge. I take it Ms. Carroll can be released?

Judge: Yes, thank you.

The hearing was concluded until the following morning again.

Day 4: Grace Vs Galway City Council

The hearing reconvened on the next day, Thursday 20th May. At the beginning of the session, I was called to take the stand for further cross examination by John Gallagher SC, for Galway City Council.

He quickly reverted back to revisit the previous day's dialogue on the topic of Patricia Philbin and the matter of her covertly recording the off-the-record conversation used in court as evidence for the council, (purporting it to be a statement from the upstairs tenant adjacent to Bríd Cummins). He went through the statement Patricia had prepared, what type of paper it was written on, and so on.

> Q. You have described Ms. Philbin as an honest and I think trustworthy person, somebody you had regard for.
>
> A. I did not have reason to say otherwise.
>
> Q. And somebody you visited while she was sick and while she was off work at home because of a broken wrist.
>
> A. As a neighbour and as a human being I did think it a gracious thing to do to drop in to see a colleague who was out injured with a broken wrist, or an injured wrist.
>
> Q. And you had no complaint about her honesty or integrity?
>
> A. No, and that is the reason that when I was asked to sign this by Patricia Philbin, and I am so sure I was asked, it was to me Patricia acting out of character, it was not a person I knew and she prefaced it by saying "Frances wants you to do it." And that's why I was not holding that against her. I understood her position. Her superior, her line manager was Frances Mullarkey and further to that the Director of Services, and when she came back the second time she said "and Ciarán wants you to do it too", knowing

250

that I had great respect for Ciarán Hayes and that all things being equal I would never question any directive given by him to me.

Q. Now, I put to you on an earlier occasion that you had suggested to her that she should remain out on sick leave as long as possible, so that Frances Mullarkey would fall on her face and you deny that?

A. I deny that.

Supermarket encounter with Patricia Philbin (1)

Q. After you left your employment with Galway City Council did you ever meet Patricia Philbin?

A. I met her once or twice in the supermarket.

Q. Where?

A. I remember meeting her in Dunnes and I remember meeting her in Claregalway.

Q. Did you meet her outside the Centra supermarket in Claregalway?

A. I did.

Q. And is there a Supervalu supermarket there?

A. There is.

Q. Did you meet her on two separate occasions in or outside the supermarkets in Galway in the latter part of 2004?

A. I am not able to remember exactly when I met the girl. I am not able to confirm. I do remember on one occasion that she was getting ready for a Christmas party so I'm not sure which year that was.

Q. Ms. Philbin recalls meeting you on two occasions in Claregalway. On one occasion she says it was outside the Centra premises is Claregalway. It was sometime after 5:00 o'clock in the evening because she was on her way home from work in Galway. She says she was coming out of the supermarket and you were going in. Do you remember that?

A. No, I couldn't give you the...

Q. The details, but you do remember meeting her?

A. I know I met her at different occasions.

Q. And did you have a chat with her?

A. Yes, because she told me she was going to a Christmas party. That's how I know.

Q. Was anything said about your previous work or about your previous colleagues or about City Hall or anything of that nature?

A. There may have been some discussion, yeah, there may have been.

Q. She will say that you said to her "how are things in City Hall?" or words to that effect.

A. Possibly.

Q. And she will also say that you said to her "Ciarán and Frances will pay."

A. I may have said that because I felt ..I have no recollection of what I said exactly but at that time I was very irate and I was very disappointed and to a former colleague like Patricia whom I trusted and whom I worked closely with. I can't remember saying it but I will not deny saying it because it would be expressing the way I felt at that time. And when I say "pay", I don't know mean financially because at the end of the day we all have to reckon with our maker and to me if you treat somebody badly, interfere with their working life, interfere with everything that they hold good, you will pay in some fashion. I don't proclaim to be a great Catholic. I say I am a Christian with values and to me there is natural justice and there is a big wheel of life and that is the way I see things.

Supermarket encounter with Patricia Philbin (2)

Q. Now, Ms. Philbin will say that she met you on another occasion and she is not sure which occasion came first, she also met you on a second occasion in Claregalway and she said that you met in either the Centra or Supervalu supermarket. It was probably after 5:00 o'clock after work. You met her in one of the aisles in the supermarket. Do you remember that?

A. I can't confirm that, I honestly can't.

Q. And she said that you said to her, you had a chat and she said "how are things?" -- you said "how are things in City Hall?" or words to that effect.

A. I am not so sure that I would be concerned all the time and I don't deny that I may have said it but it wouldn't be my opening statement every time...

Q. I am not saying it was your opening statement, I am saying that in the course of conversation that you had said something to her, "how are things in City Hall?", and she presumably answered that question. But she also says that you enquired for Ciarán and Frances and you said "they will pay yet."

A. I don't remember saying it. I will not deny saying it because it was the way I felt.

Q. And is that still the way you feel?

A. I feel we are all responsible for our actions and if I personally affected somebody's life so badly that I removed their dignity, their right to earn a living and values that were held dearly to them, I would still hold that attitude. And I am not saying this in a vindictive fashion, I am simply merely stating it as the person I am and the way I feel, and I do believe in the big wheel of life and I do believe in natural justice and that is the reason that I am here today, to bring about some kind of closure for me because I believe I did nothing wrong. Everything that I had was removed from me in the sense that my -- and I am not just talking about money, I am talking about my good name, that my integrity and that my ability to evaluate a situation was flawed. And I feel very aggrieved that I absolutely begged the Council to amend the Bríd Cummins report and accept that I did recommend a transfer and that I had nothing whatever to do with that woman's state that progressed her to taking her own life.

Q. Where has anybody said that you did anything wrong?

A. Many, many people, they believe the Council have misrepresented me in saying that I did something wrong because I didn't. As a liaison officer and when I was asked for my opinion on the situation to bring about a remedy I straight away recommended two properties that were available that nobody was living in and that would relieve the situation for both Mrs. Walsh and Paddy who were only at any time asking to have that woman transferred to ease their situation. I was making the recommendation because I now know that Bríd Cummins was not a well woman and for me at that point as a housing professional not to be able to see that there was something fundamentally wrong would say that I was either vindictive in my attitude or that my thinking was flawed.

Q. Where in any document or in any utterance has the Council or any employee of the Council made any of those allegations against you that your judgment was flawed or anything of that nature?

A. In what is now known as the Bríd Cummins report and in the questions to council, the councillors' questions to the management, two different councillors asked whether the TLO recommended a transfer or not and it is categorically stated that the TLO did not recommend a transfer. In December 2003 I identified two properties and I did make it and I begged the Council, I wrote to the manager, I met with the manager, I did everything possible to have the record amended to show that I was neither malicious, vindictive or flawed in my thinking and that I did appreciate the human dynamics.

Q. Did you tell Patricia Philbin that you had employed a private investigator?

A. No.

Q. Now, just to say that Patricia Philbin will say that you did tell her that.

A. It's ridiculous in the extreme and in fairness if that is the way Patricia Philbin wants to report or misreport or misconstrue something I said or blatantly lie about it, I have no control over it and at this point I don't feel it worth...

At this stage Mr Gallagher turned again to revisit the case of Bríd Cummins and the recording of phone calls into City Hall. A laborious dialogue ensued regarding who, how, when, where, records were taken, stored and accessed. After some time, he moved back again to the issue of what I believed to be Mr Hayes's improper instruction.

Q. But you said that what was being proposed and what you had been invited to do or were required to engage in was an exercise which would have involved misappropriation of public funds.

A. I do say that and that is the way I see it.

Q. So you saw the instructions as given by Ciarán Hayes to provide a legal service to Mr. Walsh if he wanted it as being an instruction which involved misappropriation of public funds?

A. The giving of the services of the offices of Blake and Kenny to a private citizen paid out of the public purse could not be deemed to be a proper use of public funding.

Q. Did you make any complaint about that at that time?

A. No.

Q. Did you make any complaint about that at any time after 15th of September 2003?

A. Complain to whom?

Q. To anybody.

A. No, I don't recall making a complaint about that. I was not Mr. Hayes's supervisor. As I said yesterday, the reason I wanted this discussed under oath was for a particular reason.

Q. Did you go to the manager and complain and say that this is a wholly inappropriate proposal which would involve misappropriation of public funds?

A. I did not.

Q. Mr Gallagher: I put it to you, Ms. Grace, that the first time you made that allegation was in the witness box sitting in the chair that you are sitting in now.

Covertly-maintained second file on Bríd Cummins

Q. Now, among the matters that you have complained of was the fact that you didn't have details of Ms. Cummins's health or medical condition?

A. From the time that I began to deal with Bríd Cummins in 2000, the situation was difficult and some of the behaviour was quite irrational. On her file I found nothing to tell me why this was happening and several times I said to Ciarán "do we know any more about her, is there any background?" He said there was never -- he had no further information. But at that meeting on 17/06 with Nora Walsh she said to him "do you know anything at all about this woman?" and he pointed to a file on his desk that was quite substantial. I had never seen the height of that file before and I thought there's more here than I know about and it confirmed that there was.

Q. Is this the file or does it look like the file that we are talking about? Do want to look at it perhaps? [Indicating]

A. Yes, yes, in the distance I can see it, that is the substantial file that I refer to, that size of file, yeah.

Q. I suggest to you that that file was at all times available to members of the housing staff in Galway City Council?

A. I am saying that the file I had access to was a much smaller file.

Q. Well, Mr. Hayes will say..

A. And sorry, may I see where that begins from?

Q. Yes, you may. I haven't read it myself personally but I have a copy of it. I take it that it would start at the beginning and or at the end rather and you go forwards; is that right? [Same handed] Normally there with be an application for housing accommodation, something of that nature. Is that the file? Is that, Ms. Cummins's file?

A. May I have another moment, please? With respect, your Honour, I am not trying to delay somebody. The file that I was aware of, from what I remember this was the beginning of the file that I remember because I was always wondering where the lady came from or what the story was and there is information here. I did not see this stuff, I did not have.. this was not on the file I was working with, and I notice something here as well, that the social work department in the university college hospital would have had a lot of contact, from what it says here with Ms. Cummins and I did not see that file. And may I humbly make a question, ask a question, it would be customary for applications for housing where the social workers of the Western Health Board would be dealing with them, that they would liaise with the housing worker -- the social worker in the City Council, and the City Council social worker would have maintained a number of files in relation to those situations. So I am only wondering out loud if that had been in the social work department and that's why it wasn't on the general file.

Q. You accept that that is Ms. Cummins's file?

A. I am answering the question now, I am saying that is not the file that I was working from.

Q. My instructions are that this is the complete Ms. Cummins file. Maybe the cover has changed or whatever, I don't know, but I am told that this contains all the material in relation to Ms. Cummins, including your reports.

A. I don't doubt that that is the complete file. I am saying that is not..

Q. Pardon?

A. I don't doubt, with respect, that that is the file but I am saying that that is not the file I had access to. And for the purpose of clarification, I have just realised that maybe because the information came from the social work department, that it was also contained within the social work department in the City Council offices where the social worker would have her own desk and maintain some files there with respect, Judge.

At this point in the proceedings, Ciarán Hayes stood up in his seat and leaned forward to whisper something to Mr Gallagher, who then continued:

Q. Mr Gallagher: I understand that that only applies in relation to members of the travelling community?

A. I accept what you are saying and in the interests of...

Q. So what you were just telling the Court was incorrect?

A. No, I beg your pardon, I am stating that that is not the file I had access to.

Q. No, what you were suggesting, will you accept that when I put it to you that it was only what you were recounting only related to travellers?

A. I am not sure, I didn't know the situation in relation to the files of the social work department but I did believe that where social workers in the hospital were dealing with the Council, they also dealt with the social worker in the Council, and with respect it would make very good sense that that is the way the system would run.

Q. Are you aware that there were medical reports on file which indicated that the late Ms. Cummins was...

Judge Dunne: Mr. Gallagher, I don't want to be cutting you short or Ms. Grace short in relation to anything but Ms. Grace has said several times that she never saw medical reports, she didn't see that file, she was working from a different file, so you will have to agree to disagree on that. It may well be that the Council had a full file which had all sorts of information and all sorts of medical reports but the point that is being made by Ms. Grace is that that's not the one she operated from. It may well be and she hasn't really directly said this but I think it is implicit in what she said, she saw a bigger file on the day and she said I wonder what was in that because I hadn't seen it. That is what she is saying. Now, there is no point in trawling through the practice of the Council in relation to people or what was on the file in fact or not as the case may be because the point that is being made is that there seems to have been two different files.

Mr Gallagher quickly moved onto another topic.

Q. Mr. Gallagher: And I want to put to you that a Notice to Quit was served on Ms. Cummins on 4th March 2004.

A. I will accept that.

Q. Pardon?

Judge Dunne: She said she accepts that.

Q. Mr Gallagher: You accept that, all right. And do you accept that you in fact went to Ms. Cummins's house or the vicinity of her apartment and telephoned in to confirm when she was present in her house so that she could be served?

A. No.

Q. Ms. Patricia Philbin will say that you did that, in fact that she asked you to do it, that you were asked at least to do it and that you went to the house and you said something to the effect that Bríd Cummins is in now and she can be served and she was served with the Notice to Quit by Patricia Philbin on the 4th. You deny that?

A. I deny that.

Q. All right.

A. And with respect, for the purpose of clarification, when Notices to Quit are being issued, it would normally be the arrears controllers who would be involved with that. It used to be an old Revenue collector's function. To be helpful I am suggesting that.

Q. Now, following the unfortunate death of Ms. Cummins, there were a number of meetings and reports to councillors by the then City Manager or acting City Manager, Mr. O'Neill I think in the first instance; is that right?

A. That's right, it was very public. That's right, yes.

Q. Do you remember the report that you complained about that you say that misrepresented your true position?

A. Yes, I say that.

Q. What report was that?

A. The report that was compiled by the Council for the publically elected members.

Q. Was that the report prepared and presented to the Council on 24th February by Mr. Joe McGrath?

A. Yes.

Q. I see. And do you accept that nowhere in that report are you named by name?

A. I don't accept that.

Q. Pardon?

A. I don't accept that.

Q. You don't accept that?

A. No.

Q. Your named you say as Ms. Julie Grace in that report; is that right?

A. That's right.

Q. Are you named in any manner which is incorrect or which is in any way offensive to you?

A. I believe that I am referred to in a libellous way in that I am the person referred to as the TLO who did not make the transfer recommendation.

Q. I see. But the report does not say Julie Grace did not make the transfer recommendation.

A. With due respect, with respect, the TLO who did not allegedly make the transfer was referred to as the former TLO.

Q. You had said and you complain in your Statement of Claim and indeed you have said here that you weren't aware of Ms. Cummins's medical history. Had you not spoken with a number of doctors about her and had you not received medical certificates from her?

A. I was not aware of the intensity of Ms. Cummins's psychiatric disorder.

Q. I see. But you knew she had a psychiatric disorder?

A. I knew that she had various ailments but I have answered the question, I did not know the severity and that's where the exceptional conditions would prevail in relation to a transfer.

Q. As I understood what you have just said, you knew she had a psychiatric disorder but you didn't know the severity of it?

A. And many, many local authority tenants would say they had psychiatric orders.

Q. I am not suggesting otherwise but what I put to you is that these Notice to Quit proceedings came before the District Court in the first instance.

A. Yes.

Q. You are aware of that, aren't you?

A. Yes.

Q. And I put it to you that there was no evidence offered that Ms. Cummins was legally represented in those proceedings, that no evidence was offered as to her health or condition.

A. And with respect I think that's part of the problem because Ms. Cummins didn't tell everybody about her serious -- she didn't say, or how shall I say... I do believe that she tried to mask the seriousness of her psychiatric disorder in her everyday relations with people.

Q. Mr. Gallagher: Ms. Grace, I want to put to you very specifically that you did not recommend to Ms. Philbin or Ms. Mullarkey, or Mr. Hayes at any time that Ms. Bríd Cummins should be transferred.

A. I was at the meeting in on 17/06/03 when Ciarán Hayes's views on the matter were abundantly clear. Nora Walsh asked him, she said "well, for Christ's sake will you transfer that woman" and he said "no, nothing would

262

make her happy", and the meeting of this minutes the decisions. But he did make an observation that if he were to buy an apartment in Salthill for Bríd Cummins that she wouldn't be happy and he was refusing point blank to make a recommendation. With respect I was not in a position to go back and argue any other points. The decision had been made by the Director of Services and I did not get further involved in the rights or the wrongs of the recommendation until December 2003 when my opinion was asked by the City Manager.

At this point the lunchtime period had been reached again, and the court adjourned for one hour. On return to the witness box, Mr Gallagher resumed questioning me, resuming a dialogue that had already taken place with Mr Hogan previously in relation to the Bríd Cummins situation.

Q. Mr Gallagher: You have agreed with me that you did not furnish a written report on Ms. Cummins's proposed transfer or your recommendation to a superior official that she be transferred.

A. It was not a written report.

Q. And I suggest to you that there was no house agreed with Mr. Tierney.

A. I do not agree with that. It was not an agreement, it was, to be clear, the manager asked me if there were any properties available then that would meet Ms. Cummins's needs and I identified two properties.

Q. And you suggested two.

A. Two different properties and we had a long discussion about the property in St. Anthony's Terrace in Bohermore and he asked me if I was sure that that was available and I said I was, that I was aware of that property; that a family called [Name redacted] had left it...

263

That bungalow I recommended was left vacant. Housing management was not aware that this house had been vacant for approximately twelve months, and the situation had only just come to light. I was not directly involved with the property as it was not my area. I learned that the person to whom it had been allocated did not take up the tenancy.

Mr Gallagher continued his cross-examination of me, wherein the dialogue of the conversation between John Tierney and I was repeated. Mr Gallagher claimed at that point, that the Mr Tierney did not agreed with me that Ms Cummins would be moved. In actual fact, John Tierney wondered if the remedy could be that simple. I told him that I believed it was worth a try.

Some days later, I accidently met the Manager in the corridor, who told me that Ciarán Hayes would not agree to that suggested transfer.

Q. Was Ciarán Hayes the officer to whom the manager had delegated his functions in relation to housing matters, including transfers?

A. With respect, you advised me this morning, Mr. Gallagher, that Ciarán Hayes was the man that made all the decisions in relation to housing matters.

Q. That's what I am saying, that the manager had delegated to Mr. Hayes...

A. That's right.

Q. The responsibility.

A. The man was Director of Services for housing, and as City Manager John Tierney decided that as the liaison person out there I would have tacit knowledge and he obviously deemed me to be fairly clued in, and he did say he was getting an enormous amount of correspondence about this and he would love to have it sorted out as quickly as possible.

Q. I suggest to you that this was a discussion and you may disagree with me, but that what happened was that you had advised that there were two properties available and clearly the decision had to be made by somebody other than yourself.

A. I was not in a decision-making position at all, absolutely correct.

Mr Gallagher then reverted back to earlier testimony regarding the relevance of additional medical information relating to Bríd Cummins in the bigger file.

Q. What happened in relation to Ms. Cummins and the eviction or the court proceedings relating to the eviction occurred long after you had left the Council.

A. That is so. Had I had sight of those documents while I was working for the Council, I would have progressed and I would have recommended a transfer for Ms. Cummins on the basis of her serious medical issues.

Q. What documents are you now aware of that you weren't aware of before you left the Council that would have caused to you do that, to make a written recommendation?

A. The realisation that Ms. Cummins was a patient of Prof. Tom Fahy.

Q. I see. So the fact that she was a patient of a particular doctor would have caused to you do that?

A. With the knowledge that I have in that area, I know that Ms. Cummins would not be a patient of Prof. Tom Fahy if she was suffering from a mild mental illness.

Q. What was she being treated for by the professor do you know? Was she being treated for depression?

A. Anybody being treated by Prof. Tom Fahy is in a serious mental state.

Mr Gallagher went through records and memos and letters from doctors on behalf of Bríd Cummins over the years of her tenancy. This was an exhaustive exercise, and was difficult to see where the merit was as the woman was deceased and the Coroner's Court had already ruled on the cause of death. He went on to summarise the defence's case:

> Q. Mr Gallagher: All right. Ms. Cummins [sic], I just want to put it to you formally that three members of the board who interviewed you will give evidence and will reject your allegations about the conduct or the behaviour of the chairman and will deny emphatically that you were not afforded fair procedures and that you were not treated appropriately, fairly, with good manners and that they were dispassionate and utterly impartial in their assessment; that they did not know you, did not and do not bear any malice or ill will against you, and that your impression is mistaken and that your complaints are unfounded. I should also say that whilst evidence denying and contradicting much of what you have said will be given by other witnesses, including Mr. Hayes, Ms. Mullarkey, Ms. Philbin and others, that none of them bear any malice or ill will against you, they wish you well, Mr. Hayes stands over the reference which he gave to you, but they do take issue and disagree with the allegations that you have made. They say that they are unfounded and insofar as there may be something that I have missed in the affidavit or the reply to particulars in an allegation, I want to put it to you that my witnesses disagree with your evidence, will take issue with your evidence and suggest that your proceedings are misconceived and will suggest that you are not entitled to any of the relief which you claim. Thank you very much.

> Q. Judge Dunne: Do you want to comment?

> A. I disagree and I maintain that I am bringing a case in good faith. I am telling the truth.

Judge Dunne: Thank you.

Mr Gallagher was then handed up some photographs in the courtroom, which commenced a renewed conversation in an extension of cross-examination to again question me about the filing system in operation at City Hall. It appeared that these photographs were of the 'Cardex' filing system as it operated at that time, not as it operated years previously when I worked in the section. He endeavoured to get my agreement on procedures that operated, of which I could not know, as I had not worked at City Hall for six years by this time. He persisted for some time in pursuit of a disagreement about the way housing files were maintained in the cardex. He described a system that sounded very loose in operation to me, and different from the regulated system I had worked with during my time working in City Hall.

This exhaustive session of intense questioning came to an end after this. The next witness called was Cllr Catherine Connolly.

Examination of Witness Connolly by Mr Hogan SC

Q. Mr Hogan: Thank you, Ms. Connolly.

You might just tell the Court your present occupation.

A. I am a practising barrister on the western circuit.

Q. And can you say whether you occupied any position in Galway City Council in the period 2003/2004?

A. I was first elected as a city councillor in 1999. I was elected again in 2004 and I was elected the Mayor of Galway in 2004. I am a current member of the City Council in a different ward than I stood in initially.

Mr Gallagher: Sorry, Ms. Connolly, would you mind moving in just a bit closer. Thank you.

A. Sorry.

Q. Mr Hogan: So you were Mayor of Galway in 2004?

A. From 2004 to 2005.

Q. Now, first do you recall the demise of Ms. Cummins?

A. I do.

Q. Can you say whether it was a matter of some controversy in the Council?

A. Without a doubt. It was hugely controversial, it was tragic and it affected me personally and it affected an awful lot of people in Galway.

Q. Now, can I ask you whether in 2003/2004 you knew Ms. Grace?

A. Yes, I knew Ms. Grace as a Tenant Liaison Officer certainly, yes. I would have been aware of her. She would have been a larger-than-life character. I wouldn't have known her personally but I would have known her in my capacity as a city councillor.

Q. And can you say up to the termination of her employment in June 2004 whether you had dealings with her?

A. I would have had dealings with her.

Q. How many councillors are there, were there?

A. There are 15 councillors on Galway City Council.

Q. And would the identity of Ms. Grace have been known to those councillors?

A. It would, yes. In fact that would be the only Tenant Liaison Officer that I would .. Peter Duffy rings a bell in my head but I heard it yesterday as well, but of all the Tenant Liaison Officers, it would have been Julie Grace that I would have had contact with, not very often but in relation to tenants or housing applicants or clarifying something in relation to housing matters.

Q. And why does Ms. Grace's name perhaps resonate with you in this way?

A. I would have known her as a Tenant Liaison Officer. I actually didn't know she lost her job. I don't even think I was aware of the interview process at the time. So my contact with her was entirely in relation to housing applicants or tenants.

Q. Now, we know that Ms. Cummins passed away in early December 2004.

A. 6th December.

Q. And that was after Section 62 to proceedings had been commenced by the Council.

A. That's right.

Q. You say you were Mayor of Galway at the time and what of the immediate response of the councillors to Ms. Cummins's death?

A. If I could tell you my own reaction, it was one of shock. I learnt it on a Monday night and I have to say I used unparliamentary language when I heard it. I chaired a controversial meeting. The meetings at the time were difficult in the sense that we were putting through a city development plan. It was a difficult year for all of us. We were under pressure and there were extra meetings until 12:00 o'clock at night. On the night that I heard about Bríd Cummins's death, it was a regular meeting. It started at 7:00 o'clock at that time and I chaired that meeting and when it was over sometime after 9:00 o'clock the director approached me directly. There was a long table and I was chairing the meeting, the meeting was over and he said "Bríd Cummins is dead, Mayor."

Q. And just for the sake of the record, the director being?

A. Ciarán Hayes. That's how it came to my attention on that Monday night.

Q. Had you previously been aware of Ms. Cummins?

A. I had made representation for her. I have the correspondence here and it's on file as well. My initial contact, and this is again just from checking the file, I would have no recollection of the dates except it's on file, I wrote a letter in February '03 making representations for her in relation to a transfer to John Tierney, the City Manager. I had a meeting with John Tierney and Bríd Cummins in May. Again it's on file, it's 5th or 6th May.

Q. '03?

A. '03. Bríd Cummins, again I didn't know Bríd Cummins on a personal level, I simply knew her making representations to me. We went in to John Tierney and we met in the City Manager's office and she outlined why she wanted a transfer and he said he would get back to us in two weeks. Again I don't remember that date but I see it's on the file that he assured us because there is an internal memo where he refers "I undertook to get back to Alderman Connolly within two weeks". I wouldn't have a recollection of that time frame.

Q. Moving forward, just back to December '04, we know and it's not in controversy but a report was commissioned and that was put by Mr. Gallagher to Ms. Grace.

A. I'll tell you, there was shock in Galway City at the death of Bríd Cummins. I have to say there was shock on part of the officials as well. We began to ask questions and the acting City Manager, unfortunately we were in a period of transition and it was an acting City Manager and he gave us a report in December '04. We were unhappy with that report and we asked for further information and we got a second report. So there are two reports in December '04 outlining what happened. We were unhappy with that and I think in fairness the majority of councillors were unhappy with that. We came to a situation where we asked for an independent inquiry. It went to a vote and the majority didn't support that but what they did support was that each councillor would be allowed to ask as many questions as they wanted and that's how that book of questions and answers..

Q. To which I will come now in a moment but can you say that there was concern on the part of officials understandably as a result of the death of Ms. Cummins?

A. Yes, certainly.

Q. Apart from the fact that Ms. Cummins appears to have died in tragic circumstances, can you say why there was such concern?

Mr Gallagher: I think perhaps the witness can say why she had a concern rather than speaking for 15 councillors.

MS. JUSTICE DUNNE: I think that's fair enough. What do you think, Mr. Hogan?

Mr Hogan: The witness has said that she understood that the officials had concerns and she was somebody who as Mayor of Galway at the time interacted with these individuals.

MS. JUSTICE DUNNE: I would suspect that she is in a better position than most of us to articulate what the concerns abroad at the time were having regard to her position as a public representative. So presumably she is in a position to answer the question. I appreciate she can articulate her own but she presumably was aware of other concerns as well, Mr. Gallagher.

Mr Gallagher: May it please, Judge.

Q. Mr Hogan: Ms. Connolly, I was asking you why in your opinion the officials had concerns?

A. Maybe I am misleading you inadvertently. They were shocked, they were certainly shocked and they were concerned in relation to what happened. That certainly came across. I think they were angry that there was such publicity about it, I don't what the term is, I don't know but they certainly

271

weren't happy. I myself having made representations, having written two detailed letters, the second one in March '04 directly to the City Manager, I must say I was horrified. It was my opinion that this death shouldn't have happened. It was my opinion that she should have got a transfer. I had appealed personally for that transfer on more than one occasion and I have no idea to this day why she didn't get a transfer.

Q. Can you say whether the failure to effect a transfer was a matter then which caused anxiety at the time?

A. Yes, certainly. Certainly amongst the general public there was an outpouring of anger, certainly on the local radio station in response to me going on and indeed the solicitor who acted for her in due course went on and a number of poets and so on, there was on outcry from the public that something could happen in the midst of the Celtic Tiger that somebody would die as a result of -- and, sorry, to add to it, Ms. Bríd Cummins herself went on the radio, I didn't hear it but that also caused on outcry of compassion for her and she described her despair on the local radio after both cases.

Q. Now, can I ask you just to take a look at page 54 of the question and answer session.

A. Yes.

Q. "Why was no consideration given of a former Liaison Officer's report that a house was identified and agreed with John Tierney for Bríd Cummins to move to and overruled by the Director and was there an order in writing to confirm this?"

And then you have the response: "The former City Manager did not agree with the former Tenant Liaison Officer to transfer Ms. Cummins."

A. Yes.

Q. Now, can you say these questions and responses were put I think in February 2005?

A. That would be correct.

Q. Now, can you say in February 2005 who did you understand the first line to refer to?

A. That was Julie Grace.

Q. You knew that at the time yourself, you understood that at the time?

A. Yes, that wouldn't be an issue, we'd know that was Julie Grace that was the Tenant Liaison Officer.

Q. And would the councillors have known this?

A. They would, yes.

Q. And would anybody familiar with the issues have known who this referred to?

A. I'd say so. She was known as the Tenant Liaison Officer that was the Tenant Liaison Officer for that area in Galway City.

After a discussion about her meeting the City Manager Mr Tierney to advocate for a transfer for Bríd Cummins, Mr Hogan went on to question Ms Connolly about her interpretation of a statement - made in the (Bríd Cummins) 'Report to Councillors' file – given in answer to a Councillor's question to management about the transfer request being denied:

Mr Hogan: Ms. Connolly, in February 2005 when you received this report, what did you understand the first sentence to say?

A. That she had made a recommendation for...

Mr Gallagher: Sorry?

273

A. I beg your pardon, that she had made a recommendation for a transfer.

Q. Mr Hogan: It says: "The former City Manager did not agree..."

A. You see I would have made presumptions there because I had met the City Manager and I met him in May '03 and I believed he was actively looking at a transfer -- sorry, he was actively looking at the request for a transfer because Bríd Cummins and I went in to speak to him. So I believe that he was actively looking for that. So when I read that report and read it again yesterday and when I read it at the time, I would have just taken that for granted because I felt he was positive in relation to giving her a transfer.

Q. But you said just a moment ago that you understood that Ms. Grace had recommended a transfer but the first sentence is; "The former City Manager did not agree...."

A. Yes, I see that, yes.

Q. Then it goes on to say: "Further, the former Tenant Liaison Officer did not recommend a transfer for Ms. Cummins but explained to both Ms. Cummins and her doctor that Ms. Cummins did not qualify for a transfer."

A. Yes, I see that as well.

Q. And what did that convey to you at the time?

A. I couldn't tell you, at the time I couldn't tell you but I have read it and I read the file yesterday and I see that Ms. Grace said that she didn't fit the criteria of what she referred to and I checked the file as you read it and that was 2001. I just noted the date on it.

Q. And in your view can you say whether anything had occurred relevant to Ms. Cummins's case from 2001 onwards?

A. I wasn't familiar with Bríd Cummins from 2001 onwards. I am now familiar with it because I have looked at the file. What I can clearly say is my experience, if that's of help to the Court or if it's relevant, she made

274

representations to me, as I said I went in with her to the City Manager in May '03. I believed he was positive. There was absolutely no discussion of anti-social behaviour. That sticks out in my mind and it sticks out in my mind as I read the file. She was making her concerns known as to why she wanted to move. I searched the file for a record of that meeting; it's not on the file. Now, I don't know whether that occurred to me at the time but I have had a chance to look at it today and yesterday on the train and I can't find a note of that meeting, although it's recorded that there is a meeting and it is accepted that there is a meeting. I remember John Tierney being open and positive. Certainly he did not say he was giving her a transfer. We went away from that meeting believing he was open in relation to it.

The other letter from me then, you jump forward to March '04 and it's on file and it is a two-page letter and it's pretty strong from me in relation to what has happened in the meantime and why she hasn't got a transfer and I am appealing for sense to prevail in relation to the transfer and I outline..

The witness, Ms Connolly explains to the Court how she advocated to the City Manager John Tierney on foot of a request by Bríd Cummins. She highlights how there is correspondence involving her, which is missing from the file that management provided to Councillors.

Q. MS. JUSTICE DUNNE: That's a letter from you, is it?

A. Yes, the second letter from me in March '04. I can go through it. It's a long letter, it's a page and a half and I am pointing out the absurdity. I think I use the word bizarre or absurd in the way that the matters have proceeded. I outline the various letters and I say listen, you're asking for this woman to appeal back to a director who has already said she's adequately housed, whom we have brought the matter to your attention and that's on file. So there was a huge sense of frustration. What had happened at some stage along the line was Bríd Cummins had issued proceedings, an Equity Civil Bill in relation to the state of the house and the City Manager responded to that and said that from now on he would deal with the matter now that an Equity Civil Bill was in being, he would deal with the matter through his solicitors.

Q. Mr Hogan: If we just continue on with this response: "The former City Manager did not make a decision to transfer Ms. Cummins. Had he done so, it would not have been within the remit of the Director of Services to overrule such a decision."

Then could I ask you to look at one other answer, which is page 46, question 51: "Whose decision was it to terminate the tenancy and seek repossession?"

A. Page 46?

Q. Page 46, question 59.

"The decision to seek an excluding order to terminate the tenancy and seek repossession of the premises were executive decisions. The responsibility for such decisions lie with the City Manager and Director of Services in accordance with the City Manager's powers under the Local Government Act 2001 to delegate such functions. The Director of Services made all decisions in this case."

A. Yes, I see that, I have that highlighted.

Mr Hogan went on to question Ms Connolly about whether Mr Tierney exerted his executive power, or if he devolved this down the line, in regard to Bríd Cummins's transfer request.

Q. And what does that tell you or does it tell you anything as to who made the decisions in respect of whether to grant or not to grant a transfer?

A. Well, that answer is clearly saying it's the Director of Services. However, that would come as a surprise to me and somewhat of a shock to me because I was appealing to the City Manager as the ultimate manager in a situation that was extremely difficult. There were complaints on both sides. So that answer I don't accept...

Q. MS. JUSTICE DUNNE: When you say there were complaints on both sides, who do you mean by that?

A. In relation to Bríd Cummins and in relation to her neighbour, the Walshs.

Q. Mr Hogan: Can you say whether the City Manager, Mr. Tierney, had within his power or gift to effect a transfer?

A. Absolutely. The City Manager is the person in charge.

Q. What would you say if the City Manager was advised, if it were to be the case that the City Manager was advised that a transfer should be made, albeit that that transfer is made verbally? Would the City Manager be the appropriate person to receive such a recommendation, albeit a verbal one?

Q. Sorry, let me rephrase the question. The evidence has been given that a verbal recommendation was made by Ms. Grace to Mr. Tierney to effect a transfer in December '03. She has been cross-examined to some extent by Mr. Gallagher in a way that suggests that the more appropriate person to make this recommendation to was to do it in writing to the Director of Services, and I am asking you from your experience and your position as Mayor at the time in 2004 whether the City Manager was an appropriate person to make a recommendation to, albeit a verbal one, in respect of a transfer?

A. The City Manager would be the ultimate person that would make the decisions in Galway City. Listening to the evidence and reading this and my own experience, the word I used at the time was that it was 'Kafkaesque'.

It is even more so when I read through the file now. We appealed to the City Manager in May. I wrote in March 2004. To me as a public representative it was very difficult because Bríd Cummins had made representations to me as did Nora Walsh, and I had to say to Nora Walsh when she rang up this is very difficult because I have already received representations but I do feel in fairness to both sides that there is a solution and that was in view of the meeting with John Tierney. I said I can't talk about it because I have already received representations, extremely difficult, and that was as fair as I could be that there was a solution in sight.

It was clear from this testimony from the former Mayor of Galway, that the City Manager had the 'ultimate power' to recommend the transfer. However, he elected to not use it.

Cross-examination of Witness Catherine Connolly

Ms Connolly cross examined by Mr Gallagher on her evidence. He questioned her about the complaints made against Bríd Cummins by her adjoining neighbours. The former mayor went through the chronology of her representations to the council management on behalf of Bríd Cummins. A letter of response from John Tierney was read aloud:

Q. "I have reviewed the file and respond as follows: Firstly, the position of the City Council was indicated by Mr. Hayes previously and the opinion that Ms. Cummins was adequately housed was noted in correspondence to the Ombudsman. No formal decision issued to Ms. Cummins until Ms. Martin's letter of 11th November 2003. This letter issued subsequent to an inspection of 5A Munster Avenue by officials of the Council on 3rd November at which Ms. Cummins was present. I noticed that Ms. Cummins did not subsequently appeal that decision despite being advised of her right to do so. The issuing of the Notice to Quit is a separate matter having regard to complaints about Ms. Cummins's behaviour as a tenant. Given that Ms. Cummins has failed to deliver up possession of the house, this case will proceed to court in the normal way. I trust this clarifies the matter for you.

Yours sincerely, J. Tierney, City Manager. I should have said, Judge, that this letter is to be found on page...

MS. JUSTICE DUNNE: I have it.

Q. Mr Gallagher: 191 of the book. So Mr. Tierney was making it clear to you that so far as he was concerned he was supporting the steps that were being taken to evict Ms. Cummins at that time.

A. Yes.

Q. And insofar as Mr. Tierney was concerned, that remained the position until he left Galway in the following August.

A. During the summer of that year.

Q. And he was replaced in due course then by the present manager, Mr. McGrath.

A. Joe McGrath.

Q. Who furnished the report of 23rd February 2005 to the councillors? That's the report you have before you and the documentation supporting it. They were the 280 pages of the file. So you got the complete file so far as you are concerned I take it?

A. I am not so sure about that because there is no record at all of my meeting with the City Manager in May of '03. I don't see any record of it whatsoever.

Q. I see.

A. Again it's only going back on it...

Q. We don't know whether the manager made any note of it or not.

A. Well, he was a great man to make a record. He always had a book with him. No more than myself, I am a great woman to take notes.

Q. Was anybody else present?

A. No.

Q. Except the three of you.

A. The three of us.

Q. So if there was a failure to make a record of the meeting or memo of the meeting, it was the manager's failure?

A. I'm just saying it's not there.

Q. In any event, you had no doubt as and from 30th April or 1st May that he was supporting the decision that had been taken by the Director of Services?

A. Yes.

Mr Gallagher continued to cross-examine Ms Connolly about local authority procedures and her previous evidence was confirmed in detail. At the end of cross-examination, Mr Hogan asked if the witness could be released. The judge declined, indicating she had her own questions. Cllr Connolly was then questioned by Justice Dunne.

Q. MS. JUSTICE DUNNE: Ms. Connolly, just going back to what you said, I think you made a comment to the effect, and I may have misheard it so please forgive me if I did, that there was something about Mr. Tierney commenting to the effect that there was a Civil Bill issued.

A. Yes.

Q. MS. JUSTICE DUNNE: Do you recall saying something about that?

A. Yes.

Q. MS. JUSTICE DUNNE: And that he would have nothing further to do with it or something along that line.

A. Yes.

Q. MS. JUSTICE DUNNE: Could you just bear with me until I find exactly what you said. My note is that she had issued proceedings herself, that the City Manager said he would deal with issues in relation to her. Isn't that what you were saying or am I misunderstanding it?

A. At some stage I became aware from the City Manager that as a result of the Equity Civil Bill that was issued, that that was it, that any further communication was going to be through the solicitors.

Q. MS. JUSTICE DUNNE: I see. Now, just bear with me. The reason why I asked is that as I understand it you are saying you met with Mr. Tierney in May of 2003.

A. That's correct.

Q. MS. JUSTICE DUNNE: Now, the Equity Civil Bill was issued or dated 9th April. In fact it is issued from the Circuit Court Office on 17th April 2003 and that's before your meeting. Now, obviously I don't have a date when it was served. Maybe somebody can tell me. I am just puzzled by that comment given that you had a meeting after the date of issue.

A. I wasn't aware of any Civil Bill.

Q. MS. JUSTICE DUNNE: At the time of the meeting.

A. No.

Q. MS. JUSTICE DUNNE: It may be that it wasn't served at that time.

A. And certainly John Tierney didn't draw it to our attention but equally our meeting was in relation to Bríd Cummins's difficulties and her absolute desire for a transfer and at no at that stage of that meeting was any anti-social behaviour brought up.

Q. MS. JUSTICE DUNNE: Of course if I am correct in my recollection of the Circuit Court Rules, the position in relation to the issue of a Civil Bill is that it is regarded as having been issued after service. It's rather unusual, it's not like a plenary summons.

A. It's changed since.

Q. MS. JUSTICE DUNNE: Yes, but that is only now.

A. That's right.

Q. MS. JUSTICE DUNNE: That's in the more recent legislation, yes. So at the time that it was issued, if one takes that as being accurate, one would accept presumably that it must have been served by 17th April 2003, which would be before your meeting.

A. Yes, the meeting was on the 6th and 7th May.

Q. MS. JUSTICE DUNNE: And you certainly weren't aware of any anti-social issues?

A. I beg your pardon?

Q. MS. JUSTICE DUNNE: You weren't aware of any anti-social issues involving...

A. I would have been aware, I would have been aware at some stage after that from a phone call from Mrs. Walsh.

Q. MS. JUSTICE DUNNE: But not at the time of the meeting?

A. No. There no discussion. It was Bríd Cummins talking about her problems and why she wanted a transfer. As I say, Mrs. Walsh rang me then and I explained my difficulty but I thought there would be a positive solution that would make both of them happy.

MS. JUSTICE DUNNE: Thank you very much.

The judge then offered a further opportunity to both legal sides, asking if they had any further questions for the witness, before releasing her. Mr Gallagher had one more question for Cllr Connolly, regarding the lack of any court hearing in relation to civil proceedings Bríd Cummins had initiated against the council for lack of repairs to her property (before the Council initiated eviction proceedings against her).

Q. Mr Gallagher: I am instructed that those proceedings never came to a conclusion.

A. Well, Bríd Cummins died.

Q. The equity proceedings.

A. She died.

Q. Yes, but they never came to a conclusion.

A. I think that's the reason.

MS. JUSTICE DUNNE: Well, they couldn't. She died.

Q. Mr Gallagher: But never came to court.

A. But she died, that's the reason.

The witness was then excused.

Mr Hogan expressed his fears that the case was taking somewhat longer than was anticipated, and asked the judge when the next session would be resuming. Justice Dunne outlined her busy schedule for the upcoming days. She noted that Mr Gallagher had ten witnesses to call for the defence in this case, and there was still one plaintiff witness remaining to be called. She advised that she was pencilling in a further three days at the beginning of June, which both Senior Counsel agreed to. The hearing was then adjourned to recommence on Wednesday, 2nd June 2010.

Day 5: Grace Vs Galway City Council

On returning to the High Court after the two weeks of recess, a new Court room was assigned. This time Justice Elizabeth Dunne was hearing the action in a different building on the complex. This was a less austere courtroom, which I learned was where the family courts were normally heard. On this first morning back, the first witness being heard was the Psychologist. He was examined and cross examined by both sides.

He explained the effects of what had happened to me as a result of the shame and indignity of not being allowed to continue to work in the professional area that I was qualified and experienced in, and had committed so much in through associated voluntary work. He gave evidence of the trauma suffered, how this was treated by him.

Application by Galway City Council to strike out the case
Immediately after this evidence, Mr Gallagher announced to the court that he was asking for a:

> "Non-suit at this stage, and I do so in circumstances where if you refuse my application it is my intention to go into evidence".

For me this meant that the Council were asking the judge to consider all of the evidence given so far in the case. This application was asking the Judge to decide whether all of my evidence to this point was truthful. This was a manoeuvre by the Defence team seeking to have the case thrown out. He cited the legal basis for this, using previous case law:

> "The question for the trial Judge is whether assuming that the trial or fact was prepared to find that all the evidence of the Plaintiff was true and taking the Plaintiff's claim at its highest, the Defendant has a case to meet".

Mr Gallagher then proceeded to summarise the arguments made in the case to-date, seeking to minimise them and indicate the lack of a right to proceed any further. He set out to counter all of the arguments put forward by my Counsel, and challenge every element in the Statement of Claim.

After this lengthy process, Mr Hogan stood up to summarise the main claims of the case again for the Court, to challenge the application for non-suit.

> On such an application that is for a non-suit the question for the trial Judge is whether assuming the trier of fact was prepared to find that all of the evidence of the plaintiff was true, and taking the plaintiff's case at its highest, the Defendant has a case to meet". So, Judge, if one looks at the complaints and the evidence that was given by the Plaintiff in this case, in my respectful submission, that threshold is easily surpassed by the Plaintiff.

During this presentation of the claims, legal debates ensued about technical issues. The original job advertisement was presented and debate ensued about the wording used in it. He highlighted that there was an actual specification by the Council in terms of a specific requirement:

> "The candidates must hold a full clean driving licence and will be required to have access to his or their own car".

The judge stated that she was open to being convinced about the enforceability of that requirement.

> Judge Dunne: If we go further in relation to this aspect of the matter you might just look at the law in relation to employment, the role of an advertisement for jobs, and so on and so forth.

Mr Hogan: Yes.

Judge Dunne: Because I appreciate what you are saying, I understand the use of the word "must", and so on and so forth.

Mr Hogan: Yes.

Judge Dunne: We are not dealing with the interpretation of statutes, we are looking at a job specification and advertisement. There may be different views, Mr. Hogan. If you can come up with the authorities to satisfy me that it is a mandatory requirement, I will accept that, I have no difficulty with that. I accept she did not have a driving licence and they said they wanted somebody with a driving license.

Mr Hogan: I would respectfully go somewhat further and say that that was in fact a prerequisite to the application...If I am right in my assertion, I can establish that at least one, if not more people, were appointed to the post who did not have a prerequisite to that appointment. If that happened, Judge, that would be vis-a-vis my client a breach of contract because one of the implied features of this contractual relationship is that there would be a true interview process and that persons who were not qualified for the position would not be appointed to it.

Mr Hogan reminded the court, that there were higher expectations of ethical standards when it came to public recruitment.

Mr Hogan: That particularly when it is a public body involved which imports a certain of public law duty to act fairly in the context of a contractual, a state of affairs which you have proclaimed to the entire world, that if I can answer the question this way; supposing it were to be established in a hypothetical case that a public authority had set down a criteria for interview had gone through, invited people to apply for a particular position, and that it turned out that the entire thing was a sham, and that there was no proper interview at all, and that there had been a predetermined

286

outcome, and to add insult to injury, one of the persons among the people who were appointed the position were not qualified according to the stated criteria.

I pose the question rhetorically, is it to be said that the party, the person who is a victim of this, could be told that they have no remedy at law at all, that this was simply purely an invitation to treat and created no contractual entitlements? In my respectful submission the very fact that the parties changed their position by applying for a post did so by virtue of an implied contractual representation of two things: That the interview process (a) would be fair, and (b) that nobody would be appointed to the post who was unqualified.

An extended dialogue continued between Mr Hogan, the Judge and Mr Gallagher about the contractual legalities of parties applying for jobs and matching or mismatching the job specification. Again this finished with the judge inviting Mr Hogan to research and present employment case law findings to establish the compulsion on the Council to adhere to their own job advertisement criteria. This brought proceedings up to lunch time again.

On return to the session in the afternoon, Mr Hogan presented the details of a previous case he believed to be closest to the particular point, for legal argument. This took up a significant period of time, which by the end of extended description and details resulted in Mr Hogan contending:

"That a stipulation in a job advertisement is capable of giving rise to legal consequences and is not just simply a mere puff or a mere statement of intent, or dare I say it, bluster, of something of that kind."

It was now at a critical juncture for me, as to whether a prima facie case had been established by my legal team. The judge would decide.

> Judge Dunne: What I propose to do in relation to the application that has now been made is to consider the matter overnight and I will rule on the matter in the morning.

Day 6 - Adjudication: Thursday, 3 June

I remember very clearly the anxiety, fear and dread of facing the court that June day. As the long line of Council officials breezed into Court that morning, there was a bright super-confidence on display and smirks being shared between them. I noticed that one female executive was wearing a bright candy-striped blazer and was swinging her hair in delight, as though she was about to board a flight to a sunny destination. I felt very afraid. I feared my family home could be in jeopardy if all of this went against me. I tried to push out from my mind the frightening and potential prospect of the cost of these past days in the High Court. All I had done was to tell the truth and stand up for what I knew was right.

I regretted having the tea and toast earlier in the morning. I prayed the judge would see the injustice of this entire situation. I watched the Judge's door at 11.15. Within minutes she came in with her court staff. I felt numb. This small courtroom was packed, and yet I felt very isolated. I noticed the attendance for the first time in the case of a fellow Galwegian, the Principal Solicitor of Blake and Kenny; Mr Michael Molloy. My mind flashed back to only a few years previously, when his brother Bobby as Minister for Local Government had personally presented me with one of my qualifications in Housing. I hadn't spotted Mr Molloy in court before now. He was sitting beside his solicitor Gregory McLucas, who had been in attendance for the Council with John O'Donnell and Mr Gallagher all of the other days.

The Judge commenced reading her adjudication. She referred to the application for a non-suit before her, at the request of Mr Gallagher. She summarised the issues in the case to-date. She outlined that he had indicated should his application be unsuccessful, he was proposing to go into evidence. She declared that she was considering whether the plaintiff had made out a prima facie case in respect of the case before the Court. Justice Dunne accepted that as per the case cited by Mr Gallagher, she too was considering this case "at its highest point from the point of view of the plaintiff's evidence". In effect, if she considered that any of my evidence was untrue at this stage, the case was to be thrown out and Mr Gallagher would be awarded his non-suit application on behalf of Galway City Council.

The judge went over the arguments submitted, and commented:

> "There is no doubt that the plaintiff is very unhappy with the situation in which she finds herself. By all accounts she seems to have been doing a good job, something reflected in the reference provided to her by Galway City Council, which they still stand over to this day. Other evidence given on behalf of the plaintiff is supportive of this view."

She went to address the issues at the heart of this case.

> The difficulty I have in dealing with the plaintiff's claim in respect of the claim for wrongful dismissal is this: As I have already mentioned, the plaintiff was aware of the application by the council for funding for the creation of permanent posts. She, and her union, were involved in discussions on this issue. Up to this time, the plaintiff and her colleagues had fixed term contracts. Her three-year fixed term contract came to an end in September 2003, it was extended, as referred to previously, by means of a further extension and that was referred to in the letter of the 11th September 2003 to which I have already referred, which stated that the council had objective grounds provided for in the legislation to justify the renewal of the contract of employment which currently expires on the 28th of September 2003, until the permanent filling post of tenant liaison officer. Thus, it was clear, that the plaintiff's position was always going to be terminated once the new positions were filled. That being so, I cannot accept that the plaintiff

has made out a prima facie case that she has been wrongfully dismissed. It seems, in truth, to me, that the essence of the plaintiff's complaint is that she failed to be appointed to the new position or post.

At this point, my heart sank heavily. It was not what I was hoping to hear. This was the main plank of the action compiled by my Counsel. I was stunned. I heard the judge continue:

Nevertheless, having said what I have said in relation to wrongful dismissal, the plaintiff, in my view, has made out a prima facie case to the effect that the interview process was flawed, unfair and unsatisfactory. In saying that, I am taking the plaintiff's case at its highest and I must make it clear that I am doing so solely for the purpose of considering the application now before me.

I think there is a claim in the proceedings which will allow this aspect of the plaintiff's claim to be continued, although it is perhaps not entirely clearly set out in the pleadings. I did make a comment at an early stage in these proceedings to the effect that the case seemed to me to be more about the interview process and alleged failings in that process rather than a wrongful dismissal action.

Processing this information; my heart utterly lifted! The judge had listened and was satisfied about the irregularity of the interview process. The council were not going to get away now with their non-suit.

Justice Dunne continued with her opinion of the defamation aspect claimed in the case. In summary, she adjudicated that not enough evidence had been produced to her satisfaction in pursuit of this. However, she was permitting the case to proceed for hearing to the next phase:

Accordingly, I propose to allow the action to proceed on the basis of the plaintiff's claim in respect of a cause of action which relates to, and this is how I see the case, that can be made, relation to the claim for deliberate abuse of power or misfeasance in public office, which I relate to the conduct of the interview process and damages for loss of opportunity. Which; seems to me to flow from the ruling that I have given in relation to wrongful dismissal.

Given the circumstances of this case, the ruling that I have made, the likely length of the case, the damages, if any, to which the plaintiff might be entitled, if she succeeds and the level of costs already incurred and to be incurred, I would strongly urge both sides at this stage, to consider their position and to see if there is any way of avoiding further costly, expensive and difficult litigation.

Mr Hogan stood up and confirmed that the Court's ruling had been noted. He asked for an opportunity for both sides to consult with their respective clients. The judge confirmed that this was appropriate, and added some further comments:

I do accept that there is a case being made by your client... there is an issue there is relation to the whole interview process. How that transpires will depend on the evidence in relation to that. And I include in that whole issue, the allegation of some kind of animus. And I don't exclude that for a moment, so may I be clear on that particular point.

Mr Hogan acknowledged this and other issues, and all parties withdrew to the adjacent rooms, provided for client consultations.

Negotiation Room

I adjourned to the consulting room with my son, solicitor, senior and junior counsel, and their devil (apprentice barrister). The pros and cons of the situation were discussed. The judge had decided that I did have a case to be answered. However at this point, after six days attending the High Court where four witnesses had been heard, an even longer session was anticipated in examining and cross-examining all of the other ten witnesses, declared for the City Council.

Notwithstanding this, the avenue now opened for the next stage of the case, reality for me was that the other side were now insulated with the continuing largesse of the public purse, to stay in court for as long as they desired. It was clear that this would be quite some time.

I was in a quandary. I wanted the Council management to justify why they had turned on me, the motivations for the animus exercised against me, and particularly the identities behind it.

I rationalised the whole situation at this stage and carefully considered what the judge had advised. I was hearing her. In contemplation of continuing further with this action against Galway City Council, and being afforded the opportunity to cross-examine the ten witnesses declared for the Council, one stark fact overrode all others, - the Council were spending freely with the public purse. They could spend as much time and money as they liked to protract the case into stratospheric costs. For an ordinary citizen like me, this was gambling against insurmountable odds.

An agreement was arrived at between the parties and the judge returned to the courtroom to note the outcome.

High Court Result

Mr Hogan read out the agreement as follows:

> I am authorised to say ... the parties have agreed the following:
>
> 1. The action can be dismissed.
>
> 2. The parties agree to bear their own costs.
>
> 3. The council cannot dispute Ms. Grace's evidence that she made an oral recommendation in December 2003 to the City Manager recommending the transfer of the late Bríd Cummins.
>
> 4. The plaintiff accepts that she did not make any written recommendation in respect of the late Bríd Cummins that she be transferred.
>
> ...this is the agreement reached by the parties.

The judge commended the agreement, and made her final comments:

> I am delighted the parties have been able to reach an agreement and an accommodation about that aspect of the matter and about the other aspects of the matter. Very good. And thank you for taking on board what was said, because, as I mentioned earlier, it would be unfortunate if somebody, at the end of this case was burdened with a very significant order for costs. Thank you.

My good name and professional integrity was confirmed in the Irish High Court, which was of utmost importance to me. I did not expect a personal apology for what was done to me by the Council.

However, in the aftermath of Bríd Cummins's death, and after the revelations during my court action where more daylight shone on the mishandling of her case, not one official, executive, or government representative has offered any apology or explanation for their behaviour.

It is perplexing as to how my good deed of visiting a colleague and neighbour, who was out sick after falling in the council car park, was twisted to make it look as if I had some ulterior motive.

I was horrified that such a perverse portrayal was alleged in attempting to make my sincere gesture at the time look like some kind of cynical act, in their defence of the case against them. It was surreal to hear such misconstructions under these serious circumstances.

Considering these were serious High Court proceedings, it seemed strange that Ms Philbin offered up the only attack in the case on my good name and character.

Ironically, this was in stark comparison to what the Director of Services was advising about me. He physically stood up in the court room to advise the Court through Mr Gallagher that he would still personally stand over the positive reference that he had written for me, and was prepared to continue to stand over it.

Unfettered Access to Legal Services

The executive management in Irish local authorities are financed and entitled to engage and retain legal services; as extensively and as often as they desire. I believe this is a dangerous power. It seems violently imbalanced against the individual. Is this distribution of a powerful resource questionable from a human rights perspective?

In the current local authority structures, the theory being underpinned is that 'might is always right'. This is grossly inequitable and unfair. Further, it is arguably perverse that taxpayers' contributions to the exchequer can be used negatively against them when a challenge against an executive's decision is warranted. There are many reported examples of wasteful litigation in local authorities all around the country. Who benefits from this system?

Would it be reasonable and reassuring for citizens if rates and receipts for legal procurements for all public bodies were published for public visibility?

In Bríd Cummins's situation, she was frustrated for years by Galway City Council in the denial of a housing transfer and/or the repairs where she was advised by an independent consulting engineer who examined her flat. His written advice was:

> "I am of the opinion that you are living in substandard and potentially very dangerous (electrically) housing conditions."

Ironically, in line with the Council's own transfer policy, full disclosure of the medical facts on the covertly maintained second file entitled Bríd Cummins to the transfer many believe would have saved her life.

As a former European civil servant, Bríd believed in engaging officially with the system. Her strong letters to the Council indicated her journalistic training. After she initiated a civil equity bill against the council for failing to complete housing repairs on her rented property or to grant a housing transfer, they did not engage in a timely manner. Her attempts were no match for the powerful resources of the City Council and their access to unlimited external legal services and advices. The executive who denied her requests had knowledge about her fragile state of mind. Unfortunately this was not made known to frontline workers like me.

The Council hosted a conference entitled 'Prevention of Homelessness and Tenancy Sustainment' in Galway and invited bona fide experts to speak on best practice. At the very same time, they were turning a vulnerable, single and un-resourced woman onto the streets. They wrote to advise her that they would be denying her access to the homeless services. They wrote to the Superintendent Welfare Officer in Community Care to advise they were evicting Bríd for anti-social behaviour, thereby frustrating her access to private rent allowance. All of this applied even if she gave up the keys and left.

If she had refused to hand over the keys, the released records show that the Council's own legal services were already in communication about another sanction:

> If it necessary to bring a Committal/Attachment Notice of motion, please revert to me. I enclose herewith Fee Note and many thanks for briefing me in this case.
>
> [25/11/04 Letter from Counsel John O'Donnell BL to Blake & Kenny Solicitors, Record #239, Report to Councillors]

The need for accountability by local authorities in purchasing legal services is minimal. This power is facilitated further due to the exemption of legal services from European Directives of Procurement. Whilst other professional services purchased by the State are regulated in accordance with 2004/18/EC (the 'Public Sector Directive'), there is a specific special exemption made for legal services. It has been uniquely categorised as an Annex 'IIB service' and is therefore not subject to the full scope of the Directive.

It is a feature of local authorities that annual audits are performed by the Department of Local Government auditors. Their published annual reports highlight executive matters that need attention. The audits for every City and County Council are published and made available to view on the Department of Environment web site. They are what they say they are - merely recommendations. This point is confirmed by the fact that the same recommendations for improved practices to particular local authorities can be repeated from year, to year, to year.

Absent legislation for recruitment in local authorities

Selection of interview panels for public service positions is a key power in Ireland. This power is invested with a few executives. Ireland has a well chequered history of cronyism and nepotism in public appointments. I believe the engagement of supposedly 'external' interview boards facilitates an outwardly wholesome and ethical-looking vehicle for local authority staff selection and recruitment.

Ms Justice Dunne clearly identified the absence of legislation surrounding recruitment and selection practices in local government. She highlighted that job advertisements published in newspapers for positions in local authorities have no legal standing. They are merely wish lists.

Essential criteria may infer a meaning in the English language, but not in legal terminology. One can only imagine the number of potential candidates that do not apply for advertised positions, in the belief that stated criteria in job advertisements for local authorities means something. In fact, stated essential criteria are not a barrier to entry at all.

This arose directly in my own legal case against Galway City Council, where a stated lack of qualifications, relevant experience, a full driving licence or driving experience did not hamper the candidate selected by an external interview panel and ratified by management in being ranked as the number one candidate in recommendation for one of the three positions. It is a key requirement of the Housing Estate Liaison Officer post that a lot of driving in and around city estates is necessary.

Concerned citizens and well-informed journalists regularly report and are mesmerised about the appointment of friends and family to public service positions in Ireland. Appointees often succeed over 'best-for-the-job' candidates with superior qualifications, experience, aptitude or professional work experience. Now it is clear how this is legally facilitated – by the absence of statutory legislation.

Despite many personal requests for action since my court finding, there appears to be no political appetite in government to regularise the position by addressing the judicially cited absence of legislation, in the public interest.

Once again, guidelines for best practice are and continue to be merely that – 'guidelines'.

A statement commonly attributed to the Irish political philosopher Edmund Burke (1729–1797) claims that "All that is necessary for the triumph of evil is that good men do nothing."

Summary reflection

"I didn't feel like I was given a chance to put my side, it was very one-sided. It was very much in the Council's favour. I think an opinion was formed even before we went into court, and I felt that (you know) I would like to give my side of the story. I felt that I had been victimised and bullied and intimidated because I had a case pending against Galway City Council, and I really feel that that was part of it.... "I mean they were painting me to be some kind of monster. I have never done any of the things that I was accused of. Absolutely outrageous. They had no evidence, they had no proof. Nothing."

Bríd Cummin's live radio interview after losing appeal of eviction order

"I do believe in the big wheel of life and I do believe in natural justice and that is the reason that I am here today, to bring about some kind of closure for me because I believe I did nothing wrong. Everything that I had was removed from me in the sense that my -- and I am not just talking about money, I am talking about my good name, that my integrity and that my ability to evaluate a situation was flawed. And I feel very aggrieved that I absolutely begged the Council to amend the Bríd Cummins report and accept that I did recommend a transfer and that I had nothing whatever to do with that woman's state that progressed her to taking her own life."

Sworn evidence of Julie Grace to the High Court (2010)

"POWER DOES NOT CORRUPT MEN; FOOLS, HOWEVER, IF THEY GET INTO A POSITION OF POWER, CORRUPT POWER."

GEORGE BERNARD SHAW (1856–1950)

Alternative Dispute Resolution

Within the confrontational structures of legal frameworks, disputants are disadvantaged by having decisions taken out of their hands. Parties have to accept outcomes that are decided on, outside of their control. This is apart from the public airing of sometimes sensitive or private matters.

As a qualified and experienced mediator in my own company, I am a passionate believer in the merits of the mediation process to resolve disputes, without the need to engage in protracted, stressful and expensive litigation. Through a mediation process, disputants can agree on their own unique solutions, designed and arrived at entirely by themselves.

Using the skills of a good mediator, seemingly intractable disputes can be resolved in a cost-effective, timely, non-threatening and non confrontational forum.

Acknowledgements

Many thanks to the *Galway Advertiser*, the *Connaught Tribune Group* of newspapers in Galway City for permission to republish some of their newspaper articles, and thanks to Galway Bay FM for permission to publish a transcript of Bríd Cummins's on-air interview.

Special thanks to Liam Staunton & Co., Solicitors, Sea Road, Galway, for their professional representation, integrity, trustworthiness and zeal in representing me in the High Court. I highly recommend their honest brokering to anyone needing a competent and reliable solicitor in Ireland.

I also wish to remember the late Jarlath McInerney, Solicitor, of Eyre Square, Galway. He is fondly remembered and missed for his decency, humanitarianism and professionalism. Jarlath always did his best for his clients.

Thank you to all of the people that I encountered in the writing of this book, who encouraged and supported my endeavour.

Finally, it is important to acknowledge the immense courage and struggle of Bríd Cummins, who maintained her dignity to the very end. I hope this work gives some comfort to her family and friends.

"May she rest in peace and may heaven be her bed".